The
Canadian Tax and
Investment Guide

The
Canadian Tax and
Investment Guide

Henry B. Zimmer

M&S

Canadian Cataloguing in Publication Data

Zimmer, Henry B., 1943–
   The Canadian tax and investment guide

ISBN 0-7710-9077-3

1. Tax planning – Canada – Popular works.
2. Income tax – Law and legislation – Canada – Popular works.
3. Investments – Law and legislation – Canada – Popular works.
I. Title.

KE5682.Z82Z5 1993   343.7105′2   C92-095526-6
KF6334.ZA2Z55 1993

Typesetting by M&S
Printed and bound in Canada

McClelland & Stewart Inc.
The Canadian Publishers
481 University Avenue
Toronto, Ontario
M5G 2E9

ACKNOWLEDGEMENTS

This book is dedicated to the many executives, professionals, and business owners who have attended my seminars and have encouraged me to put it all in writing.

I wish to thank my good friend Dr. Norman Schachar, who was kind enough to read the text for the first edition of this book, then titled *The New Canadian Tax & Investment Guide,* and whose valuable criticism helped me to keep sophisticated and technical material simple.

I also would like to acknowledge the efforts of Frank Solomon, formerly of Revenuc Canada, who helped me put together the chapter on dealing with the tax collector.

To my darling Jo
Who taught me that there is more to life than the Tax Act.
The reality is so much greater than the fantasy.

CONTENTS

INTRODUCTION

On June 18, 1987, former finance minister Michael H. Wilson introduced his long-awaited tax reform. The major thrust behind his program was to implement a general decrease in both personal and corporate income tax rates without any substantial loss of government revenue. Many tax incentives and loopholes were therefore eliminated, and middle and upper-income taxpayers were forced to bear the brunt of cutbacks in deductibility of automobile expenses, home offices, entertainment costs, and a lower dividend tax credit. Over the past few years, the taxable percentage of capital gains was adjusted from one-half to three-quarters. Most tax shelters fell by the wayside, although contribution limits to pension plans and registered retirement savings plans were extended.

When the last edition of this book was completed in June 1988, most of these changes were brand new and had not yet been implemented. Now, the new rules are firmly in place and it's time for a revision that explains all of the up-to-date opportunities that still exist.

This edition also takes into account recent economic trends that affect investment strategies and provides a digest of the important tax changes made in the last few years. There is still a great deal to work with! Because the overall economic climate indicates that we are in for a turbulent decade, the key to your own financial survival is flexibility, especially in the area of tax planning. Many of the larger economic struggles have been and will be fought in the taxation arena, for taxation is like a chess game. The government makes a move and it then falls upon taxpayers and their advisers to make countermoves. Remember, each individual is entitled to order his or her affairs within the framework of the law to pay the least amount of tax possible.

While many of the discussions in this book will be familiar to you if you have read any of the previous editions, the new approaches and new material will be just as useful. As I have indicated so many times before, *if you can pick up just one new idea each year, your savings can be many thousands of dollars.*

CHAPTER 1

Your Silent Partner

What This Book Will Do for You

This is not a book to assist you in preparing your tax return. Nor will it save you money if you read it just before you file. By then, it will be too late. Tax planning is a twelve-month-a-year exercise, one that should take place every time you are up for a pay increase, or manage to put away $1,000 for investments, or think about starting (or buying) a business.

If you have bought this book, you probably already realize that you are paying too much tax. Any Canadian whose taxable income reaches $30,000 will begin to pay almost 40% out of each additional dollar of earnings to a silent partner – Revenue Canada.

If you are earning $200,000 or $300,000 a year, things tend to fall into place by themselves. You can afford the best professional advice and you may be able to use certain tax write-offs. If you are a business owner, you may use a corporation for sheltering income. However, for the vast majority of people, who earn less than a six-figure income, many of these opportunities are not as accessible. Any legitimate advantage in dealing with the silent partner should therefore be pursued. To some extent this is difficult, since the government is the one that makes up the rules of the game. However, if you learn the rules, playing the game can be fun as well as profitable.

Certainly, the situation today is far better than it was a few years ago. There is the new lifetime capital gains exemption which allows every individual Canadian to accumulate up to $100,000 of total capital gains on most property tax-free. Farmers and small business owners may benefit from limits that are five times higher than those available to other Canadians. Also, over the next five years the maximum allowable contribution to a Registered Retirement Savings Plan (RRSP) will be, for many people, approximately twice as much as it was in 1990 and previous years. Lower interest rates are certainly another good sign and, as in the past, Canadians may continue to rely heavily on the use of leverage to accumulate capital, by borrowing against their earning power on a tax-deductible basis in order to make investments. Each of us must use the tax system to our best advantage. This book will help you in this complex and difficult endeavour.

Actually, taxation concepts are not especially difficult to understand. Over the years, I have presented some four hundred and fifty seminars to perhaps thirteen thousand business owners, executives, and professionals across Canada. These people have shown that the average Canadian not only wants to understand how the system works, but with just a little effort, also can make the system work for *him* or *her.* All anyone needs is a translation of the tax rules into plain English.

As you read through this book, you will find that learning the tax rules is easy. Also, formulating an effective investment policy for yourself does not necessarily require a crystal ball. You don't need an accounting or legal background. You need only assimilate some facts, and use some common sense and a bit of imagination. If you are capable of reaching a 40% tax bracket, you should be able to appreciate the logic of the tax and investment suggestions that this book contains. Of course, you may choose to disregard some or all of my suggestions and think independently. However, unless you are an extremely sophisticated person and have done extremely well in the past on your own, there is no reason why you shouldn't seek independent advice from your own advisers.

When to Use the Experts

An important point must be put into proper perspective. While the cost of an hour's time with a tax accountant or lawyer can exceed $200, rarely will the development of a tax and investment planning outline take more than three or four hours in total. The actual implementation of the ideas can then be accomplished with the assistance of non-specialist advisers whose rates are considerably cheaper. Earlier in my own career, I consulted on these matters almost exclusively to small businesses and executives and in very few cases did my fee exceed $500. This is not because I undercut the competition, but because I left the implementation of my proposals to my clients' regular advisers.

What if you don't think that you have a problem? You will still find that a tax and investment check-up is important. In the same way that it is worthwhile for you to go to your physician for a physical check-up at least once a year, a periodic tax and investment check-up can save you money by detecting problems and outlining planning opportunities that you may not even know exist. While $200 an hour sounds expensive, a fee of a few hundred dollars is not costly if you can save considerably more.

The key to proper planning, however, is to ask the right questions. Since the price for legal and accounting services is high, many business owners, executives, and professionals have expressed to me a desire to educate themselves to discuss tax and investment matters intelligently – especially since accountants and lawyers often have difficulty coming down to a layperson's level. As one of my clients said to me several years ago, "I've got to learn what this is all about. After all, it's *my* money."

How to Use This Book

This book is a collection of the topics with which I have dealt in seminars on tax and investment planning all over Canada. I have found speaking to the public extremely gratifying. Once, an Edmonton businessman said that he had learned more in one day from me than he had from his accountants in eleven years, and a Vancouver doctor told me, during the first coffee break in the morning, that he had already absorbed enough to cover the cost of my seminar and the loss of a day's earnings. Invariably, I was asked by participants to produce a book in order to cover the material that I teach. I therefore wrote *The New Canadian Tax & Investment Guide,* which was published in the fall of 1980.

But the government keeps changing the rules and this has compelled me to revise my *Guide* approximately every two or three years. With each update, I become more and more dismayed by the suggestion that I made on page 5 of the first edition – "a tax plan, once initiated, should be effective for many future years." Fortunately, I also suggested that the ongoing benefits of any program are dependent on the general structure of the tax laws remaining the same. I, for one, never dreamed that the rules could change so greatly in only one decade.

So here is the 1993 update. There is still room for planning that uses fringe-benefit programs, such as group health and life insurance packages, employee loans, and business-pleasure trips, where the value of these benefits is often much more than a (fully taxable) raise in pay. Although some of the tax advantages have been lessened, a good fringe-benefit program is still important.

Chapter Nine takes an in-depth look at the lifetime capital gains exemption and explains how your benefits from this exemption can be increased with effective tax planning. There are some excellent opportunities for aggressive individuals to take multiple advantage of this legislation. In Chapter Eleven, you will also be brought up to date on the tax-deferral advantages of personal-service companies, especially for doctors, dentists, and commissioned salespeople. Some tax changes made several years ago plugged certain loopholes previously used by various executives and athletes, although a consultant capable of earning revenues from different sources can still avail himself or herself of the benefits of incorporation.

Chapter Six explains the rule changes that have taken place over the last few years in the real estate area. In addition, the topic of life insurance as a tax shelter will be covered. As in the past, I must emphasize the importance of first finding a good *investment* before concentrating on tax-shelter aspects. Then, you can use the information in this chapter to take advantage of any shelter an investment may provide. Certainly, recent changes have eliminated some of the shelter features of real estate investments. As I predicted several years ago, in the short run (without these tax incentives) real estate values did, in fact, fall substantially. Today, however, with lower interest rates, we have a new situation. If you understand the scenario that is now unfolding in this country, you will find that large profits are still obtainable. An understanding of the tax rules will then enable you to retain as much of these profits as is possible.

Another chapter explores ideas for maximizing investment yields by splitting income with family members. Important changes to these guidelines have been made necessary by recent federal budgets. You will also be alerted to some of the misconceptions pertaining to investment yields, which can result from erroneously trying to apply U.S. guidelines to Canada. For example, U.S. rules do not differentiate between the earning of interest and dividend income. However, for most Canadians in 40% or 45% tax brackets, a Canadian dividend is worth at least one and a quarter times as much as an equivalent yield of Canadian interest on an *after-tax* basis. Thus, if a stock pays an 8% dividend, this is equivalent to pre-tax interest of 10%.

I will show you that for many individuals, the difference between buying a blue-chip Canadian stock and investing in a term deposit or Canada Savings Bond is only a 2%–3% net annual cash difference in favour of the interest-bearing security. However, when you take capital appreciation potential and the capital gains exemption into account, the balance will often swing in favour of share investments.

We will also examine the major tax-planning concepts for owner-managers of private companies. Significantly higher RRSP limits necessitate brand new guidelines for salary-dividend policies so as to optimize after-tax retentions in any active business situation.

For anyone planning to buy a business, I will explain how there is a "right way" and a "wrong way." Without proper planning, anyone who buys the shares of a Canadian private company could be *overpaying income taxes by more than $45,000 for every $100,000 of the purchase price*. With proper planning, this needless tax can be legitimately eliminated. Other material introduces estate-planning concepts, such as the points that a will should contain, and suggests some guidelines for a commonsense approach towards allocating assets to family members.

Before we go any further, however, a word of caution is in order. My intention is not to replace your accountants and lawyers. Nor am I trying to turn you into a "tax expert." My purpose is to show you what is available so that when you sit down with your own advisers, at least you have a common starting point. After having read this book, you should be able to discuss specific matters with the professionals who are there to assist you in implementing the proposals that I suggest. In many cases, your own advisers will be able to make important modifications suitable to your own specific circumstances.

Another word of caution is also warranted. The contents of this book are based on the tax law in force at the end of 1992. There are, however, some tax changes that will no doubt be made in 1993, although these are expected to be very minor. In other words, keeping up with the tax rules is an ongoing process. *This book is your starting point.* Beyond checking out specific tax-planning concepts with your own advisers, I strongly recommend that you keep up to date by reading digests of budget proposals, which appear in publications such as the *Financial Post* or the *Financial Times*. If there are important modifications before any laws are passed, your own accountant should be able to explain the relevant changes a few days after they are made.

It is also important to understand how to evaluate tax changes properly. Before becoming excited about a legislative amendment or an opportunity for planning, always compare the tax theory to the actual dollars of tax cost or saving, as the case may be.

In addition to saving taxes, I hope that you will learn *tax awareness* from this book. One thing I have learned over the years, is that there is no such thing as permanent or long-term investment policies. You must be aware that the economy fluctuates at all times and also cultivate political awareness. Perhaps, most important of all, you must learn to think in terms of after-tax dollars and discount additional income that you receive by the tax burden of earning it.

To take a common example, most of us who earn employment income from one source or another receive cost-of-living increases. If the cost of living goes up by 6% in one year, then a 6% raise is often received exclusive of merit increases. However, for most of us, a raise in pay will now translate on an after-tax basis to only about sixty cents on the dollar. Thus, our 6% cost-of-living increase becomes only 3½% in our pockets. It is true that to the extent that certain of our costs are fixed, we may be unaffected by increases in the cost of living. For example, how many of us envy our neighbours who have owned their homes for the last twenty or twenty-five years and were thus "immune" to the jump in house prices in the late 1970s? Nevertheless, 6% still equals 3½% – maybe not in mathematics but in "real life" arithmetic.

As you increase your understanding of the Canadian tax structure, you will also become aware that while certain loopholes have, in fact, been blocked, other valid opportunities for planning will always present themselves. Parliament giveth, Parliament taketh away . . .

CHAPTER 2

Minimize Your Salary and Maximize Your Benefits

Whether you own your own business or work for someone else, you probably derive at least a portion of your income from salary. In general, you should only draw as much salary as you need to meet your particular living requirements after income taxes. Once you earn sufficient salary to pay living expenses, the next step is to look for fringe benefits. These benefits can actually be worth more than a salary increase, since your employer can provide goods and services that you want without the full impact of taxes otherwise payable on an equivalent amount of salary.

This chapter will deal with some of the more common and readily available fringe-benefit programs you can obtain by virtue of employment. Naturally, if you are self-employed, you are more likely to be able to take advantage of these opportunities than if you have to ask someone else for them. However, as you will see, it is often advantageous for the employer as well to provide some of these benefits, because the cost may be less than salary or about the same.

However, you must be careful. While most fringe benefits are, in fact, benefits, remember their status is always subject to change. Thus, even if you have an established fringe-benefit package, you should review it annually to ensure that it is the right one under the circumstances. For example, the company car that was such a bonus a few years ago may no longer be a viable "perk" for many individuals. Because of the major tax changes in this area, I will deal with company cars first.

Company Cars

For many years the best benefit you could have obtained from employment was a company car – an automobile owned or rented by your employer, who covered all operating expenses as well. In order to enjoy this benefit, however, it was always important that each employee have at least some business requirement for the vehicle that would justify the cost to the company providing it.

Technically, Revenue Canada has always insisted that employees report a taxable benefit for personal use of a company car. In theory, a reasonable calculation of such a benefit would reflect any personal use operating expenses paid for by the employer. In 1972, however, in order to eliminate the complex bookkeeping required to segregate these costs on a car-by-car basis, the Income Tax Act adopted the concept of a minimum stand-by charge, that is, a benefit based on *availability* for personal use. Actually, two formulas were incorporated into the Income Tax Act. If an automobile was owned by the employer, the benefit was computed at 1% per month multiplied by the original cost of the car multiplied by the number of months of availability. If the car was leased, the computation took into account one-third of the monthly car rental (exclusive of insurance and maintenance) multiplied by the number of months of availability. These formulas were certainly straightforward and allowed Revenue authorities to easily verify the taxable benefits. The formulas took into account availability of the car for personal use, not actual use.

To understand why a company car was considered the best available fringe benefit in the 1970s, let's take some simple numbers and apply them to the minimum stand-by charge formula in use until 1982. For example, assume that a $15,000 car was owned by an employer and was available to a particular employee. Under the formula, the taxable benefit was $1,800 ($15,000 × 1% × 12 months). If the individual was in the 50% tax bracket and had $1,800 added to his or her income, the only annual cost was a maximum of $900. Therefore, for an out-of-pocket cost of only $75 a month, the employee had a $15,000 car available throughout the year for which the employer paid all the expenses. What better benefit could one ask for? Most executives were certainly willing to forgo increases in pay (which would be fully taxed) in favour of a $15,000 car at a cost of only $900 a year.

Unfortunately, the government saw fit, starting about ten years ago, to *double* the tax benefit under the minimum stand-by charge formulas. Where an automobile was owned by an employer, the benefit became 2%

of the capital cost of the car per month. If the automobile was leased, the benefit became two-thirds of the lease cost. There is one minor concession that applies if an employee uses a company car less than 1,000 kilometres a month for personal purposes and the car is used at least 90% for business. In such case, the formulas permit the employee to reduce the benefit for tax calculations. The workings of the stand-by charge formula are illustrated in Figure 2-1. The example assumes that a $15,000 car is owned by an employer and is provided to an employee throughout the year.

Figure 2–1   **If Automobile Is Owned by Employer**

	Case One	*Case Two*
Capital cost	$15,000	$15,000
Number of months available for employee's use	12	12
Total kilometres driven	16,000	24,000
Personal use in kilometres	1,600	12,000
Taxable benefit calculation*	$\dfrac{\$3,600 \times 1,600}{12,000}$	$\dfrac{\$3,600 \times 12,000}{12,000}$
Taxable benefit	$480	$3,600

Formula:

$$2\% \times \text{capital cost} \times \text{no. of months available} \times \frac{\text{no. of personal km. (max. 12,000)}}{1,000 \times \text{no. of mos.}}$$

You can see that in Case One, since the car is used only 10% of the time for personal purposes, the benefit is only $13\frac{1}{3}\%$ of the total maximum benefit of $3,600. In the second example, on the other hand, the full $3,600 has to be reported as income even though the automobile is only used half the time for personal purposes. This is because in Case Two the individual does in fact get a full 1,000 kilometres a month of personal use.

If the government had simply decided to double the taxable benefit under the formulas, most individuals would still probably consider a company car as the best available fringe benefit. However, the government also decided in 1982 that a stand-by charge or availability benefit is *not enough.* In addition to the formula computations, the actual use must also be considered where an employer pays an employee's operating expenses for personal use. In other words, the total taxable benefit is now the sum of *two* calculations – the stand-by charge as shown above *plus* an operating benefit. The operating benefit takes into account the actual operating expenses in relation to personal kilometres driven. Its workings are illustrated in the example in Figure 2-2.

Figure 2–2   **Effect of Second Tax on Company Cars**

Capital cost of automobile	$15,000
Total operating costs	$ 3,625
Number of months automobile available to employee/shareholder	12
Total kilometres driven for the period	24,000 km
Personal kilometres driven for the period	12,000 km

Operating benefit:

$$\frac{12,000 \text{ km}}{24,000 \text{ km}} \times \$3,625 = \qquad\qquad\qquad \$1,812.50$$

Stand-by charge:

$$\$15,000 \times 2\% \times 12 \text{ months} \times \frac{12,000 \text{ km}}{1,000 \text{ km} \times 12 \text{ mos}} = \qquad \underline{\$3,600.00}$$

Total benefit $\qquad\qquad\qquad\qquad\qquad\qquad$ $\underline{\underline{\$5,412.50}}$

Comparable benefit in 1981:

$$\$15,000 \times 1\% \times 12 \text{ months} = \qquad\qquad\qquad \underline{\underline{\$1,500.00}}$$

As you can see from this simple case study, the total benefit is $5,412.50 – almost four times as much as the equivalent benefit for 1981, when administrative practice was to refer to the stand-by charge alone (at that time 1% per month).

In 1984, the government introduced an optional alternative for calculating the taxable benefit pertaining to operating costs for a car provided by an employer to an employee or shareholder. Instead of calculating the actual benefit with reference to specific costs incurred and the actual personal distance driven, the operating benefit may be computed at the rate of 50% of the stand-by charge pertaining to that automobile. In other words, if the employer decides to ignore actual operating costs, the stand-by charge becomes 3% per month of the cost of the car (if the car is owned by the employer) multiplied by the number of months the car is available for personal use by the individual employee. For a leased car, the total taxable benefit becomes an amount *equal* to the rent paid by the employer, instead of two-thirds of this amount.

With this new alternative, the total taxable benefit calculated in Figure

2-2 would become $5,400 ($15,000 × 3% × 12) instead of $5,412,50, a difference of only $12.50.

Effective 1988, where an employer-owned motor vehicle is provided to an employee, the election to include in income an additional one-half stand-by charge for employer-paid operating expenses for the vehicle, in lieu of itemizing the expenses, is only available where the automobile is used at least 50% for business purposes.

Capital Cost Allowance (Tax Depreciation) Restrictions and Other Recent Tax Changes

Today, only the first $24,000 of the cost of a passenger vehicle used for business purposes is eligible for capital cost allowance. An equivalent reduction also applies for the deductibility of lease payments for passenger vehicles worth more than $24,000 at the time a lease is entered into. This rule basically restricts deductible lease payments to $650 a month. The actual formula is:

the lesser of:

(a) $650 per month; and

(b) $\dfrac{A \times \$24,000}{0.85\ B}$

where

A = actual lease costs for the year, and
B = the greater of: $28,235, and the
     manufacturer's list price for the
     automobile plus provincial sales tax.

The maximum deduction for carrying charges on money borrowed to purchase a passenger vehicle is also limited to $300 for each month during which the loan is outstanding. These rules apply to all passenger vehicles acquired after August 31, 1989. For vehicles acquired between June 17, 1987 and August 31, 1989, the limits were $20,000, $600, and $250 respectively. (Capital cost allowance on an automobile is 30% per annum on a declining balance basis, except in the year of acquisition when it is limited to one-half of the amount normally allowed.)

By definition, a "passenger vehicle" to which these rules apply generally includes automobiles, station wagons, and passenger vans designed to carry not more than nine persons and intended for use primarily on highways and streets. The definition does not include an ambulance or an automobile acquired primarily for use as a bus or taxi or in connection with funerals or a limousine or automobile acquired for hire in the course of a rental or leasing business.

If an Individual Uses His or Her Own Car for Business

In some cases, the taxable benefit from a "company car" may exceed the real value to an employee. This could happen if the employee uses the car primarily for business but also has, say only a 20%–30% personal usage. Such limited personal use should not really attract a full taxable benefit – but it does!

As an alternative, an employee can provide his or her own car and deduct business-related costs to the extent that they are not reimbursed. However, it is obviously to an employee's benefit to derive as much reimbursement as possible.

The Income Tax Act does, however, limit the amount of reimbursement that can be paid by an employer to an employee on a tax-free basis to whatever is "reasonable in the circumstances." While this amount may vary, depending on fluctuating gasoline prices, or perhaps road conditions, a reimbursement of around 25¢ per business kilometre would probably be accepted without any concerns.

In general, after August 31, 1989, an employer may not deduct reimbursements exceeding 31¢ per kilometre for the first 5,000 kilometres of business distance per employee per year and 25¢ per kilometre thereafter.

Tax-Planning Guidelines

In the next few pages, I would like to provide some guidelines for tax planning for three groups of individuals:

1. Employees
2. Self-Employed Taxpayers
3. Owner-Managers of Canadian-Controlled Private Corporations

Guidelines for Employees

Where an employee of a business must use an automobile in the performance of his or her duties, there are generally two possibilities. Either the business provides the individual with a company car or the individual uses his own vehicle. Where the individual provides the vehicle, it is likely that business expenses are reimbursed.

If the employee has some control to decide whether or not to accept a company car, comparative calculations should be made to determine if a company car is worthwhile. As I explained previously, where a company car is provided, there is a double taxable benefit. First, the minimum stand-by charge applies as a taxable benefit based on availability for personal use. The stand-by charge is 2% per month multiplied by the original cost of the car, multiplied by the number of months the car is available for personal use during the year. Thus, if a car is available evenings and weekends throughout the year, the stand-by charge becomes 24% of original cost (or two-thirds of the rent if the car is leased).

Over and above the stand-by charge, there is an operating benefit based on personal kilometres as a percentage of total kilometres, where the operating expenses for personal use are paid by the employer. As long as the car is used at least 50% for business use, a shortcut may be taken by having the operating benefit deemed equal to one-half the stand-by charge. In other words, in many instances, the total taxable benefit derived from a company car is either 3% per month of the original cost or the entire rent paid, in cases where the car is leased.

As an alternative, an employee can provide his or her own car and deduct business-related costs to the extent that they are not reimbursed. However, it is obviously to an employee's benefit to derive as much reimbursement as possible. This is because a reimbursement is worth one hundred cents on the dollar, while a deductible expense still costs at least fifty-five cents on the dollar (for an individual in a 45% tax bracket) after the recovery of taxes. As mentioned previously, reimbursements of 31¢ per kilometre for the first 5,000 kilometres of business distance driven and 25¢ per kilometre thereafter are considered reasonable. These amounts should be adequate to compensate an employee for both operating expenses and the portion of the cost of the car offsetting business-related depreciation.

Guidelines for Self-Employed Taxpayers

For someone who is self-employed and uses an automobile in the course of his or her business activities, there does not seem to be a whole lot of choice. This is because the self-employed person is a single entity and there is not the flexibility of being able to take into account the tax position of more than one taxpayer. The available expense deductions would be calculated based on business distance over total distance driven. Revenue Canada requires that a mileage log be kept to substantiate business usage. Beyond keeping such a record, my only concrete advice is that it would be extremely expensive today for a self-employed person to incur expenses in connection with a car costing more than $24,000 or leasing at more than $650 a month. One suggestion is that, if a self-employed person has two cars, he or she should try to use one of them almost exclusively for business purposes and use the other for personal driving.

Guidelines for Owner-Managers of Canadian-Controlled Private Corporations

Perhaps the greatest flexibility in tax planning is reserved for the owner-manager of the Canadian-controlled private corporation. A Canadian small business generally pays a tax of not more than 20% of its annual business profits of up to $200,000. Therefore, one alternative is to get the corporation to buy a company car for the owner-manager, using what might be termed "80¢ dollars." In terms of required "earning power," it would be a lot cheaper for the corporation to acquire a car than for an individual to buy the vehicle if his or her other income already results in a (top) 45% tax bracket. The individual would then only have "55¢ dollars" available to make the purchase.

As shown in Figure 2-3, a business can afford to pay for a $15,000 car using only $18,750 of "earning power." The individual owner would, on the other hand, need around $27,000 of additional gross salary (assuming he or she is already in a 45% tax bracket) to net the same $15,000. So there is a tremendous saving in earning power if you own a business and the corporation purchases a car.

Figure 2–3   **Pre-Tax Dollars Required to Purchase $15,000 Car**

	Gross Earnings	Taxes Payable	Net Cash Flow for Car
Ownership by corporation in most provinces	$18,750	$ 3,750 (20%)	$15,000
Ownership by individual	$27,000	$12,000 (45%)	$15,000

Where, however, an owner-manager wants to drive an expensive vehicle, a significant tax problem arises. Specifically, the corporation will be limited to capital cost allowance on the first $24,000 of purchase cost while the taxable benefit for purposes of the stand-by charge calculations will be based on actual costs. The corporation will be permitted to deduct all operating expenses, although the individual will have to pay tax on the personal portion. Nevertheless, the opportunity to acquire an automobile using "80¢ dollars" is still quite attractive.

There is, however, a possibly more viable alternative, and that is for the corporation to *lend* after-tax retained earnings to the individual owner-manager to buy his or her *own* car. As long as the car is used by the individual in the performance of his or her duties as an employee of the corporation, Canadian tax law allows a car loan to a shareholder-manager to be repaid over a reasonable period of time. This would probably be between three and five years. (Loans to employees and shareholders are discussed further on in this chapter.)

A loan to buy a personal car would provide today's dollars to the individual, although the repayment would be made with dollars that would presumably be worth somewhat less because of inflation. The individual owner-manager would have to take into income each year a taxable benefit based on the amount of the loan outstanding multiplied by the prescribed rate of interest (which is presently 8%). Over and above the taxable benefit from "imputed interest," under the scenario where the company lends money to the owner-manager, the individual would pay all operating expenses for both business and personal use. However, he or she could then charge the employer a reasonable amount for reimbursement. Again, if the company pays between 25¢ and 31¢ per kilometre for business usage, this would be considered a tax-deductible and reasonable allowance. Over a three- or four-year period, the owner-manager could then pay off a substantial portion of the car loan by offsetting the debt against the charge made to the employer for business usage.

As is the case with an employee, it would now certainly pay to make comparative calculations. Is it more advantageous for the individual owner-manager to have a company car, resulting in a double taxable benefit along with CCA restrictions at the corporate level, or should the individual borrow money and provide his or her own car? Again, under this alternative, the individual would not attempt to write off any expenses but would simply amortize part of this loan (with imputed interest costs) and pay operating expenses out of a kilometre charge to the corporation.

While providing guidelines is a relatively straightforward exercise, an actual decision cannot be made without a detailed analysis that compares alternative costs on a case-by-case basis.

For larger companies, it would generally be more expedient for the owners to lease automobiles for key executives, as long as each car's value does not exceed $24,000. The employees could sign agreements stating that in the event of resignation or dismissal, they would assume the balance of the leases. (If an employee is not financially stable, the company would presumably withhold this benefit.) Since turnover is greater among new staff, company cars could be reserved for employees who have attained high income levels and a certain length of service.

More on Tax Planning for Company Cars

Depending on how much business driving you do relative to your personal use, your employer (or your own company) may still want to provide you with a company car. If so, there are several other planning points you should consider. First, if your lifestyle is such that you take an annual one-month vacation and you leave your company car at home, I suggest you park it in the employer's parking lot instead. Under these circumstances, the car cannot be said to be available for personal use during the time you are away on holiday. It appears to me that you are entitled to approach your employer to have your taxable benefit recalculated accordingly. Similarly, if your job requires you to travel extensively and you leave your car for several days at a time at an airport parking lot, you are also entitled to have your benefit reduced since, on those days, the vehicle cannot be said to be available for personal use.

Consider, as well, your position if you are driving a company-owned car that is several years old. Remember that the benefit for tax purposes is based on original cost. It might pay to have the employer sell the car to a leasing company at book value (cost minus depreciation) and lease it back for a further two or three years at a relatively cheap rate. Your taxable benefit will then be based on the leasing cost instead of the original cost.

Another interesting opportunity for effective tax planning is to buy a company car at the cheapest price possible and to settle for a reduced trade-in value. For example, what if your employer is buying you a $24,000 car and is entitled to a $9,000 trade-in on your old company vehicle? In these circumstances, the car dealer must receive a cheque for $15,000 to complete the purchase. Why not structure the deal so that the new car costs only $20,000 and a mere $5,000 trade-in allowance is provided for the old one? If this is done, the dealer would still receive $15,000 in cash but your taxable benefit would now be based on a car that has a smaller cost. Of course, you must use some discretion. I would not recommend that the dealer actually sell the new vehicle to the business for less than cost.

Loans to Employees and Shareholders

In the last section, I touched briefly on the idea of having a corporation lend money to an individual to buy a car to be used, at least partially for business. Now, I would like to explore the topic of loans to employees and shareholders in more detail.

If a business makes a loan to an employee, there are no requirements in the Income Tax Act governing the repayment of that loan within any specific time – as long as the employee is not a shareholder of the corporation. Thus, a loan from an employer to an employee can be made for an indefinite period and can remain outstanding as long as both parties agree. If the loan is ever forgiven, the forgiveness of debt would, at that time, create income from employment.

Where an employee is also a shareholder, there are, however, some very strict repayment rules that apply when a loan is made. The reason for these rules is that the government does not want shareholders borrowing money initially taxed at comparatively low corporate rates without the imposition of personal taxes. In the absence of any special rules, a corporation with profits of $10,000 would have around $8,000 of funds available for shareholders' loans after paying Revenue Canada taxes of about 20% of its profits.

The general rule on shareholder loans is that if a loan is outstanding on two successive year-end balance sheets of a company, it is *retroactively* included in the shareholder's income. Thus, the maximum length of time that a loan can remain unpaid is two years less one day. (The "two years less one day" would only apply if the loan is taken out on the first day of a company's fiscal year.)

You cannot subvert the system by simply repaying a loan just before the deadline and borrowing back the funds. Other provisions within the Tax Act provide that a "series of loans and repayments" is equivalent to not having repaid the loan at all. In addition, you cannot have various family members take loans to extend the length of the borrowing. A loan to a member of a shareholder's family becomes the equivalent of a loan to the shareholder directly.

There are four specific exceptions to the above rules, which provide a shareholder with an opportunity to borrow money for an extended period of time. These exceptions are:

- A loan made in the ordinary course of business by a corporation whose ordinary business consists of making loans.
- A loan made to a shareholder who is also an employee to acquire shares of the corporation out of treasury (i.e., previously unissued shares) under a stock-option or stock-purchase plan.
- A loan to acquire an automobile to be used by a shareholder-employee in the performance of his or her duties.
- A loan to a shareholder-employee to acquire or construct a house to live in.

In all cases, the Income Tax Act requires that a reasonable repayment schedule be decided upon at the time the loan is made and that it be subsequently followed.

The first exception is of limited significance. It is in the Act in order to prevent unfair tax treatment of an individual who borrows money from a chartered bank in which he or she has a few shares. Thus, if I deal with the Royal Bank of Canada and borrow $40,000 for business purposes, it would be somewhat ridiculous for me to have to consider that amount as income if, by coincidence, I have one hundred shares of Royal Bank stock in my investment portfolio.

The second exception, however, is very important when it comes to "buying into" a business – whether that business is privately owned or whether the stock-option or purchase plan involves a public company. It appears that the government wants to encourage employees to become shareholders of (or extend their shareholdings in) corporations that employ them. Thus where a corporation makes a loan for this purpose, a reasonable period may be used in order to effect repayment. It must be stressed, however, that the exception applies only to *previously unissued shares* and not to shares acquired by an individual from another shareholder.

Until recently, the third exception has been of minor significance because the greatest benefit from employment was always a company car. Thus, a loan to an individual to buy his or her *own* car was of limited use. However, as explained previously, a company car will now result in a double taxable benefit, one based on availability and the second based on use. For many Canadians, the balance now swings over in favour of personal ownership. In these circumstances, the employer could lend the individual money to buy a car – even if he or she is a shareholder – and the employee could then charge the business for actual business use.

While the value of loans for cars must be assessed on a case-by-case basis, it is clear that the best tax deal emanates from the fourth exception, which is a housing loan. The first advantage of such a loan arises because corporate tax rates tend to be significantly less than personal rates. Where the employer is a privately owned corporation, around eighty cents out of each dollar of profits up to $200,000 a year is left over after tax. These funds can be used as an advance to the owner-manager for purposes of buying or building a home. This is much cheaper than using approximately fifty-five cents out of each dollar of after-tax *personal* earnings.

Figure 2–4   **House-Purchase Alternatives**

Personal after-tax funds:

Salary to shareholder-employee	$100,000
Less: Personal taxes of 45%	45,000
After-tax funds available to purchase a home	$ 55,000

Corporate after-tax funds:

Earnings taxed in corporation	$100,000
Less: Corporate taxes of 20%	20,000
After-tax funds available to shareholder as a loan for a home	$ 80,000

The second advantage is that the employee-shareholder gets the use of corporate dollars *today,* which he or she must repay over a period of time, presumably with "cheaper" dollars because of inflation. A reasonable repayment program for the principal portion might be ten or fifteen years.

If you own a controlling interest in an incorporated business, I suggest that you speak to your advisers with regard to such a loan *before* you purchase or build any residence. The residence need not be a city home. A country house (or second home) will also qualify, as long as it will be owned primarily for personal use and could not be construed as a rental property.

Note that this very generous provision in the Income Tax Act permitting such a loan applies only in situations where a house is being built or bought. It does not apply to the refinancing of your present home. However, if your intention is to make a major extension to an existing residence, it may be possible to get an advance ruling from Revenue Canada allowing a company loan for that purpose under the same favourable tax conditions.

"Imputed" Interest on Loans

Before 1979, I would have classified a non-interest-bearing or low-interest loan as the best of the employment benefits. This is because there was no requirement that interest be charged on loans to either employees or shareholders – or that interest be calculated as a taxable benefit. All this changed on January 1, 1979, and further modifications were made in 1982.

According to the current rules, if interest is not charged by an employer, it must be calculated at a set rate adjusted quarterly based on prevailing treasury-bill rates and added on to the T-4 slip as a taxable benefit. During most of the last few years, the prescribed rate of interest was between 9% and 14%.

Where a loan is used for the purpose of acquiring shares in the employer's company under a stock option or stock purchase plan, the requirement to treat calculated interest as a taxable benefit does not really present any hardship. This is because interest calculated as a taxable benefit on share-purchase loans also qualifies as a tax-deductible carrying charge against the investment itself. Therefore there is no net tax cost as a result of such a loan.

There are also special rules that apply when an individual receives an interest-free or low-interest housing loan (i.e., at a rate lower than the prescribed rate) to assist the employee in relocating to maintain employment or to begin a new job. Under these provisions the taxable benefit is calculated as the difference between the prescribed rate and the interest rate actually charged, multiplied by the amount of the outstanding loan. However the calculated interest on the first $25,000 is exempt from tax for the first five years of the loan. The exemption applies in the same circumstances as the tax rules governing the deduction of moving expenses. These require the new residence to be at least 40 kilometres closer to the new job than the old residence.

Where housing loans are made in circumstances other than employee relocation, there is a taxable benefit. However, if a loan actually bears interest at prevailing market levels, a taxable benefit will not apply.

Let's now look at housing loans other than those specifically for relocation.

Planning for Housing Loans

Remember that at the time the government introduced the tax changes on housing loans about ten years ago, interest rates were moving up. As a result, the legislation brought in a rather important alternative to simply receiving a taxable benefit. These rules provide that there is no taxable benefit if the rate of interest on a housing loan is equal to or greater than the prescribed rate of interest in effect *at the time the loan was made*. This would protect the individual from increases in interest rates after the loan is received. However, if the term of a loan is greater than five years, the tax-exempt status of the loan with respect to interest is adjusted to the then current prescribed rate at the end of each five-year period.

These provisions now set the stage for some interesting tax planning. As we move further into this decade, general interest rates have now declined to the point that the taxable-benefit calculation rate is only around 8%–12%. The chances of a substantial decline in interest rates below today's level appear quite remote; it is more likely that over the next few years interest rates will escalate as the government is forced to borrow more and more money to meet its rising deficits.

In the past, most individuals have chosen to live with the taxable benefit without paying any interest to their employers. A few years ago, at the time when the rate of calculated interest was 16%, the common thinking was that paying 8% out-of-pocket in taxes (16% multiplied by 50% tax bracket) was preferable to actually paying non-deductible interest to an employer. In fact, this was the planning which I recommended in some of the earlier editions of this book. Now, however, it appears to me that this thinking is obsolete.

By definition, a home-purchase loan includes not only a loan made to an employee or shareholder to acquire a home, but also a loan made to repay a loan or debt to acquire a home in the first place. In other words, a loan made to *replace* a home-purchase loan is itself treated as a home-purchase loan.

Suppose you are an individual in a 45% tax bracket and you have a $50,000 non-interest-bearing loan towards the purchase of your home. If the calculated interest rate stabilizes at 11%, your annual taxable benefit becomes $5,500 and your out-of-pocket tax cost is $2,475. Let's say you now renegotiate your home-purchase loan for a five-year period and actually agree to pay to your employer $5,500 a year – the going rate of interest at the time the loan is renegotiated. At the same time, your employer gives you a $5,500 raise in pay.

From your employer's perspective, the $5,500 interest income and $5,500 additional salary expense offset one another. However, from your point of view, the $5,500 increased salary represents a net take-home pay of $3,025, although you would then be laying out $5,500 of after-tax money to pay the interest on your loan. When the smoke clears, you are still out-of-pocket $2,475. This is the same exact amount that you would be paying if you continued to submit to a $5,500 annual taxable benefit on which your tax liability is 45%.

In other words, matching a loan payment to your employer with an equivalent raise in pay produces no adverse tax consequences to the employer and the net after-tax cost to you, the employee, is the same. What, then, is the advantage? It will simply *stabilize the actual tax cost of the loan to acquire your house for the next five years.* Thus, for example, if interest rates move back up to 16%, you would not have to worry about an $8,000 taxable benefit (16% × $50,000) and a $3,600 tax bite (45% × $8,000) in comparison to a cost of only $2,475.

Figure 2–5   **Home-Purchase Loan Alternatives**

Alternative 1

Interest-free loan of	$50,000
Taxable benefit (11%)	$ 5,500
Out-of-pocket cost (45% × $5,500)	$ 2,475

Alternative 2

Interest-bearing loan at 11% of	$50,000
Interest charged by employer (non-deductible)	$ 5,500
Net proceeds from $5,500 raise (55% × $5,500)	(3,025)
Out-of-pocket cost	$ 2,475

Employer's position

Interest received	$ 5,500
Raise in pay to employee	(5,500)
Net effect	Nil

Of course, no one knows for certain in which direction interest rates are going to move. If the calculated or imputed rate drops as low as 6%, you might be a bit unhappy because you would now be overpaying. On the other hand, there does not appear to be any restriction against a further (downward) renegotiation for a five-year period beginning at that time. And yet, as I mentioned previously, what if rates go back up to 16%,

18%, or even 20%? The opportunity to stabilize your out-of-pocket cost should be well worth your while. This is illustrated in Figure 2-5 above.

Private Health-Care Programs

One of the most common and yet valuable fringe-benefit programs is an employer-sponsored private health-care (including dental services) package. Under such a program, the employer pays for insurance, which reimburses the employee if his or her family incurs medical or dental expenses not covered under provincial medicare. Such costs could include prescription drugs, eye glasses, and dental care. In 1981, the government proposed that employer contributions to such programs would become taxable. Because of public outcry, however, this proposal was retracted.

A private health-care program thus continues to be a valuable benefit for two reasons. First, the cost of group coverage for insurance is much cheaper than personal coverage. Second, where an individual pays the costs of medical or dental services (not covered by medicare) the payments are only considered for tax purposes to the extent that they exceed the lesser of around $1,500 and 3% of annual net income. Thus, most Canadians would not obtain worthwhile tax relief from medical expenses if these were paid for personally. In addition, remember one of the cardinal rules of tax planning – *a reimbursed expense is worth a hundred cents on the dollar while a tax-deductible expenditure only results in a recovery of slightly less than half the outlay.*

Holiday Trips, Including Travel Expenses
for an Employee's Spouse

Revenue Canada officials take the position that the value of a holiday trip, prize, or incentive award must be included in an employee's income as a fringe benefit – even if the person paying the costs is a customer or supplier of the employer. Travel benefits include the expenses of an employee's spouse as well. However, within this rather general framework there are a number of exceptions. The most important would be the case where a holiday trip can be combined with a valid business purpose. Where a business purpose exists, the taxable benefit can be reduced or even almost eliminated in some cases.

A friend of mine who is a chartered accountant was asked by a Canadian client of his to prepare a report on the tax consequences of investing

in U.S. real estate. My friend informed his client that although a significant amount of research could be done from Canada, it would still be
advantageous for him to meet with a tax accountant or lawyer based in
the United States to discuss some of the finer points involved. The client
readily agreed. It so happened that my friend was invited to a family wed-
ding in Los Angeles that was scheduled to take place within the following month. It doesn't take much imagination to guess where my friend
made arrangements to meet with a qualified U.S. tax practitioner.

Another case involves a privately owned real-estate-brokerage house,
which has offices in major cities in both Canada and the United States.
This firm services many clients from both Europe and the Orient who
want to invest in North American real estate. For several years, this particular company has had a policy of providing a rather interesting fringe
benefit to employees. Each year, commissioned salespeople who reach
their quotas are rewarded with free trips. In year one, the employees
based in western Canada go east while the eastern employees go west. In
year two, the Canadian employees go south to the United States while the
U.S. employees come north to Canada. In year three, the trip is to Europe,
in year four to the Orient, and in year five to Hawaii.

In each case, the employee is required to file a detailed report on his or
her return. The report must compare real estate prices in the places that he
or she has been to those at home, and the employee must, as well, list con-
tacts that he or she has made in the other city or cities. These reports are
kept on file by the company. Not long ago, Revenue Canada officials did
an audit at the company's head office. They proposed to allow the first
four trips as being for business only, without any taxable-benefit implications, while they decided that the fifth years's trip to Hawaii should be
treated as a fully taxable benefit.

The company objected on behalf of its employees, stating that many
investors are buying real estate in Hawaii and that there is as much business justification for that trip as there is to one anywhere else. At one
point, the company's controller asked my advice. I suggested that the
company back off and allow its employees to be taxed on the value of the
Hawaiian trip. My reasoning was simply that even if they could convince
Revenue Canada to allow, say, 30% as being for business purposes, the
authorities could just as easily change their minds and contend that 40%
or 50% of the other four trips was for pleasure. Sometimes, a compromise with Revenue Canada officials will save more in the long run –
especially when one takes into account the professional fees incurred in
handling a dispute. I don't know if the controller took my advice, but in

any event, my message should be clear. Wherever possible, combine business and pleasure. As a general rule, I suggest that you avoid business meetings in both Florida and Hawaii since Revenue Canada appears to take a very negative attitude to expenditures incurred in these two locations.

If you take your spouse on a business trip, Revenue Canada's general outlook is that the costs of taking the spouse are a taxable benefit. The exception is where your spouse accompanies you at the specific request of your employer and primarily for purposes of enhancing the employer's business efforts. In this case you should obtain written instructions from your employer requiring you to bring your spouse on a trip. The letter should indicate that it is anticipated that there will be meetings in the evenings involving customers, clients, or suppliers and their spouses, and that your spouse is expected to contribute to these meetings by promoting the employer's activities. This letter could be extremely useful during a subsequent Revenue Canada audit – but it will only work where there is an arm's-length relationship between you and the employer. This means you cannot be related by blood, marriage, or adoption. If an employee also happens to own the business, there is no great advantage in getting the individual in his capacity as president of the company to sit down and write himself a letter requiring that he take his own spouse away on business.

When it comes to the employer paying the cost of bringing spouses along to conventions, Revenue Canada's attitude appears to be somewhat mixed. In many cases, the authorities will add on taxable benefits when participants take their spouses along, although, in recent years, many organizations seem to have been making efforts to eliminate or reduce the tax exposure. Most convention agendas now make bona fide attempts to include the spouses of participants in business-related sessions. At one convention where I was a speaker, there was a specific program for spouses on stress management. At another convention, a former colleague of mine from the University of Calgary spoke to the association members' spouses on how to interpret financial statements of small businesses. Many of my own programs on personal financial planning are suitable for both spouses.

New Rules for Business Meals
and Entertainment Expenses

Government tax policy reflects the fact that business meals and entertainment also involve an element of personal consumption and, therefore, some part of their cost should properly be characterized as a personal and/or non-deductible expense. Thus, the deduction for business meals (including food and beverages) and entertainment expenses (such as accommodations at a resort and tickets for the theatre, a concert, athletic event or other performance), is limited to 80% of their cost.

The 80% limitation also applies to gratuities, cover charges, room rentals at a hotel or a resort to provide entertainment, and the costs of private boxes at sports facilities. As well, the tax restrictions apply to the cost of meals while travelling to attend a convention, conference, seminar, or similar function. To the extent that an individual is reimbursed for the business meal or entertainment, the 80% limitation applies to the person who makes the reimbursement. As an alternative to the 80% limitation, employers have the option of including 20% of meals and entertainment costs as a taxable benefit to their employees. In cases where food, beverages, and entertainment expenses at a conference, seminar, or convention are not specifically detailed as part of the fee, the regulations deem $50 to be the actual cost of food, beverages, and entertainment for each day of the event. Thus, $10 per day is considered as either a disallowed business expense or as a taxable benefit.

You should note that the 80% limitation on business meals and entertainment expenses does not apply to the costs of meals or recreational events provided by an employer for the general benefit of all employees or to the cost of a restaurant, hotel, or airline of providing meals to customers in the ordinary course of business. Another exception applies for meals and entertainment expenses related to an event where the primary purpose is to benefit a registered charity.

While most (high-bracket) individuals are not particularly happy with these rules, you should note that 80% of legitimate entertainment and promotion costs continue to be tax deductible.

If you ascribe to the old adage that "misery loves company," note that similar restrictions on business-related entertainment expenses also apply in the United States, Australia, and the United Kingdom.

Discounts on Merchandise Ordinarily Sold
by an Employer

If you obtain a discount on merchandise ordinarily sold by your employer, Revenue Canada does not require you to include the value of that discount in your income. Presumably, keeping track of such discounts would involve an effort more costly than the dollars lost to the government coffers. Thus, if you are in a position to take advantage of such discounts because, for example, you work for a retail company, feel free to do so.

Note, however, that special rules have always applied to the construction industry. Where an executive is able to acquire a home built by his or her employer, and the cost is less than its fair market value, most of the District Taxation Offices try to label a portion of the difference as a taxable benefit. The amount of the benefit is, of course, subject to negotiation. If you work in the construction industry and are able to benefit from the purchase of a company-built home, avoid any disputes by purchasing at a price that would give your employer at least a small profit margin.

While on the subject of construction companies, I strongly suggest that you stay away from the practice of letting your company pay for improvements to your own residence while charging off the cost of these expenditures against job-construction projects. Anybody who does something of this nature is committing fraud, which is punishable by severe penalties.

Recreational Facilities and Club-Membership Dues

In an attempt to cut back on expense-account living, Parliament passed a law twenty years ago prohibiting the deduction as a business expense of membership fees in any club providing dining, recreational, and sporting facilities. Thus, if an employer pays these membership fees, they are non-deductible even if the facilities are used for proper business entertainment and promotion. Although the membership fees are automatically disallowed, house accounts (for green fees or the actual cost of meals and beverages) are at least 80% tax-deductible if it can be shown that these specific accounts arose in the course of business entertainment.

When the above rules were brought in, Revenue Canada was faced with an administrative dilemma. If the department were to adopt the policy of taxing these memberships as a benefit to individual employees, then a double-tax situation would arise. (This results any time an expense is disallowed to an employer, while the outlay is also taxed as a benefit to an individual.) In order to circumvent double taxation, Revenue Canada issued an Interpretation Bulletin exempting employees from having to include these benefits in income. Officially, the exemption only applies where an employee uses the facilities *primarily* to further the employer's business objectives. Administratively, however, it appears that the department has taken a rather lax approach in enforcement. Therefore, club memberships paid for by a company can be an excellent benefit for senior executives. This is especially true where the individual is in a substantially higher tax bracket than the corporation that employs him or her.

The benefit is even greater where the individual happens to be a major shareholder of the company as well. Again, as is the case with company cars, less earning power is needed to pay for a club membership on an after-tax basis where the corporation bears the cost. This is illustrated in Figure 2-6.

Figure 2–6   **Pre-Tax Earnings Needed to Pay Club-Membership Dues of $800**

Personal Earnings:	
Salary to individual	$1,450
Less: Incremental taxes at assumed 45% marginal bracket	650
After-tax funds for membership dues	$ 800
Corporate Earnings:	
Profit retained by small-business corporation	$1,000
Less: Taxes at 20%	200
After-tax funds for membership dues	$ 800

Stock-Option and Stock-Purchase Plans

Where an individual is employed by a *public* corporation and the individual obtains the right to acquire shares of his or her employer company out of treasury, the tax rules consider this to be an employment benefit. Until 1984, the amount to be added to income was the *full* difference between the price to be paid for the shares and their fair market value at the date the employee exercised his or her option. (The fair market value of the shares on the date the option was granted was not relevant for tax purposes.) This can be illustrated by a simple example:

Fair market value of each share	
at the time the option is exercised	$20.00
Less: Option price to be paid	14.00
Benefit from employment (per share)	$ 6.00

Any further appreciation in value was treated as a capital gain.

For stock option programs initiated after February 15, 1984, by public corporations, the taxable benefit on the eventual exercise is now limited to *three-quarters* of the difference between the option price and the fair market value of the shares at the time the option is exercised. This reduces the tax cost of a stock option program compared to the rules applicable to previous plans. The new rules apply *provided the exercise price for the shares is not less than their fair market value at the time the option was granted.*

Technically, the full amount of an option benefit, even for "new plans," has to be included as part of income from employment. However, there is a deduction in arriving at taxable income equal to one-quarter of the stock option benefit included in computing income from employment in the first place. This is provided that all the other conditions referred to in the last paragraph apply.

Where the option is for shares in a public corporation, the fact that a taxable benefit arises is not too onerous. These shares generally tend to be marketable and it is usually possible for some of the shares to be sold in order to pay taxes on the benefit. In addition, since these shares are saleable, an employee can often borrow money to pay the taxes by using the shares as collateral.

Stock-option plans are thus quite attractive for employees of public companies who are able to acquire shares at less than the going trading price. Although the individual must contend with a taxable benefit at the time the option is exercised, any future growth beyond that point is treated as a capital gain – only three-quarters of which is potentially taxable. A capital gain will only arise at the time the shares are sold, and the gain may in fact be insulated from tax by using the lifetime capital gains exemption. (See Chapter Six.)

During the early 1970s stock-option programs were rarely, if ever, used with respect to *private* corporations. This was for two major reasons:

- Shares of private companies are not marketable. Thus, an employee cannot sell some of his or her shares to pay taxes.

- Shares of private companies are not readily pledged as collateral for bank financing. Accordingly, an individual faced with a tax liability would be hard-pressed to borrow against his or her shares for the purpose of making payment.

In mid-1977, however, Parliament decided for the first time to differentiate between option plans granted by public corporations and option plans of Canadian-controlled private companies. An employee of a private company is now permitted to buy (previously unissued) treasury shares at literally *any price* from one dollar up to fair market value. As long as the employee continues to hold these shares in his or her own name for at least two years after the date of acquisition, no taxable benefit need be calculated. The only tax consequences that will arise occur at the time of sale. Three-quarters of the difference between the actual purchase price and the selling price becomes taxable at that time. Part of this amount (the growth in value after the shares are actually purchased) will be treated as a capital gain eligible for the lifetime exemption.

Thus, it is theoretically possible for key employees of Canadian-controlled private corporations to acquire substantial interests in their employer companies for as little as one dollar. The only requirement that must be adhered to (in addition to the two-year minimum holding period) is that the employees must deal at arm's length with the controlling shareholder or shareholders. Because of the very generous tax treatment afforded employees of Canadian private companies, a share-interest in the business is definitely one of the key benefits to be negotiated wherever possible.

From the standpoint of the controlling shareholder, admission of key employees as "partners" can be a very viable alternative to an outright sale. Consider, for example, the case where a person has built up a business and now wishes to retire. Unfortunately, no one within the family wants to assume the responsibilities of administration. The owner could, in such circumstances, issue sufficient shares to one or more key employees so that they wind up with, say, 25% of the equity. These key employees would remain as custodians and would receive salaries for their continued efforts. In addition, if the business does well, 25% of the profits from all future growth will accrue to their benefit, while the rest of the profits would remain within the family of the retired owner.

Disability Insurance

If an employer pays for disability insurance on behalf of an employee, there need not be any taxable benefit reported at that time. However, if the employee is ever disabled, he or she will pay tax on the disability benefits received.

However, if the employer chooses to add the disability premiums to an employee's income as a taxable benefit or forces the employee to pay them directly, this is also acceptable. In such circumstances, any disability benefits received are tax-free.

Often the employer pays the cost of short-term disability insurance (i.e., up to six months' protection) while employees pay for long-term coverage. This ensures the receipt of tax-free income in the event of a long-term illness.

Financial and Other Counselling Benefits

Employers sometimes pay for the cost of financial and other counselling benefits on behalf of employees. Revenue Canada issued an Interpretation Bulletin several years ago that exempts group financial counselling (such as seminar participation) from inclusion as a taxable benefit. However, the costs applicable to personal financial counselling (including preparation of personal tax returns) must be added to an employee's income if payment has been made by an employer.

On the other hand, three types of counselling services paid or provided for by an employer specifically do *not* have to be taken into account in calculating employment income. These are:

1. Counselling in respect of an employee's physical or mental health,
2. Re-employment counselling for employees whose employment is being terminated, and
3. Retirement counselling for employees age fifty or older, or where the counselling is given in any two-year period that includes the employee's retirement date.

Such services as tobacco, drug, or alcohol counselling, stress management counselling, and job placement and retirement counselling are also not treated as taxable benefits.

Other Benefits

Two other fringe benefits that should be considered are travel passes and discount rates for transportation-company employees and subsidized board and lodging in remote work locations. While at one point the government proposed to tax these benefits, they subsequently backtracked, and these perks essentially remain non-taxable. Airline passes available to airline employees are now only taxable if the employee travels on a space-confirmed basis and pays less than 50% of the economy fare available on that carrier for that trip on that day of travel. The value of the benefit is the difference between 50% of the economy airfare and any amount reimbursed to the carrier for that trip. Employees of bus and rail companies are not, however, taxed on the use of passes. Moreover, retired employees of transportation companies are not taxed on pass benefits under any circumstances. An employee in the travel industry is certainly better off with a "cheap" holiday as a bonus instead of using a fully-taxed raise in pay to subsidize a vacation.

Similarly, there is also an excellent incentive for an engineer or other highly skilled employee to accept an assignment in a smaller community where large industrial plants or resource-development facilities are located. Such an individual would be well advised to negotiate a smaller salary in exchange for subsidized board and lodging.

Where an employer owns a vacation property which is used by an employee, it is the opinion of Revenue Canada that the taxable benefit is the amount that the employee would have had to pay a third party for equivalent accommodation less any amount the employee actually pays to the employer. The authorities do recognize that the taxable benefit may be reduced where there is conclusive evidence to substantiate that the employee was involved in direct business activities during the holiday or vacation.

Getting the Competitive Edge

There are many opportunities to capitalize on the differences between the tax rules pertaining to an employee's income and those pertaining to an employer's income. For example, certain expenses are at least 80% tax-deductible when incurred by an employer but are not deductible at all to employed individuals. Although it is difficult to generalize, a concrete example should serve to make this point.

Convention Expenses

Under the tax rules, convention expenses are not a proper deduction in arriving at employment income. Thus, for example, when an individual attends a trade or professional convention and bears the cost personally, these expenses would not be deductible unless the individual is self-employed.

Consider an individual who wishes to attend a particular trade or professional conference. He or she asks an employer to subsidize the costs, but the employer refuses on the grounds that it is contrary to company policy. The employer, however, says that the employee may go if he or she is willing to take the time off as part of the annual vacation. If the employee is tax conscious, he or she should then suggest that the employer pay the costs of the convention and reduce his or her salary accordingly.

From an employer's standpoint, it makes no difference whether an amount is paid as a salary or as a convention expense. The full payment in either case can be written off for tax purposes although 20% of meal costs will have to be reported as a taxable benefit to the employee. However, where an employer pays convention costs and reduces an employee's salary, the employee gets a much smaller amount reported on his or her T-4 slip than the full-value of equivalent salary. Having less income to report in the first place is equivalent to having a higher income offset by a tax-deductible expense.

This is a prime example of getting the competitive edge – finding a situation where an expense is deductible to an employer that would not be deductible to an individual employee.

Tax Avoidance Versus Tax Evasion

The previous example falls under the definition of effective tax *avoidance*. There is nothing fraudulent about arranging your affairs to produce the smallest tax bite possible in any given circumstances. There is, however, a fine line of distinction between tax avoidance and tax evasion. Evasion is something that you should stay away from since this is an offence punishable under both common and criminal law. To illustrate the difference, here is a short story outlining one of my favourite examples of evasion.

There is a privately owned appliance store that operates in a major

Canadian city. Over a period of twenty or twenty-five years the owner of that store got to know his regular customers quite well, and he eventually came up with a very interesting idea for promoting sales. When a customer who owned a business came in to buy, say, a television set for personal use, the store owner would approach him or her with the suggestion that he could invoice the television to the customer's business as an air-conditioning unit. The customer's business could then pay for the set and could also obtain a tax write-off through future depreciation. From the appliance dealer's standpoint it wouldn't make any difference to his cash flow, but from the customer's position, getting a company to pay (on a tax-deductible basis) for a personal expenditure would be an excellent benefit.

Somehow or other, Revenue officials caught on to what was happening. They did an audit of the appliance dealer's operations and compared sales invoices to related shipping documentation. Naturally, the discrepancy became apparent. The invoices described air conditioners sold to companies while the shipping documentation was for television sets delivered to personal residences. Both the appliance dealer and all the customers who had participated in this particular venture lived to regret this little scheme.

Tax fraud is, of course, subject to severe penalties. Granted, it is often difficult for a layperson to differentiate between permissible avoidance and punishable evasion. Usually, if you are in doubt, listen to your stomach. The more queasy you feel about a particular manoeuvre, the more likely it is that you are crossing over into forbidden territory. When in doubt, consult your own advisers. That is one of the reasons you have them. In the meantime, use your imagination. I am sure that most business owners and executives can find ways to get that competitive edge *legitimately.*

CHAPTER 3

Tax Planning for the Commissioned Salesperson

There are several strategies that commissioned salespeople can use when planning their affairs so that they take maximum advantage of the Canadian tax rules for the recording of income and expenses. In this chapter, strategies are discussed for commissioned salespersons who are employed as well as those who are self-employed. Strategies are also outlined very briefly for the self-employed commissioned salesperson who may be able to benefit from incorporating his or her activities. These latter considerations will be discussed in much more detail in Chapter Eleven.

Employment Versus Self-Employment

Tax planning for the individual who receives income from commissions must start with a determination of whether the person is employed or self-employed. It is important that this be decided, because if you are self-employed, you do not necessarily have to report your income on a calendar-year basis. If you are considered to be carrying on your own business, you can initially pick any year end that you want, as long as you are then consistent in following years. As I explain further on, this allows for regular tax deferrals. Also, if you are self-employed, the Income Tax Act tends to provide much more liberal expense deductions than if you are an employee. So, again, the first and perhaps key distinction is to determine whether you are an employee or an independent contractor.

If you are considered an employee, the company for which you work is required to deduct Canada or Quebec Pension Plan contributions as well as Unemployment Insurance premiums. If there is any problem in determining your status, you are allowed to request a specific ruling, which is valid not only for Canada Pension and Unemployment Insurance but also for income-tax purposes. To make an application, you must file Form CPT-1 and the related questionnaires, which you can obtain from your local District Taxation Office.

Some of the major criteria in distinguishing whether you are an employee or self-employed include the following:

- Are you an officer or director of the company that pays you?
- Are you prohibited from performing your services for other businesses during the same period in the working day?
- Does the company that pays you have a preferred call on your time and efforts?
- Are you required to furnish your own office or does the business which pays you provide you with a place to work?
- Do you have to report on a regular basis to a representative of the business that pays you?
- Are you required to cover your territory within a specified time or with specified frequency?
- Are you required to meet a quota to retain your position?
- Are you guaranteed a minimum amount of compensation irrespective of your commissions?
- Are your expenses reimbursed by way of an allowance?
- Are you required to perform all services personally?
- Do you have a draw against anticipated earnings?
- Are you covered under various fringe-benefit programs such as a registered pension fund, group insurance, profit sharing, and so on?
- Can your services be terminated at will by the business that pays you?

No one factor or combination of factors is necessarily conclusive except that if the answer to most of the previous questions is "yes," you are probably going to be considered an employee. On the other hand, if you are an independent contractor, you are thus self-employed.

Examine Your Gross Revenues –
Timing of Income Recognition

Once you have established your status, the next step is to look at your gross revenues. If you are employed, your gross revenues would presumably include salary or wages as well as commissions. As an employee, your commissions are normally taxable in the calendar year they are received. In other words, employment income is calculated on a cash basis. This is an important consideration because it gives you, perhaps, the first opportunity for planning. Let's assume that you make a very large sale in December 1993. You have already enjoyed a very good year and you recognize that your commission on this sale would be taxed at approximately 45%, the top marginal tax bracket in most provinces of Canada. If you can arrange with your employer to defer the payment of your commission until January 1994, you won't have to account for this income until the subsequent year. If you expect your tax bracket to be lower in 1994, you might gain a substantial advantage. From your employer's perspective, delaying the payment of a commission by one month has no effect for tax purposes. This is because the employer calculates income on an accrual basis and can claim a deduction at the point in time that the liability is incurred, even if it is paid a bit later.

On the other hand, you should note that Revenue Canada takes the position that if you receive advances against commissions, they are *also* taxable in the year that they are received, even if they are only earned subsequently. Again, you may have an opportunity for planning. For example, if 1993 is a relatively bad year for you but you are expecting a significant improvement in 1994, you might ask your employer for an advance in 1993 against 1994's commissions. It's true this will accelerate the payment of your taxes but you may get the advantage of paying in a lower bracket.

If this type of planning appeals to you, I think an hour or so with your own accountant towards the end of the year, but before December 31, would be time and money well spent. My point is that a commissioned salesperson generally has more flexibility than most employees.

If you are self-employed, you must report your income on an accrual basis. This means you are taxable when your income is earned, irrespective of whether it is received before or after the time it was earned. However, a self-employed person is entitled to adopt an accounting period other than the calendar year. In the first year that you carry on a business, you can pick any year end that you want. After that time, all year ends must remain constant unless you get approval for a change from the Minister of National Revenue. Usually a good valid business reason is required for such an approval to be granted.

What is the advantage of selecting a year end other than the calendar year? The answer is the opportunity to defer taxes for as much as a full year on an ongoing basis. For example, let's assume that you are an employee of a particular company until March 31, 1993. At that point, you decided to go into your own business as an independent commissioned agent. You can pick as your first year end any time from April 1, 1993, to March 31, 1994.

Assume you earn a very large commission in mid-November 1993. You might pick October 31 as your first year end. Thus, when you file your 1993 return in April 1994, you would only report your employment income for the months of January, February, and March and your profit from your self-employment for the period April through October. In other words, your big commission for the month of November 1993 would only become income in 1994 and you would only have to report this income on filing your 1994 tax return in April 1995. This is a significant tax advantage. However, once you have established an October 31 year end, all year ends thereafter would have to be October 31.

This is only one of many possibilities. As an alternative, you could pick January 31, 1994, as your first year end. Under these circumstances, when you file your 1993 tax return, you would only have to report your employment income for the months of January, February, and March. Your 1993 income from your entire period of self-employment (in other words, April through December) would only be taxable in 1994. Again, your taxes would be paid in April 1995.

If you become self-employed in the middle of a particular year, you don't have to make a decision on when your first year end is going to be until the following March or, if you're prone to waiting until the last minute, even early April. In other words, you've got the benefit of hindsight, although you should make your decision before your next tax return is due the following April 30. In my last example, a decision on what year end to adopt should really be made no later than mid-March or early April 1994. This way, a proper tax return for the 1993 year can be prepared before the April 30, 1994 deadline.

Again, spend some time with your accountant. It would be well worth your while, though, to have available for your accountant's consideration a summary of your income earned on a month-by-month basis and a schedule of related expenses. With this information and some trial-and-error calculations, your accountant can help you make a year-end timing decision that is to your maximum advantage.

So, to summarize everything I have said to this point, your first step is to determine whether you are employed or self-employed. Step two is then to recognize the point in time at which your gross income is subject to taxation, regardless of whether you must report on a cash or on an accrual basis.

Fringe Benefits

If you are an employed commissioned salesperson, it is likely that you are receiving benefits beyond wages, salaries, and commissions. Most fringe benefits are included in income at their value to an individual employee. Some common fringe benefits include holiday trips, prizes, and incentive awards as well as travelling expenses of an employee's spouse, tuition fees for courses, and premiums under provincial hospitalization and medicare programs.

One of the most common fringe benefits allocated to commissioned salespeople is a company car. If you drive a company car, your income for tax purposes will include a two-part benefit, the first calculated on availability of the vehicle and the second based on operating expenses. The double taxable benefit from company cars was discussed in detail in Chapter Two. I suggest that, in at least some cases, it may be more to your advantage for you to provide your own automobile and to charge your employer between 25¢ and 31¢ per kilometre. This allowance would, of course, cover not only the business operating expenses but also that portion of the capital cost of the car applicable to business-related usage.

You should be aware that there are a few employee benefits that are not taxable. For example, if your employer provides you with a distinctive uniform that you are required to wear while carrying out your duties, this does not constitute a taxable benefit. Similarly, if your employer pays for laundry and dry-cleaning of such a uniform, this is also not taxable. A good example of such an arrangement can be found in the case of a number of national real-estate companies that provide their salespeople with distinctive blazers.

Perhaps the most important non-taxable benefit for the commissioned salesperson is the use of recreational facilities. If your employer provides you with a paid membership in a club that provides dining, recreational, or sporting facilities, this is not taxable as long as it is to the employer's advantage for you to be a member of the club. In other words, if you use these facilities to entertain customers, clients, or prospective customers or clients, there are no adverse tax consequences for you.

Deductibility of Expenses

Let's now turn to the deductibility of expenses that may be claimed against income from commissions. I will make some general points first which are applicable primarily to employed salespeople and I will then provide some detailed comments on specific expenses, highlighting some of the major differences between being classified as an employee versus a self-employed person.

First of all, an employed commissioned salesperson is allowed to claim "salesmen's" expenses if he or she can answer yes to four specific questions as follows:

1. Are you paid, at least in part, on a commission basis?
2. Are you required to pay your own expenses pursuant to your contract of employment?
3. Are you involved in selling property or negotiating contracts?
4. Are you required to carry on your duties of employment away from your employer's place of business?

Those who do qualify for a claim under salesmen's expenses should note that if they receive an allowance for travel expenses, they can record that allowance as income and then claim actual expenses as an offset. The other option is to ignore the allowance and disregard actual travel costs. The option that provides the greater benefit for tax purposes is the one that should be selected.

For many commissioned salespersons, the most contentious item is the question of carrying on duties away from an employer's place of business. For example, if you are involved in selling furniture or appliances, you may not qualify for a claim for salesmen's expenses because you would not ordinarily be required by your employer to involve yourself with customer visits. However, if you are engaged in selling carpeting or draperies and you must make customer calls, then you would likely qualify.

The one area where the Revenue authorities appear to be reasonably lenient is in connection with securities salespeople – in other words, individuals who sell stocks and bonds on a commissioned basis. The problem here is that a securities salesperson generally operates via the telephone. In other words, he or she may not spend much time away from the employer's place of business during the working day. However, the Revenue authorities seem to allow an expense claim, provided that the employer requires the salesperson to contact clients away from the employer's place of business. Since many securities salespeople feel that face-to-face contact with clients and prospective clients is an important segment of their activities, and since successful securities salespeople tend to spend significant amounts of money on entertainment and promotion of clients outside normal business hours, it appears that this condition can be satisfied.

If an employed salesperson claims salesmen's expenses, there are a couple of points that should be noted. First, the expenses claimed cannot exceed the amount of commissions received in the year with the exception of capital cost allowance (depreciation for income-tax purposes) on an automobile used by the individual in performing his or her duties, along with interest expense on money borrowed to acquire that car. In other words, with the exception of capital cost allowance on a car and interest expense, you are not permitted to claim a commission loss for the year. You should reread the section in Chapter Two which outlines the various restrictions on the deductibility of car expenses.

If you don't want to make a claim under the category of salesmen's expenses, you may claim your travel expenses only. Travel expenses will include capital cost allowance and finance charges on an automobile used in the performance of your duties. However, if you claim under the travel-expense rules, you may not include items such as advertising, entertainment, or promotion.

Once you determine that you qualify to claim salesmen's expenses, it is necessary to examine what your expenses are and to what extent these may be deducted. If you are an employee, you are limited to those expenses specifically called for under the Income Tax Act. The next part of this chapter will highlight some of the differences between claiming expenses as an employee versus claiming them when you are self-employed. But first, please note that if you are an employee, you may generally only deduct expenses in the year they are incurred. In other words, you may not carry forward amounts expended in prior years even if your income was too low for you to obtain any substantial benefit. There is an exception for home office expenses, which is discussed later on in this chapter.

Car Expenses

For most commissioned salespeople, car expenses are probably the largest single expense deduction. The rules for keeping track of and claiming expenses appear to be the same whether you are employed or self-employed. Of course, in dealing with car expenses at this time, I make the assumption that you are using your own car, not an automobile provided by someone else. The rules pertaining to automobile expenses have been explained in Chapter Two.

Travel Expenses

For some commissioned salespeople, whether employed or self-employed, a second major expense category is travel expenses other than car expenses. Travel expenses would be incurred while away from home overnight on business and would commonly include hotel accommodations, transportation by way of bus, train, taxi, or airplane, as well as meal costs. When it comes to meal costs, there is an important limitation that applies to employed salespeople. Specifically, a meal is only deductible as a travel expense if you are away for more than twelve hours from the municipality in which your employer's business establishment is located. Thus, to claim travel expenses, you must ordinarily be away from home overnight. Of course, if your meals are taken in the company of clients or customers, even within the municipality in which your employer's business is located, you may be able to claim your expenses as business promotion instead.

As already explained in Chapter Two, the deduction for business meals (including food and beverages) and entertainment expenses is limited to 80% of their cost. The 80% limitation also applies to gratuities, cover charges, room rentals to provide entertainment at a hotel or resort, and the cost of private boxes at sports facilities. The same restrictions apply to the cost of meals while travelling, or attending a convention, conference, seminar, or similar function.

Business Promotion

Business promotion involves a wide variety of expenses, including advertising and entertainment. Common advertising costs include giveaway items such as calendars, pens, and samples, as well as the cost of business cards, newspaper ads, flyers, and printed pamphlets.

Business entertainment includes the costs of meals (to 80% only) and certain expenses incurred in conjunction with the use of recreational facilities. Membership fees in any club that provides dining, recreational, or sporting facilities are not tax-deductible, regardless of whether you are employed or self-employed. However, the actual expenses of *using* recreational facilities, such as green fees, or the costs of food and beverages, are at least 80% deductible if these costs are incurred as part of legitimate client entertainment.

Promotion expenses will include gift items, such as a bottle of liquor to a customer or client, or (very common in the real-estate industry) a house-warming gift to a family that buys a house from a real-estate agent. Another (80%) tax-deductible promotion expense is tickets to sporting events. I caution you, though, that if you wish to claim gifts and/or the cost of sporting-event tickets, you should keep careful track of who the recipients are. If you can't substantiate that the beneficiaries are clients, customers, or potential clients and customers, Revenue Canada may disallow your claims.

An Office in the Home

From the standpoint of a commissioned salesperson, one of the most difficult areas is a claim for expenses incurred in conjunction with an office in the home.

There are several conditions that must be met for either an employed or self-employed commissioned salesperson to maintain successfully a deduction for home-office expenses. First and most important, the Income Tax Act specifies that an *employed* individual must be *required by his or her contract of employment* to maintain an office at home to be eligible. If the office is not required, then Revenue Canada is at liberty to disallow all expenses, even if otherwise legitimate.

Even if you pass the test of having a home office required by your employer, there are several other criteria that will be considered in judging your claim. First, under Canadian tax law, there are no specific guidelines relating to those types of expenses that may be deducted in conjunction with a home office. It is commonly accepted, however, that deductible expenses include rent, Capital Cost Allowance, mortgage interest, property taxes, insurance charges, maintenance, repairs and utilities costs, and depreciation on furniture and equipment attributable to a business. Until a few years ago, a deduction was permitted for home office expenses, even in cases where these expenses were somewhat incidental to business activity.

In 1988, however, new rules were introduced which now limit the deduction for expenses to those circumstances where maintaining a place of business in the home is *necessary* for the conduct of business. A self-employed person *or* employed commission salesperson is only allowed to claim a prorated portion of home expenses if the space is used *exclusively* on a regular or continuous basis for the purpose of earning business income. To qualify, the home office must then *also either* be the taxpayer's principal place of business *or* be used on a regular basis for meeting clients and customers.

In addition, home office expenses incurred in a year are deductible only up to the income for the year from the endeavour for which the office is used. Any deductions disallowed in one year as a result of this rule are treated as home office expenses incurred in the next subsequent year.

Even if you qualify to claim a deduction for home office expenses, I do *not* recommend that you write off Capital Cost Allowance, since this claim could jeopardize your special "principal residence" exemption from capital gains tax at the time your house is sold.

Other Allowable Expenses

If you maintain an office at home (even if these costs are non-deductible), you are likely to incur telephone expenses. Revenue Canada adopts the position that only long-distance phone calls related to business are a proper deduction unless you have a separate business line. If a separate business line is maintained, all telephone costs would then be tax-deductible.

Whether you are employed or self-employed, you are also permitted to claim professional or association membership dues as well as license fees necessary to maintain a professional status. Association entrance or initiation fees are, however, considered capital outlays and are not tax-deductible.

Salary to an Assistant

One of the trickiest areas is a claim for salary expenses. Again, the problem only arises if you are employed on a commission basis. An employee is only allowed to deduct salary expenses paid to an assistant or substitute if these payments are *required* through the contract of employment, even if the employee can substantiate that payments (not actually required) were bona fide and that services were in fact rendered. This problem does *not* arise if you are self-employed. Your claim for salaries is much less likely to be scrutinized closely.

If you can claim salaries and wages, they may include amounts paid to your spouse or to other family members. However, if you are making payments to a member of your family, you must be very careful to ensure that you can show that these payments are in fact reasonable. Reasonable is considered to be the amount that you would otherwise have to pay an outside party to perform the same services. You should also note, whether you are employed or self-employed, that salaries paid to others are subject to tax deductions at source, including Canada or Quebec Pension Plan and Unemployment Insurance premiums.

The Cost of Supplies

Another area where the Income Tax Act closely regulates expenses deductions by an employee is the subject of supplies. Again, a deduction for supplies consumed may only be claimed if the purchase of these supplies is required pursuant to a contract of employment. If you are self-employed, this restriction does not apply. Supplies include such items as pens and pencils, appointment calendars, diaries, stamps, paper-clips, and stationery, but not furniture.

Conventions

Another major difference between employed and self-employed commissioned salespersons pertains to convention expenses. Convention expenses are never deductible against employment income; they are only a proper deduction against income from a business. If you are employed and you are required to attend a convention or sales conference, you do not have to add reimbursement costs into your income. However, if you receive a non-deductible allowance to cover your expenses, your allowance would have to be reported as a taxable benefit and you expenses would not be deductible.

If you would like to attend a convention, essentially at your own expense, you might ask your employer to pay the expenses directly on your behalf and to reduce correspondingly the rate paid to you as gross commissions. Your employer could claim these convention expenses as a deduction as part of his or her business activities, and if you show a

Figure 3–1   **Sample Schedule of Salesman's Expenses**

Automobile expenses*
  Gas and oil
  Repairs and maintenance
  Insurance
  Parking
  Licence
  Car washes
  Short-term rentals
  Lease payments if car is leased
  Capital cost allowance if car is owned
  Interest expense on money borrowed to purchase car

Travel expenses other than automobile
  Hotel accommodations
  Transportation by bus, train, taxi, or airplane
  Meal costs away from home (80% only)

Advertising, entertainment, and promotion
  Give-away items (calendars, pens, samples, etc.)
  Business cards
  Newspaper ads, flyers, and printed matter
  Entertainment of customers and clients
    Meals (80% only)
    Certain recreational costs (other than membership fees)
    Tickets to sporting events (80% only)
  Gift items (liquor, etc.)

  Office at home**
    Utilities
    Telephone (long-distance expenses only, unless you have a separate
      business line)
    Cleaning
    Minor repairs
    Mortgage interest – only if self-employed
    Capital cost allowance – only if self-employed

  Professional membership dues and licences

  Salaries of an assistant**
    Including salary costs (UIC; CPP & QPP)

  Office supplies**
    Pens, pencils, appointment calendars, diaries, stamps, paper clips,
      and stationery

Convention costs – only if self-employed – up to two conventions a year
   (only 80% of certain costs qualify).

Accounting fees and the costs of tax-return preparation

*Note the restrictions for expensive vehicles.
**An employed commissioned salesperson must be required to incur these expenses
under an employment contract or they are non-deductible. Note the other restrictions
that also apply.

smaller gross income from commissions, this would be the equivalent of
a higher income coupled with a deductible expense. This is certainly one
of the many grey areas in the Income Tax Act and I caution you to get professional advice before implementing any planning steps. If you are
involved as a commissioned salesperson in either the life insurance or
real estate industry and you are employed by a company, I suggest that
you speak to representatives of that company so that a suitable policy
regarding conventions can be set up on a company-wide basis. As mentioned several times already, only 80% of certain convention-related
costs, such as meals, are tax deductible.

If you are self-employed, you are permitted to deduct most of the costs of
up to two conventions a year, provided that these conventions are spon-
sored by a business or professional organization and were attended by
yourself in connection with a business that you carry on. You need not be
a member of the organization sponsoring the convention, but to qualify
for a deduction, your attendance must be related to your business.

The Income Tax Act specifies that you may only claim convention
expenses at locations consistent with the territorial scope of the organization holding them. Generally, this means that a Canadian business would
be bound to hold its convention activities somewhere in Canada if the
business is national in scope, while if the organization is provincial, the
convention should be held in that particular province. However, since
many organizations are multinational, there is no rule that would deny a
convention-expense deduction for reasonable costs incurred outside the
country.

As a general rule of thumb, I recommend that if you wish to claim the
costs of two conventions, one of them should be located in Canada and
one may take place outside the country. Revenue Canada does, however,
take a rather dim view of conventions held in exotic locations such as the
Bahamas or Hawaii, but then again, as long as there is a good business
reason, there is no real cause for disallowance.

If you combine attendance at a convention with a vacation trip, you should prorate your expenses on a reasonable basis. Also, if you are accompanied by your spouse or children, the costs you incur for these people are generally not deductible.

Accounting Fees

Finally, a few words about accounting fees, including the cost of preparing an income-tax return. Revenue Canada has issued an Interpretation Bulletin that indicates that fees incurred for advice and assistance in preparing and filing tax returns are deductible in computing income from a business, if the business is of sufficient scope to warrant legal or accounting expenses. Accounting fees incurred by an employed commissioned salesperson are also considered to be tax-deductible, if they are reasonable in the circumstances and the individual is making a claim of salesmen's expenses.

Rules for Making Income-Tax Remittances

As I mentioned at the beginning of this chapter, if you are employed, it is incumbent on your employer to deduct income taxes at source from commissions paid. If you are self-employed, under current tax law you must make quarterly instalments on the last day of March, June, September, and December. Only the difference between the instalments which you have paid and your actual tax liability is due the following April 30 when your tax return is filed. Instalments are required if you had taxable income in the previous year and tax was not deducted at source from at least three-quarters of your net income. You are exempt from instalments, however, if your federal income tax for either the current year or the previous year does not exceed $1,000. Generally, in your first year as a self-employed salesperson, you will not be required to make any tax instalments. These matters should be reviewed annually with your own advisers because insufficient instalments are subject to non-deductible interest charges.

In 1989, a new penalty was introduced on deficient instalment payments. Before, the Income Tax Act only imposed an interest charge at a prescribed rate set quarterly on late or deficient instalments. The penalty is now an additional one-half of this interest charge, to the extent that the interest charge exceeds $1,000. Paying taxes promptly therefore becomes a top financial priority for high tax-bracket individuals.

Incorporation

Incorporation of a commissioned sales agency is only feasible if you are, beyond the slightest shadow of a doubt, self-employed and you receive your gross commission revenues from more than one source. When I refer to more than one source, I mean that you are paid by at least two, if not more, independent entities. It is not sufficient that you yourself service many customers or clients. Instead, the products that you sell must be provided by at least two independent businesses.

Incorporation provides several important tax advantages. First, there is the ability to split income between members of your family. Even if your family members are not active in your business, you can make them shareholders in the corporation and split income by way of dividends. This is explained in Chapters Eleven and Thirteen. Alternatively, any profit not required by your family to meet living expenses can be retained by the corporation. Corporate tax rates for small businesses range around 20% on active business income of up to $200,000 annually, which is substantially less than the rate of tax applicable to individuals at middle- and upper-income levels. Then, as the retained earnings of a corporation accumulate, the funds represented by these earnings can be invested on your behalf. You are far better off investing about eighty cents on the dollar than reinvesting only fifty-five or sixty cents on the dollar after personal taxes. You should note, however, that there are restrictions governing the use of small-business tax rates. These are covered in Chapter Eleven, which highlights the important rules that must be followed.

In most cases, the question of whether or not to incorporate cannot be resolved without the assistance of professional advisers. You will, no doubt, pick up some good ideas from Chapter Twelve, "Tax Planning for New Business Ventures." However, you should still make use of the services of your own accountant and lawyer. They should be able to explain your tax position to you and also quantify the benefits that you may hope to derive from incorporation. Since every individual's income, expenses, family situation, and living requirements are different, you cannot simply rely on generalities or on what your friends are doing when it comes to making your own business decisions.

CHAPTER 4

Postponing Your Income

Planning for Retirement, Loss of Job, and Transfers Outside Canada

If you are a business owner or executive aged fifty-five or older, you should be giving some thought to planning for retirement. In this chapter, I will show you that a knowledge of the tax rules can certainly be helpful. Even if you are under the age of fifty-five, this material describes opportunities for tax savings that you might have if you ever become a non-resident as a result of a job transfer outside Canada, or if you become unemployed after several years of service to a company.

The basic theme of this chapter is the conversion of income from salary into a "retiring allowance." We have already seen that a raise in pay is simply taxed in your top marginal bracket. With respect to retiring allowances, there are other options – and even a relatively young person may become eligible to receive such payments.

In passing, you should note that Chapter Ten contains a general discussion of *all* aspects of planning for the retirement years. This chapter concentrates on earned income only.

Before reading any further, you should note that several years ago former finance minister Michael Wilson dealt a severe blow to salary-deferral arrangements. I therefore suggest that you read the following material very carefully to determine what has been blocked and what planning is still available.

Non-Statutory Deferred Compensation Programs

For tax purposes, it may be said that there are two kinds of deferred compensation. The first is referred to as "statutory" deferred compensation. This means that specific rules governing these concepts are set out within the Income Tax Act. Statutory deferred compensation programs include retirement savings plans and employer pension plans, which will be dealt with in Chapter Five. The second type of deferred compensation is "non-statutory." Non-statutory means that these plans are not covered specifically within the framework of the Income Tax Act. Actually, non-statutory deferred compensation is based on a *voluntary negotiated agreement* between an employee and an employer.

In the first half of the 1980s, non-statutory deferred compensation programs (also commonly referred to as employee benefit plans) gained increasing popularity. A program of this nature is an arrangement under which an employer makes contributions to a trustee who at some future time would make payments out of the plan to participating employees. Before Mr. Wilson's February 1986 budget, a participating employee was not taxed at the time the contributions were made by the employer and was only taxed on payments received. An opportunity therefore existed for a participating employee to defer taxes on income that would otherwise be taxed on an ongoing basis. The advantage was that an employee could then have one hundred cents on the dollar of employer contributions earning income for him, instead of as little as only fifty cents, had he or she received salary on which taxes were payable immediately.

The major drawback of an employee benefit plan, however, was that the employer would not get a deduction for the contributions until payments were actually made to the participating employees. Nevertheless, ideal circumstances to use employee benefit plans existed if the employer was a non-taxable entity such as a hospital, school board, or any non-profit corporation. Moreover, corporations which were profit-making entities also used employee benefit plans if they were not currently taxable because of operating losses or because they had significant tax deductions.

To block the use of such programs, any remuneration payable to an employee after February 25, 1986, is now required to be included in income in the year that the income is *earned* and not in the year in which it is received. Deferred salary is then deductible immediately to the employer. A salary deferral arrangement is defined as "any arrangement between an employer and employee that has as a main purpose the deferral of remuneration otherwise payable in the year to the employee for services rendered in the year or preceding years." The definition of salary-deferral arrangements explicitly excludes pension and other registered plans as well as certain "prescribed arrangements" including those governing teachers' sabbaticals and compensation for services as a professional athlete.

These rules do not apply to remuneration payable under an agreement in writing entered into on or before February 25, 1986. However, for all intents and purposes, an employee benefit program can no longer be used for future income-deferral arrangements. There may still be some opportunity for a company to acquire a life insurance policy on the life of an executive which is designed to produce a growing cash value. It then appears possible to transfer the ownership of that policy to the individual upon retirement. It remains to be seen whether this will become an approved method of deferring a portion of the individual's compensation.

Retiring Allowances

While non-statutory salary-deferral arrangements have recently been blocked, this does not necessarily mean that a *retiring allowance* program cannot be incorporated as part of a tax plan between an individual employee and the company that he or she works for.

The term "retiring allowance" is defined in the Income Tax Act to include three types of payments:

- a payment in recognition of long service;
- a payment in respect of loss of office;
- certain other termination payments.

Much of the discussion in this chapter involves only the first of these three types of payments. The other two will be dealt with last, in the section on payments for loss of one's job.

In spite of the many recent tax changes, there do not appear to be any guidelines in the Income Tax Act as to how much can be paid out by a corporation as a retiring allowance. In 1981, however, Revenue Canada did issue an Interpretation Bulletin which suggests that a payment of up to two-and-one-half years' salary would be reasonable in cases where the individual is not a member of a registered pension plan or deferred profit-sharing program.

In addition, there are no specific guidelines as to how old an employee must be in order to receive a retiring allowance. *A payment in recognition of long service does not tie in to either a specific age or to a specific length of service with the employer.*

There are several advantages to receiving retiring allowances. First, by simply retiring *early* in a given taxation year, an individual may be able to take a substantial portion of the allowance into his or her income and gain a significant tax advantage.

It is important for you to understand the difference between *marginal tax brackets* and *effective taxes* – the marginal rate is considerably higher. On the first $100,000 of a retiring allowance, for example, the tax bite is only about $35,000 if this is an individual's *only income* in the year of retirement. The *effective* tax rate thus becomes 35% rather than the 45% *marginal* rate that most business owners and executives must contend with annually. There can be an absolute tax saving of 10% as long as the recipient can organize his or her affairs to keep other income in that year small.

A retiring allowance may qualify, in whole or in part, for a transfer into a Registered Retirement Savings Plan (RRSP). For years of service before 1989, the law allows a tax-deferred transfer of retiring allowances to an RRSP of up to $2,000 for each year in which the individual was covered by a registered pension or deferred profit-sharing plan and $3,500 for each year of service with no pension coverage. For service subsequent to 1988, however, a single limit of $2,000 per year of service applies. Thus, if an individual has thirty years of service with an employer, there is a considerable amount that would conceivably qualify for "rollover" treatment.

One advantage of an RRSP transfer is that funds do not have to be withdrawn from such a program until the beneficiary reaches age seventy-one. In the meantime, the investment income earned by these funds accrues and compounds on a tax-deferred basis. At current rates of interest, any amount put into an RRSP at age sixty five would increase by 50% by the time the beneficiary reaches the age of seventy-one.

The major drawback to the concept of a retiring allowance is that a corporation may not be able to fulfill its commitment at the time of an individual's retirement. If, for example, an employer goes bankrupt any time before an employee is due to retire, the employee does not have any protection. If a written agreement is actually made between an employee and employer, this may be construed as a "salary-deferral arrangement," the use of which has, as explained previously, been blocked. Thus, retiring allowances may no longer constitute an effective planning technique for employees of medium-sized and large corporations, especially where there is an arm's-length relationship between the individual and the employer.

Retiring Allowances for Owner-Managed Businesses

However, a retiring allowance can be extremely useful in planning for a smaller owner-managed business – especially where the executives (owners) have confidence in their own ability to ensure that their company will be sufficiently solvent to meet its future obligations. In addition, a retiring allowance can be an excellent vehicle to assist in passing on the ownership of a small business to other persons, such as one's children or key employees. In recent years, the retiring allowance has become increasingly important for the owner-managed business. Several years ago, the Income Tax Act was changed so that corporations are no longer permitted to have large special pension-plan programs restricted for the benefit of owner-managers. Then, subsequent tax amendments restricted deferred profit-sharing programs where a principal shareholder is a beneficiary. In other words, the owner-manager of the Canadian small business is limited to contributing to a personal RRSP each year (or participating in a modest pension plan) and cannot avail himself of the larger statutory plans available to many other taxpayers. Fortunately, the retiring allowance can make up for this inequity. The following example will explain how – even though the numbers would now require some revision because of the new rules.

Several years ago, I was asked by another Montreal chartered accountant to assist him in tax planning for one of his clients. The client was a construction company owned by two brothers, both of whom were in their early sixties. Each brother had been drawing a salary of $100,000 a year for the previous five years and the company had earned $500,000 of profits in its fiscal year that ended June 30. Without any planning, the first $150,000 of corporate profits would have been taxed (at that time) at approximately 25%, while the remaining $350,000 would have been subjected to taxes of about 50%.

The owners of the company were somewhat upset because construction starts had dropped dramatically following the year end because of a severe recession. By the time the accountant called me in as a consultant, it was already early December. I met with him and his clients, and at that meeting the two expressed a desire to retire. They felt it would be a while before the construction industry would recover and they really did not want to continue in the business. They decided, however, not to wind up the company but to sell it to a son of one of the brothers.

Given these facts, the first recommendation I made was that the company change its year end to December 31. (New ownership is one of the valid business reasons that the tax authorities accept for a change in the year end.) It was as of that date that control would pass over to the buyer, and an audited financial statement was required in any event. There were no significant construction activities during the six months ended December 31, and for all intents and purposes, the operations showed a break-even position. However, as of December 31, I suggested that the company pay out $175,000 of retiring allowances to *each* of the two brothers. The brothers legitimately retired as employees, resigned their directorships and offices, and sold their shares.

The retiring allowances totalling $350,000 created a business loss for that fiscal period. The tax rules at that time provided for an automatic one-year carry-back of any business loss that could not be applied against other income in the current year. By carrying the loss back one year to the fiscal period ended June 30, the revised net profit became only $150,000 – coincidentally the specific amount that then qualified for a 25% low rate of corporate tax. This resulted in a recovery of $175,000 of corporate taxes otherwise payable. The brothers then transferred most of their funds into RRSPs, thus deferring significant amounts of tax.

In the case of an owner-managed business, such as in the preceding example, the retiring-allowance arrangement has one additional benefit. *It makes the corporation whose shares are being sold easier to sell.* In the preceding example, the payment of $350,000 reduced the tangible assets of the corporation by $175,000 ($350,000 minus $175,000 of corporate taxes recovered). Whatever price would otherwise have been paid by the son of one of the brothers to acquire the company consequently became that much less. For example, if the value of the corporation before the retiring allowances was $1 million, these payments reduced the value to $825,000.

A retiring allowance can thus be an integral part of *any* purchase and sale of a private business where the vendor shareholder-manager(s) will also be leaving the employ of the company. Retiring allowances can in fact make a private corporation easier to sell – they reduce the net tangible assets of the corporation.

Figure 4–1   **Simultaneous Retirement and Sale of Business**

		Fiscal Year Ended	
2 Brothers		*June 30*	*Dec. 31*
2 × $100,000	Salaries		
	Corporate profit	$500,000	—
2 × $175,000	Retiring allowance		$(350,000)
	Loss	(350,000) ◄———	350,000
	Revised profit	$150,000	

RRSP   RRSP

You should note that, as I explained before, the maximum amount that can be transferred into an RRSP is limited to only $3,500 for each year of service before 1989 and $2,000 per year thereafter. However, if we assume that each of these two brothers was with the company for thirty years before retirement, as much as $210,000 ($105,000 each) could have been "tax sheltered" in an RRSP – even under the new rules. Also, if the retiring allowance was set up on the books of the company as a liability on December 31, and was only paid on January 1 of the following year, the tax cost of the remaining $70,000 per person could be minimized by the brothers having arranged to keep their other incomes for the subsequent year relatively low. Thus, the concept of retiring allowances is still as valuable as before for owner-managers.

Planning for Non-Residency

As I mentioned earlier in this chapter, a retiring allowance can be useful not only when you attain normal retirement age but also as a method of tax planning for non-residency. This is because a "payment in recognition of long service" does not tie in to any specific age requirement. To be effective, however, I suggest that there should be a minimum term of service of at least five to ten years *before* the employment relationship is severed.

At this point, it would be useful to review one or two tax-planning ideas that are generally applicable if you are contemplating leaving Canada. First, the Canadian tax system makes a sharp distinction between residency and non-residency. A resident of Canada is taxed on world income. A non-resident is only taxed (at normal graduated tax rates) on employment income from Canadian sources, self-employment income (i.e., business income), and certain Canadian capital gains. However, when property income (such as interest, rents, royalties, or annuities) is paid to a non-resident, it is subject to a special flat-rate tax of not more than 25%. A "part-year" resident of Canada is taxed on world income during that portion of the year that the person is resident. During the other portion of the year, there is no Canadian tax obligation as long as the individual does not have Canadian-source employment, business, or certain capital gains incomes.

With this background, the first major tax-planning idea is to leave Canada, whenever possible, early in a given taxation year. The advantages can best be illustrated with another short case analysis.

One year in late November, an executive with one of the Calgary-based oil companies came to me for some tax counselling. He was being transferred by his employer to a related corporation operating in Australia. Among other things, the executive wanted to know what tax planning he should do before leaving the country. When he told me that he was booked to leave Calgary in the last week of December, I immediately asked whether or not his departure could be postponed until the first week of January. The man shrugged his shoulders and indicated that if there were tax advantages, a postponement could certainly be arranged.

I then asked him what benefits he was entitled to by virtue of severing his relationship with the Canadian company. He began to calculate his accumulated sick leave and vacation pay. In total, these came to approximately $8,000. His other income for the year was approximately $70,000 – already sufficient to put him into a 45% marginal tax bracket. I explained that adding a further $8,000 to the first $70,000 would produce effective taxes of 45% on the incremental income. However, by leaving during the first week in January, the $8,000 would then be taxed all by itself and the cost would only be about $1,200. Australian taxes would not apply to income earned before the executive took up residence in that country. By leaving one week later, he could obtain an absolute tax saving of $2,400:

	Year One	Year Two
Incremental income	$8,000	$8,000
Less: Taxes thereon (Year One: 45%)	3,600	1,200
Net income	$4,400	$6,800

This particular executive then went so far as to suggest to his employers that they "accidently" remove him from their payroll as of December 15. He also suggested that the "mistake" could be found in early January.

In this manner, he hoped to move his last two weeks' salary from one year to the next in order to compound his tax advantages. The people in charge of payroll were receptive in theory, but they still rejected the idea. Apparently, this company was so large that it was "over-computerized." It was explained to my client that if he were removed from the payroll, the company would never be able to get him back on again. Using the old adage that a bird in the hand is worth two in the bush, my client agreed to receive his normal salary when it was to have been paid in the first place. However, the $8,000 of severance pay and other benefits were in fact moved into the following year because he delayed his actual departure from Canada.

This example also explains the importance of retiring early in a given taxation year, even if you are not planning to leave the country. Usually, your income in the first year of retirement will be much less than your income in the last year of full employment. Therefore, by retiring early in a given year, you can derive large tax savings with respect to severance pay, accumulated sick-leave payments, as well as the last year's vacation pay.

Let us now return to the opportunities to use retiring allowances in conjunction with non-residency. Assume that you are an executive employed in Canada by a company that either has or expects to have an affiliated (but legally separate) corporation operating in another country. Fo simplicity's sake, let's assume the other country is the United States. The president of your company calls you in and asks whether you would be interested in moving to Dallas or Denver as a branch manager for the U.S. company. If you accept such a transfer, there are some excellent chances for tax planning.

You could ask that your present salary be reduced for the current year by an amount equal to $2,000 for each year of service with your employer ($3,500 for years of service before 1989 if you were not a member of either a pension plan or deferred profit-sharing plan). The Canadian company could pay this to you as a retiring allowance just before your departure and you could take the money and purchase an RRSP.

RRSP Payments to Non-Residents

Having "rolled over" your retiring allowance into an RRSP, your worst exposure to Canadian tax would be a flat-rate withholding tax of 25%. This is the requirement under the Canadian Income Tax Act whenever

RRSP payments are made to a non-resident. This is significantly less than the marginal income-tax rates on executive salaries in Canada.

It is important to note that this idea will work only if you are ceasing to be employed by a particular company. If you are going to work for a foreign *branch* of the *same* company, the Revenue authorities will not accept the retiring allowance. This is because, in these circumstances, you would not have retired from a particular employer-company.

Even if you do not have much time to plan potential non-residency, a retiring allowance is still feasible. Assume that you are an executive with a Canadian company and receive a salary of $60,000 a year. In January, your superior calls you into his or her office and asks you to accept a transfer to the U.S. affiliate in Chicago. To keep things simple, assume that your salary for the first year in the United States would be the same $60,000 and ignore the exchange-rate differences between currencies.

Again, opportunities exist for tax planning. You could ask the Canadian company to pay you a $30,000 lump-sum retiring allowance. This would then be taxable all by itself in the year that you leave the country. Even without an RRSP rollover, your effective tax would be only around 25%! Then, during your first year of employment with the U.S. corporation, you would be prepared in such circumstances to work for a reduced salary of the remaining $30,000. This is because half of what would otherwise have been your salary has already been paid to you before leaving Canada.

Overall, the effective tax cost on a $60,000 income becomes virtually negligible. As long as the Canadian company and the U.S. company can make adjustments between themselves, there would be no real problem in setting up this kind of arrangement.

Definition of a Non-Resident

If you ever plan to become a non-resident, there are certain points that have to be considered. First, the Canadian Income Tax Act does not define the term "resident." Therefore, it becomes a question of fact whether or not an individual is or is not a resident for tax purposes at a particular time. In general, Revenue Canada takes the position that if an individual is not out of the country for at least two years, he or she will be deemed to have retained residency status if he or she was a Canadian resident before leaving. In addition, to substantiate non-residency, it is important that members of a taxpayer's immediate family accompany him or her out of the country. An immediate family would include dependent children as well as a spouse. While you are living outside the country, you are still entitled to visit. Nevertheless, the more time physically spent in Canada, the greater the risk that you will be deemed to have residency status.

In cases that have come before the courts, judges have often looked to the question of whether or not the individual maintains a home in Canada. Thus, whenever a client brings up the idea of "going non-resident," I strongly recommend that he or she sell his or her home to strengthen the tax position. If the individual is unwilling to sell, I recommend that the property be leased out on a long-term (minimum two-year) lease.

Next, you should have a reason for departing the country, such as another job or business opportunity, or perhaps the fact that you have decided to retire to a warmer climate. You should also have a valid residency status in whatever other country you are going to. In other words, if your status in that other country is only that of visitor, it becomes much easier for Revenue Canada officials to deem that you have not ceased to be a Canadian resident.

You should also close out all bank accounts for regular operating expenses. This does not mean that you cannot have Canadian investments. However, you should not maintain bank accounts in Canada out of which everyday living expenses are paid.

Finally, club memberships in golf and country clubs should be surrendered. In some cases, it may be possible to convert a normal membership into a special non-resident status.

While many clients and acquaintances have talked to me over the years about becoming non-residents, I have seen very few who have followed through – even where the tax savings would have been extremely substantial. One tends to think long and hard before uprooting an entire family and severing most ties with the past.

Death-Benefit Programs

Before leaving the topic of retiring allowances, a few comments on the tax consequences of "death benefits" would be in order. A death benefit is a payment made by an employer to a spouse (or in some cases to other dependents) of an employee who has died while in service. This type of payment can be likened to a posthumous award in recognition of long service.

Under the tax rules, the first $10,000 is tax-free to the recipient of a death benefit. Although the funds are tax-free to the recipient, the employer still gets a deduction for the full payment as a business expense.

However, there is no reason to assume that a death benefit need be *limited* to only $10,000. It must simply be reasonable. Any payments in excess of the base amount would be income to the recipient but would be subject to very little tax if the recipient has no other income in the year or years they are received. Figure 4-2 illustrates this concept using approximate 1993 tax rates.

Figure 4–2   **Effective Taxes on Death Benefits (1993)**

Death benefit (in excess of $10,000 base amount)	$35,000	$50,000	$75,000	$100,000
Federal tax (approximately)	$ 6,400	$10,400	$17,300	$ 24,600
Provincial tax (assume 50% of federal tax)	3,200	5,200	8,650	12,300
Total tax	$ 9,600	$15,600	$25,950	$ 36,900
Effective tax percentage	27.4%	31.2%	34.6%	36.9%

You should note that the law permits a death benefit to be paid out *over several years*. As long as the total payment is reasonable from the employer's standpoint, the employer gets a deduction, while the recipient can take advantage of low tax rates each year – provided other income is not substantial in relation to the annual benefit payment.

Most people think of death benefits as payments that might be made by a corporation such as Bell Canada to the widow of an employee who had died while in harness. And yet, there is no restriction whatsoever limiting to large public companies the right to pay death benefits. In fact, a death benefit can be extremely useful in tax planning for owner-managed businesses as well. What better way is there to extract a minimum of $10,000 from a corporation and have that amount received tax-free? (To benefit owner-managers, the business must be incorporated, since the concept is based on salaries previously paid. The income of a proprietor of an unincorporated business is not considered employment but is labelled as his or her personal business income.)

In the same way that a retiring allowance can be used as part of an arrangement to transfer the shares of a business from one taxpayer to another, a death benefit can also be used in conjunction with a buy-sell agreement. If the spouse of a deceased owner receives a large death benefit paid out over several years, it becomes that much cheaper for the surviving owners to buy out their late partner. The value of the business as a whole is decreased by the amount of the death benefit (net of corporate taxes recovered).

All private companies that pay salaries to owner-managers should adopt at least some kind of death-benefit program. There is everything to gain and nothing to lose.

Payments for "Loss of Office"

Although this chapter has discussed retiring allowances primarily in terms of payments in recognition of long service, you should note that the definition includes payments in respect of "loss of office" and certain other termination payments. Thus, where an employee is fired or asked to resign, a payment made by the former employer to the individual will be treated as a retiring allowance. Although such a payment is income, it also qualifies for reinvestment into an RRSP (within the limits discussed previously).

Note that where a former employee sues his or her employer for damages for wrongful dismissal, another tax change made several years ago provides that all of his or her receipts (from the suit) will be considered taxable. Under the previous law, any award, whether made by a judge or by way of an out-of-court settlement, was *not* taxed to the extent that the payments exceeded an equivalent of six months' salary. Now, even excess payments are considered as taxable income.

CHAPTER 5

RRSPs, Pension Plans, and Other Statutory Deferred Compensation Programs

In order to ensure the self-sufficiency of as many senior citizens as possible, the Canadian government encourages taxpayers to plan for their own retirement. The Income Tax Act sets out certain rules that allow earned income to be exchanged for future benefits. This deferral of income is accompanied by specific tax concessions that make it easier for individuals to finance their retirement by themselves.

The tax rules do, however, draw a distinction between encouraging realistic savings plans and the tax-avoidance possibilities that would otherwise exist if the deferral allowances were overly generous.

Recent Pension Reform

In the mid-1980s, the government introduced legislation that was eventually to result in sweeping reforms to both public and private pension plans as well as Registered Retirement Savings Plans (RRSPs). Changes were also made to both the Canada Pension Plan and the Old Age Security Act to extend coverage available to widowed and divorced persons and to strengthen these plans and improve total benefits.

Under the new pension plan and RRSP legislation, many Canadians will eventually be able to obtain post-retirement incomes of up to 2% of total career earnings to a maximum of $60,000, indexed by future changes in the average industrial wage.

Generally, individuals and their employers are now able to contribute up to 18% of a person's pensionable earnings to retirement programs.

The system incorporates a single limit that applies for contributions to both registered pensions and RRSPs. To the extent that an employer makes contributions on behalf of an individual, the individual contribution level is decreased. However, where an individual is not a member of a registered pension plan program, he or she is entitled to self-finance a personal retirement program up to new, very generous, limits. The table below depicts the phase-in of the new limits from 1991 to 1996.

Figure 5–1   **Dollar Limits on Tax-Assisted Retirement Savings**

Year	RPP	RRSP	Required Earned Income to Maximize RRSP
1991	$12,500	$11,500	$63,889
1992	12,500	12,500	69,444
1993	13,500	12,500	69,444
1994	14,500	13,500	75,000
1995	15,500	14,500	80,556
1996	indexed	15,500	86,111

Because of complexities in record keeping, there are no provisions to allow Canadians to catch up if they have not contributed to retirement plans before 1991. However, effective 1991, any individual who fails or is unable to contribute in a given year is allowed to carry over the difference for up to seven subsequent years. This is explained further in this chapter.

Other provisions within the pension amendments provide for the portability of "vested rights" when an individual changes jobs. Delayed vesting is now limited to two years only and pension benefits carry over between spouses. In the event that an employee dies prematurely, a spouse now becomes entitled to either a lump-sum amount or a percentage of the pension otherwise payable to the deceased individual. In addition, pension credits are divided in the event of marriage breakdown.

While the government's efforts to provide extended pension coverage must be commended, the complexity of the program is somewhat ironic. Although the government has moved, as part of its more recent budgets, to simplify the small-business rules affecting perhaps 200,000 Canadian businesses, those same budgets will eventually complicate the lives of literally millions of taxpayers – unless a simple system for streamlining the pension process can be devised. In this chapter, RRSPs and pension programs are discussed in detail.

Registered Retirement Savings Plans

Under the Registered Retirement Savings Plan program, an individual is allowed to set aside tax-deductible contributions if these are made in a given taxation year or within sixty days of the end of that year. For 1993, the maximum limit is 18% of *1992* "earned income" to a maximum of $12,500 less a "pension adjustment" for members of pension plan programs. The maximum limit jumps by $1,000 a year, reaching $15,500 by 1996. After that, limits will be indexed with reference to annual inflation. In each case, the "earned income" calculation is based on the "earned income" of the *immediately preceding year.*

The Definition of "Earned Income"

Effective *1990,* earned income includes:

- income from an office or employment, after deducting travel or other employee expenses, but before contributions to registered pension plans, the Canada Pension Plan, and Unemployment Insurance;
- income from royalties in respect of a work or invention where the taxpayer was the author or inventor;
- net research grants;
- alimony and maintenance payments received from a (former) spouse or common-law spouse;
- income from carrying on a business, either alone or as a partner actively engaged in the business;
- net rental income, either active or passive, from real estate; and
- disability pensions under the Canada and Quebec pension plans.

Less the total of the following:

- losses from carrying on a business either alone or as an active partner;
- net rental losses from real estate; and
- deductible alimony and/or maintenance payments.

Before 1990, earned income included all superannuation or pension benefits (including Old Age Security), death benefits, retiring allowances,

Figure 5–2   **RRSP Accumulation Projection**

Assumptions:	Earned income				$40,000
	Income growth rate (%)				6.0
	RRSP/RPP investment yield (%)				9.0
	Contribution (% of income)				10.0

Age	Projected Earned Income	Opening Balance	Investment Yield	Current Contribution	Closing Balance
35	40,000	0	0	4,000	4,000
36	42,400	4,000	360	4,240	8,600
37	44,944	8,600	774	4,494	13,868
38	47,641	13,868	1,248	4,764	19,880
39	50,499	19,880	1,789	5,050	26,719
40	53,529	26,719	2,405	5,353	34,477
41	56,741	34,477	3,103	5,674	43,254
42	60,145	43,254	3,893	6,015	53,162
43	63,754	53,162	4,785	6,375	64,322
44	67,579	64,322	5,789	6,758	76,869
45	71,634	76,869	6,918	7,163	90,950
46	75,932	90,950	8,186	7,593	106,729
47	80,488	106,729	9,606	8,049	124,384
48	85,317	124,384	11,195	8,532	144,111
49	90,436	144,111	12,970	9,044	166,125
50	95,862	166,125	14,951	9,586	190,662
51	101,614	190,662	17,160	10,161	217,983
52	107,711	217,983	19,618	10,771	248,372
53	114,174	248,372	22,353	11,417	282,142
54	121,024	282,142	25,393	12,102	319,637
55	128,285	319,637	28,767	12,829	361,233
56	135,982	361,233	32,511	13,598	407,342
57	144,141	407,342	36,661	14,414	458,417
58	152,789	458,417	41,258	15,279	514,954
59	161,956	514,954	46,346	16,196	577,496
60	171,673	577,496	51,975	17,167	646,638
61	181,973	646,638	58,197	18,197	723,032
62	192,891	723,032	65,073	19,289	807,394
63	204,464	807,394	72,665	20,446	900,505
64	216,732	900,505	81,045	21,673	1,003,223

and amounts received from an RRSP, RPP, or Deferred Profit-Sharing Plan (DPSP).

The theory behind the RRSP program is fairly simple. Contributions are made on a tax-deductible (or pre-tax) basis each year. As long as these amounts are invested in qualified investments, the income earned within an RRSP compounds on a tax-deferred basis. After several years of ongoing contributions, the available capital starts to snowball and the build-up of capital continues until retirement. At that time, the assets in the plan are liquidated and an annuity is purchased in order to provide a post-retirement cash flow. Although withdrawals from an RRSP are taxable, many individuals anticipate being in lower tax brackets after retirement than previously.

The benefits of an RRSP are substantial. Figure 5-2 depicts the potential accumulation if an individual aged thirty-five, earning $40,000 per year, contributes 10% of his or her earnings for the subsequent thirty years to an RRSP program, on the further assumption that income increases by an average of 6% each year and that the RRSP investment yield averages 9%. As you can see from the table, he or she would accumulate over $1 million by age sixty-five. If the individual can afford to wait a further five years before making withdrawals, the capital could almost double. This should be sufficient to provide a monthly income well in excess of almost anyone's retirement needs unless the inflation factor is extremely severe.

Qualified Investments

Historically, qualified investments of a Registered Retirement Savings Plan included things such as Canadian public-company stocks and bonds, Canada Savings Bonds, and mortgages. A small percentage (up to 10%) of plan assets could be held in foreign securities. In 1990, however, the allowable foreign limits began to increase by 2% each year, so that, by 1994, up to 20% of total assets may consist of non-Canadian investments.

As of 1986, retirement income programs are permitted to make *arm's-length* investments in the shares of private Canadian corporations. Up to 50% of plan assets are eligible for such investments. To encourage such investments, an RRSP is then allowed to invest $3 in foreign securities for every $1 invested in an eligible small business. The allowable foreign investment is over and above the normal foreign investment limits. The intent of this legislation is to foster small-business development in

Canada. It is questionable, however, whether too many people are willing to risk their retirement savings by making investments in small businesses that they themselves do not control. Possibly, some people may conclude that they will invest in their friends' businesses if their friends invest in theirs. Nevertheless, the risk factor is substantial and only time will tell if this type of investment gains acceptance.

Should I Have an RRSP?

One of the most common questions posed to me by executives is whether or not an RRSP is advisable, especially because of investment restrictions. Real estate is still a non-qualified investment, as are precious metals such as gold and silver, and you cannot invest to any great extent in foreign securities. Notwithstanding the limitations placed on your RRSP portfolio, my general comment is that an executive doesn't have a choice – he or she *must* have an RRSP.

Let's examine the alternatives. For anyone in a 40% tax bracket in 1993 with 1992 earned income of $41,667, it becomes a choice of either having $7,500 (18% × $41,667) earning income at a compound rate of, say, 10% each year or having 60% of the capital ($4,500) with the tax paid and earning income at only 6% (since the unsheltered investment yield would be fully taxable). Having almost twice the capital returning almost twice the rate certainly makes an RRSP worthwhile.

To summarize then, in dealing with the question of whether or not an RRSP is attractive, simply ask yourself, what better choice is there? Take a moment to study Figure 5-2. I'd be very surprised if this isn't enough to motivate you to take an RRSP seriously.

Should I Borrow Money for an RRSP?

Until a little over ten years ago, an additional advantage of an RRSP was that an individual who did not have the necessary funds to contribute could borrow for RRSP purposes and deduct the interest incurred to make the investment. This encouraged many middle-income earners to participate in an RRSP program. However, the November 1981 Budget ended the deductibility of interest on loans taken out after that date to finance RRSPs as well as other income-deferral plans.

As a result, RRSP contributions dropped after December 1981 – normally the peak time for such contributions. What few people realize even today is that borrowing money to buy an RRSP can *still* be advantageous as a forced savings program. Consider the alternatives. If the same individual who had a 1992 earned income of $41,667 borrows $7,500 in 1993 to buy an RRSP, and places his or her funds in the plan to earn (for purposes of illustration) 10%, after one year he or she will have earned interest income of $750. Even if he or she were to take all the earnings out of the plan and pay full taxes on this interest, the net yield would be $450.

On the other hand, borrowing $7,500 involves a commitment of $625 a month over a one-year period, not including interest. Given an outstanding loan of $7,500 at the beginning of a year and a balance that is reduced to zero by the end of the year, this is equivalent to owing $3,750 throughout the year (see the example in Figure 5-3). Even if the interest rate charged by a lending institution is (again, for purposes of ilustration) 14%, the cost of the loan is therefore essentially 14% of $3,750, or $525 in total. Even though this interest is non-deductible, it is still not overly expensive when compared to the investment yield on $7,500 in the RRSP *throughout* the year. In fact, the actual cost in this example is really only $75 ($450 – $375).

Figure 5–3 **Borrowing to Buy an RRSP May Still Be a Good Idea**

Funds in RRSP		$7,500
Investment yield (10%)		$ 750
	Repayment over 12 months	
Funds borrowed for 1993 contribution	$7,500	Loan reduces to $ 0
Average loan	3,750	
Interest expense (14%)	$ 525	
If interest income is deregistered:		
Interest received	$ 750	
Less: Taxes (40%)	300	
Net interest income	450	
Less: Interest expense	525	
Cost of borrowing	$ 75	

Note: If a tax refund is received in July or August and is applied against the loan balance, the average outstanding amount becomes less than $3,750. There may, in fact, be *no* net cost of borrowing.

Actually, the cost is substantially less. The previous example has assumed that the average loan outstanding throughout the year would be $3,750. If, on the other hand, a $7,500 RRSP contribution results in a tax refund of $3,000 (for an individual in the 40% tax bracket) and these funds are used when received (generally in July or August) towards an immediate reduction of the outstanding loan balance, the actual average loan throughout the year is much less. This means that the non-deductible interest expense is decreased accordingly. Therefore, in the final analysis, the cost of borrowing on a year-to-year basis for the RRSP is virtually nothing. Keep in mind that after the first year, the plan-holder would then have $7,500 available to earn compound income in subsequent years. This procedure can be repeated year after year, taking into account the new limits discussed earlier in this chapter.

This discussion contains a valuable lesson. Any time the government makes a change in the rules, you must not only examine the theory but you must also take representative numbers and see what the impact of such a change really is. On the surface, a prohibition against interest deductibility on funds borrowed to buy an RRSP seems to be a severe restriction. And yet, in the final analysis, the cost, if any, is negligible.

Carryforward of Unused RRSP Deduction Room

The government recognizes that, for various reasons, individuals may not be able to use their allowable contribution room in any given year. For example, a younger person, trying to pay off a mortgage or make a major purchase, may have to wait several years before beginning to save for retirement. Individuals with fluctuating incomes may also be unable to make use of allowable contribution room in a given year. The government has therefore decided to permit the carryforward of unused RRSP contribution room for up to seven years.

Beginning in 1991, any RRSP contribution made is automatically applied against contribution room that arose in the earliest year. For example, if you do not contribute in 1992 and 1993, but do contribute in 1994, the contribution will first be applied against unused contribution room carried forward from 1992. Revenue Canada has promised to advise each taxpayer of his or her unused contribution limits in respect of the current year and the preceding seven years. It should be noted that waiting until later years to make contributions may actually cost you money in the form of a smaller overall accumulation in your RRSP. This is because the major benefit, in the long run, comes not from the contributions themselves, but from the untaxed compounded investment income.

On the other hand, in some instances, the ability to take advantage of the unused contribution benefits can provide some substantial tax benefits. For example, consider the case of an owner-managed business that is expanding. In the early years, the owner-manager may wish to restrict his or her RRSP in order to keep the maximum dollars available for business expansion. Then, if business profits exceed $200,000 in a particular year, it may then be possible to bonus out the excess profits, thereby saving approximately 40% corporate tax. Instead of having to pay personal taxes on the bonus, it is possible that all or part of the bonus could then be sheltered in an RRSP. This may prove to be a better tax plan than having the owner-manager draw additional dollars in those (early) years when the corporation was not faced with high-rate taxation. Each case will have to be decided on its own merits. A commissioned salesperson who has an exceptional year may also find the RRSP carryforward concept extremely beneficial.

Overcontributions and Ineligible Investments of RRSPs

There are certain rules that you should note pertaining to overcontributions. If you overcontribute in relation to your "earned income," but the total contributions are not in excess of the maximum dollar limitation for the year, you may apply for a refund of any excess contributions without penalty. The Income Tax Act does, however, provide a severe penalty in any case where more than the maximum dollar limitation is placed into an RRSP for any given year. The penalty tax is 1% per month on excess contributions.

There are also regulations dealing with the purchase by an RRSP of "non-qualified" investments (e.g., non-arm's-length mortgages, excess investments in the shares of private companies, or foreign investments beyond the previously defined limits). Such investments will result in either taxable income in the hands of the beneficiary or a special tax on the non-qualified investments. If the assets of an RRSP plan are used as security for a loan, there is also a penalty that deems income in the hands of the owner.

Spousal Plans

If you agree that an RRSP is a valid means of both tax sheltering and building up investment capital, there are additional refinements that should be kept in mind. The first of these is the "spousal" RRSP.

Over ten years ago, the tax rules were amended to allow you to split RRSP contributions between yourself and your spouse. This does *not* mean that you can double up and contribute (up to) $25,000 for 1993.

However, if your own annual limit is, for example, $12,500, you can channel this entire amount into your own plan, into a spousal plan, or you can allocate between the two in any proportions (for example, 50-50, 60-40, etc.). The only way that a married couple can have more than $12,500 added for 1993 to RRSP savings is where *both* husband and wife have earned income. Thus, if your spouse has an earned income of his or her own, he or she too can contribute to an RRSP, earmarking the funds either personally, to you, or in any combination.

Let us examine a situation where a husband has an earned income while his wife remains at home looking after the children. What are the advantages and disadvantages of setting up a spousal plan? One major advantage of splitting RRSP contributions is that over a period of time, two separate pools of capital are built up. Eventually, each pool will give rise to an annuity. Since tax rates for individuals are graduated, the tax bite will be substantially less if the annuity is split so that the husband only gets part of the income while the wife gets the remainder.

The second advantage of a spousal plan relates to another important rule. As a concession for senior citizens who have had the foresight to save for retirement through deferred compensation plans, the Act provides that the first $1,000 of annual private-pension income qualifies for a 25% combined federal and provincial tax credit. (Receipts from the Canada Pension Plan or the Old Age Security Pension do not qualify for this tax benefit.) Thus, the second advantage of splitting your RRSP is to build up two annuities and to double up on the annual $1,000 pension-income credit.

The only disadvantage of a spousal RRSP occurs in the event that a couple gets divorced. Where, for example, a husband has contributed into his wife's plan, the funds belong to her. This disadvantage does not, however, appear to be too serious. In recent years most provinces have adopted family-law provisions whereby assets acquired after marriage are divided 50-50 in the event of a marriage breakdown. Thus, a court would presumably take assets held by each party's RRSP into account as part of a property settlement.

My recommendation is that a spousal RRSP should be used – as long as your marriage is reasonably solid. I don't see much point in being paranoid about what might happen many years in the future. On the other hand, if your marriage is somewhat shaky, why look for trouble? It might then be best to forgo the tax benefits of this arrangement, keeping in mind, however, that the government's legislation calls for a splitting of RRSP benefits in the event of marriage breakdown.

One word of caution. If you place funds into a spousal plan, you must be prepared to leave these dollars for at least a while. The tax rules provide that where a wife withdraws funds from an RRSP, her husband is taxed to the extent that he had made any contributions in his wife's name either for the current year or the two preceding years. This "attribution" of income is designed to prevent a high-bracket taxpayer from contributing funds (on a deductible basis) to his spouse's plan and to prevent her, in turn, from withdrawing the money practically tax-free almost immediately thereafter. You cannot beat the system by having your wife withdraw "older" contributions first. Under the above rules, the most recent contributions are deemed to be the first ones withdrawn for tax purposes. Naturally, the converse also applies when a wife contributes to her husband's plan. The attribution concept does not apply, however, if funds are withdrawn from a spousal plan after a marriage breakdown.

Bequeathing Your RRSP to a Spouse

There are also some important rules that apply on the death of a taxpayer. Essentially, if you have an RRSP at the time of your death, the value of the RRSP is included in your income in the year of death. This rule applies unless you have bequeathed your RRSP to your spouse. Ignorance of this rule can be rather expensive – especially if you were to die late in a year and have RRSP income over and above other income earned in that year. Generally, your will should provide for a spousal bequest of an RRSP. If an RRSP is bequeathed to a spouse, the spouse then has a choice:

- the spouse can pay tax on all or part of that which is received and then have a portion of the money left over; or
- the spouse can transfer funds into his or her own RRSP.

If you are a male and were to die and your wife had very little income in that year, it would probably be advisable for her to take part of the RRSP that she inherits directly into her income. In fact, she might be willing to pay taxes on as much as $100,000. This concept was dealt with in Chapter Four. The total taxes on $100,000 would amount to approximately $35,000, and on an after-tax basis, she would have about sixty-five cents on the dollar available for reinvestment.

Additional RRSP funds could then be transferred into her own RRSP. She can then wait until as late as age seventy-one before making withdrawals. In addition, by placing an inherited RRSP into several separate plans, it is quite possible for your wife to make periodic withdrawals as funds are required. For example, if an inherited RRSP were rolled into ten separate RRSPs, there appears to be no restriction against deregistering one a year for the following ten-year period. Your wife would be able to use the funds to meet ongoing living requirements at a relatively low annual tax cost.

Bequests of RRSPs to Other Beneficiaries

If you die without leaving a surviving spouse, there is still an RRSP roll-over if you leave RRSP funds to dependent children or grandchildren under the age of twenty-six. The rollover is $5,000 for each year that the dependent child or grandchild is under twenty-six at the time you die. This particular rule was passed by Parliament in response to a lobby from unmarried or divorced taxpayers who felt that they were being discriminated against. Unfortunately, for most people this amendment is probably not worth the paper it is written on.

Think about how it would apply in your circumstances if you were to die without leaving a spouse to receive your RRSP. In most cases, you would not have a substantial RRSP portfolio until approximately age fifty-five. This is because the compounding effect really only builds up in the last ten or fifteen years before retirement. When you are fifty-five, do you expect to have dependent children or grandchildren under the age of twenty-six?

(Note that there are no dollar or age limitations if a dependent is mentally or physically infirm.)

Becoming a Non-Resident

Ironically, one of the best benefits that one can derive from an RRSP is reserved for the individual who becomes a non-resident of Canada. The maximum exposure to tax on RRSP withdrawals by a non-resident is a flat rate of 25%.

Temporary Residents of Canada

The RRSP can also be an excellent tax-saving device for temporary residents of Canada. Take, for example, the situation of a doctor coming to this country to obtain specialist training. Assume that he or she takes a hospital position paying $65,000 per annum and expects to stay in Canada for a three-year period. During those three years, the doctor should invest the maximum amount possible in an RRSP. He or she would get a deduction for tax purposes and would save almost half the contribution in taxes each year. Then, when he or she leaves the country, the worst exposure to taxation would be a flat 25%. Any time one can recover forty or forty-five cents on the dollar when contributions are made and not pay more than twenty-five cents on the dollar a few years later, the saving is worthwhile.

What Kind of Plan Should I Have?

RRSPs are administered by trust companies, banks, and insurance companies. In addition, you are allowed to have a self-directed plan in which you appoint trustees (or a trust company) and the trustees make whatever investments that you as the plan-holder desire. Of course, all investments must fall within the acceptable tax guidelines discussed earlier in this chapter.

Traditionally, people tend to wait until the end of February to purchase their RRSPs for the preceding year. Many millions of dollars are spent annually by companies trying to promote their own particular plans. To attempt to compare all the different alternative investments is a full-time job for a qualified investment counsellor. Contrary to popular belief, most accountants and lawyers are not any better equipped to pick "the right" RRSP than you are. When it comes to selecting an RRSP, you cannot necessarily even rely on past performance. Remember that the performance of a particular plan is only a function of those people employed as fund managers. If a well-qualified investment analyst changes jobs, the plan that was number one last year might very well sink to number ten, while last year's poor performer can end up on top the following year.

The only concrete advice that I give is that you invest conservatively. While purists will probably try to extract every last nickel of income, I tend to believe that a 1% or 2% difference in yield is not going to make or break the average middle-income and upper-income individual in the long run. It is true that compounding at a return of 7% instead of 10% can result in a significant difference over twenty or thirty years. However, plan performances will often balance out over the long run and you may not even be aware of what you could have realized had you invested differently many years ago. So don't worry about that extra 1% or 2% unless you have the time to pursue the top performers as the list keeps changing.

Insurance Companies Versus Banks and Trust Companies

Traditionally, insurance companies that administer RRSPs tend to charge the major portion of their fees for handling your money against the initial contributions. This is called a *front-end load*. By contrast, banks and trust companies tend to charge their fees all along in smaller amounts over the entire life of your plan. I once did a study comparing what I considered (at that time) to be an "average" insurance plan to an "average" trust-company plan. Over a period of twenty-five or thirty years, there was only a negligible difference in the assets that would be available to provide a post-retirement annuity.

Thus, when a client asks me to comment on the difference, I tend to say that in the long run, there is no real difference. However, if you are a short-term resident of Canada, or non-residency is imminent, I suggest that you stay away from any plan with a front-end load. This is because, on deregistration, you may find yourself getting less money than you actually put in. So if you plan on leaving Canada in a few years, your prime consideration should be directed towards an RRSP that will yield the largest possible income initially, with the smallest administration charges. In addition, you should obtain an undertaking from the trustees that your money will be refunded on demand and, if there are any reregistration charges, these should be clearly spelled out in your agreement.

Suggested RRSP Investments

Over the years, two schools of thought have evolved with respect to RRSP investments. The first group recommends investing money in interest-bearing securities or mortgages paying the best current yields. Other advisers suggest that you might be better off investing in equity funds involving Canadian public-company securities. The proponents of equities feel that capital growth will outstrip interest yields over the long run – as long as you pick the right securities!

However, equity investments are thought by many to be unattractive because of the fact that all withdrawals from RRSPs are taxable as ordinary income. In other words, you do not get the advantage of the favourable tax treatment accorded to Canadian dividends through the dividend tax credit (see Chapter Nine). In addition, capital gains become transformed into regular income.

At the time this is being written in late 1992, the stock market is not following any encouraging pattern. As long as there is no clear-cut indication that interest rates will stay down, I think that you should be conservative and invest at least part of your money in an RRSP that earns the prevailing rate of interest. After all, investment yields in an RRSP compound on a tax-deferred basis and anything better than the inflation rate is a positive return.

Protecting an RRSP from Loss

Since large sums of money can accumulate in an RRSP, many taxpayers are concerned about the protection of their money in the event that a financial institution fails. In some instances, the Canada Deposit Insurance Corporation (CDIC) may cover potential losses. All chartered banks and federally incorporated trust companies and mortgage loan companies are members of the CDIC. Provincial mortgage loan companies and trust companies may apply for membership. While an RRSP itself is not insured, the investments held by an RRSP that qualify for the deposit insurance are covered. Qualifying investments include savings accounts and guaranteed investment certificates, as well as term deposits redeemable within five years. You should note that insurance does not apply to foreign currency deposits, such as U.S.-dollar savings accounts or U.S.-dollar income certificates.

The maximum insurance coverage is $60,000 per customer per member institution. Thus, if your RRSP is large, you may be well advised to deal with more than one institution either directly or through a self-directed plan. CDIC insurance on an RRSP is separate from CDIC insurance on investments held personally. Thus, it is technically possible to obtain maximum coverage of $120,000 from each institution. While RRSPs sold by life insurance companies are not covered by CDIC protection, an important plus in their favour is the fact that, in many cases, life insurance RRSPs are protected from creditors if the annuitant should go bankrupt. It should be noted that switching an RRSP to an insurance company just before declaring bankruptcy will probably not accomplish anything since the bankruptcy laws are designed to look through these types of avoidance transactions. The insurance industry also maintains a special fund to safeguard investors if a particular company should become bankrupt or insolvent.

Using Your RRSP to Hold the Mortgage on Your Home

In spring 1984, an important new development arose in conjunction with RRSP planning. Revenue Canada, for the first time, decided to permit a self-administered RRSP to hold a mortgage on a plan-holder's home.

As a general rule, an RRSP is not permitted to make a loan either to the annuitant or to a party that is not at arm's length. However, there is an obscure regulation within the RRSP rules that appears to permit these restrictions to be circumvented. Under this regulation, a mortgage loan becomes a qualified investment of an RRSP as long as it is insured by a public mortgage insurer and is administered by an approved National Housing Act (NHA) lender. Thus, as long as a mortgage is issued and administered under normal commercial terms, it appears that the Revenue authorities will allow this as a qualified investment.

If you are interested in investigating the possibility of your RRSP holding your mortgage, you should be aware of what the requirements are. The first step involves transferring your RRSP funds to a self-administered plan. Next, you arrange to have the RRSP make you a loan secured by a mortgage on your home. The mortgage must be administered by an approved NHA lender, but this should not be a problem since most financial institutions qualify. Finally, you must arrange to have your mortgage insured by the Mortgage Insurance Company of Canada. Once this is done, you can withdraw the funds from your RRSP as a loan, completely tax-free.

However, before you rush out to do all this, you must take care to determine whether or not it all makes sense. Keep in mind that there are mortgage-insurance fees to pay and these range from 1% to 1½% of the entire mortgage on your home. In addition, the plan administrator will probably charge a fee for arranging the various transactions.

Here is another situation in which an hour or two spent with your own accountant would be well worth your while. Keep in mind that this type of planning can be particularly attractive if you are unable to obtain alternate sources of personal financing. If the money that you withdrew from your RRSP is used for business or investment purposes, you may find that there are additional benefits. In this case, the interest that you pay to your RRSP will generally be tax-deductible even though it will accumulate within your RRSP on a tax-deferred basis.

Home Buyers' Plan

In February 1992, the Minister of Finance released draft legislation and explanatory notes outlining the mechanism for a new Home Buyers' Plan. The proposals will allow an individual to withdraw up to $20,000 from an RRSP to fund the acquisition of a "principal place of residence."

Both spouses may take advantage of the program; accordingly, up to $40,000 of RRSP funds may be used to purchase a home. These rules also apply to spousal RRSPs.

Normally, when an individual makes a withdrawal from an RRSP, such amounts are included in income. However, if an individual withdraws funds between February 25, 1992 and March 2, 1993 and acquires a "qualified home" before October 1, 1993, such withdrawals ("excluded withdrawals") will not be included in income. Otherwise, the withdrawals will be included in income in the year of withdrawal unless the amounts are repaid before December 31, 1993.

Here is a summary of the rules:

- A person must be a resident of Canada both at the time the funds are withdrawn and at the time the home is acquired.
- A home under construction is deemed to be acquired when the home becomes inhabitable by the individual.
- A condominium unit is deemed to be acquired on "first closing" (i.e., when there is an entitlement to immediate vacant possession).
- A recreational property (e.g., a cottage) which may otherwise be designated as a "principal residence" will not qualify for these rules unless it is the "principal place of residence."
- A qualifying home may be jointly acquired with one or more other persons.
- A qualifying home must be used as a principal place of residence not later than one year after its acquisition.
- A written agreement for the acquisition or construction of the qualifying home must be entered into before the time of withdrawal.
- The qualifying home must not have been previously acquired by the individual or the individual's spouse.
- A written request must be made in prescribed form setting out the location of the qualifying home.
- A prescribed form must be submitted to an issuer of an RRSP in connection with the plan. This form must be filed by the issuer with

Revenue Canada no later than 15 days after the calendar quarter in which it was submitted to the issuer.

- To avoid any amount being included in income, at least 1/15 of the total of the withdrawals must be repaid annually. The amount withdrawn from the RRSP must be repaid between 1994 and 2008. The minimum annual repayment is calculated taking into account previous repayments on a cumulative basis. If an individual repays less than the minimum annual amount, the deficiency will be included in income. This income inclusion is treated as a repayment of the loan. Future catch-up payments will not create a deduction. If a taxpayer repays more than the minimum amount in a year, the excess is carried forward and can be applied toward a future year's repayment.

- Withdrawals may be made from more than one RRSP. Repayments need not be made to the same RRSP from which the funds were withdrawn unless the home is not acquired. Revenue Canada will provide an annual statement of required repayments.

- If a taxpayer turns seventy-one before full repayment, the amounts unpaid will be included in income as they become due unless the full amount is repaid before the end of the year in which he or she turns seventy-one.

- Special rules will apply if an individual becomes bankrupt in a year.

Restriction of Annual RRSP Contributions

If a person takes advantage of this program, the otherwise deductible contribution to an RRSP between February 25, 1992 and March 1993 will be reduced. Any contributions to an RRSP as a result of certain tax-free transfers (for example, retiring allowances, transfers from a pension plan, etc.) are not affected by these rules.

The annual repayment of the loans will not be considered to be deductible premiums nor excess amounts for the purpose of calculating penalty tax. Furthermore, interest on debts incurred to finance the repayment will not be deductible.

Death of a Taxpayer

If a taxpayer dies, any unpaid amount will be included in income in the year of death unless the taxpayer's spouse assumes the deceased's position with respect to future repayments.

Ceasing to Be a Resident of Canada

If a person ceases to be a resident of Canada, any unpaid portion will be included in income unless there is a repayment of the amount before either the tax return due date or ninety days after becoming a non-resident, whichever is earlier.

Although this program is slated to expire at the end of March 1993, you should keep abreast of future developments in case the 1993 federal budget contains an extension of the deadlines.

"Cashing in" an RRSP for a Life Annuity

At one time, there was only one way to "cash in" an RRSP. The Income Tax Act required an individual, prior to reaching the age of seventy-one, to use the funds accumulated in an RRSP to purchase a life annuity from an insurance company. The annuity benefits were then taxable as and when they were received. The only available alternative was to make lump-sum withdrawals from the RRSP before age seventy-one and become liable for income tax on all amounts received. In order to protect your position against an early death, you were also permitted to modify the ordinary life annuity by adding a "guaranteed term" rider. (A guaranteed term means that payments continue for at least that length of time even if the annuitant dies prematurely. However, any time a taxpayer lives beyond the guaranteed term, the payments will continue until such time as the individual dies.) Several years ago, the maximum guaranteed term permitted under an RRSP life annuity was raised from fifteen to twenty years. In addition, you are also allowed to arrange a joint-and-last-survivor annuity program, in which payments would continue out of an RRSP until both husband and wife have died. Even the joint-and-last-survivor option may now be structured to have a guaranteed term of up to twenty years.

Over the years, the requirement that one deal only with a life insurance company at the tail end of a program did not appeal to many potential RRSP investors. Actually, the insurance companies have been somewhat unjustly maligned because of a very common misconception. If you are seventy years old and you go to an insurance company with $100,000 in your RRSP, you could probably find a company that would agree to pay you an annuity of approximately $13,000 a year if you do not opt for any guaranteed term. Of course, you would not ordinarily think that this is any bargain. If you are male, you are probably conscious of the fact that your average life expectancy is only seventy-two years. Thus, how would you feel about receiving only two years' worth of annuities, or $25,000 out of a $100,000 investment made initially?

If you agree to the above reasoning, you have fallen into a common trap. While it is true that the average life expectancy of a male would be seventy-two years, this is only for a person under forty. Once you pass the age of forty, life expectancy goes up. You will find, if you examine a standard table of mortality rates (see Chapter Ten), that a seventy-year-old male has a life expectancy of another twelve years, and that a female of the same age is projected to live another fifteen years. A male age seventy-three does not have a life expectancy of "minus one." Thus, an insurance company is not really mistreating you by offering $13,000 a year as an RRSP yield. In preparing calculations, the insurance company must budget for a twelve- to fifteen-year payout, without any guarantees. Since most people are not aware of this, insurance companies have acquired "bad reputations" somewhat unjustly over the years.

Two Additional Options: Fixed-Term Annuities and Registered Retirement Income Funds

In 1978 the government decided to allow other financial institutions to enter the RRSP annuity field and two further options were introduced:

- A fixed-term annuity may now be purchased to provide benefits to age ninety, and/or
- RRSP savings may be transferred into a special kind of investment vehicle – a Registered Retirement Income Fund (RRIF).

Typically, however, the government gave and took away at the same time. Earlier, I indicated that anyone issuing a life annuity to a seventy-year-old must be prepared to pay out over a twelve-year period. Under the fixed-term annuity to age ninety, the same initial capital is paid out over a twenty-year period. Thus, the penalty for taking a fixed-term annuity (over twenty years) is receiving smaller annual payments than under a life annuity. The fixed-term option may therefore only be attractive to those individuals with other incomes and other assets who wish to pass on estates as large as possible to their heirs. Of course, rates of return are subject to change from time to time and it is always necessary to shop around for the best possible deal before making a final decision.

Under the RRIF option, a specific minimum fraction of one's total RRSP assets – capital plus accumulated earnings – must be withdrawn

Figure 5–4 **Required Minimum Payments as a Percentage of RRIF Assets for RRIFs Established after 1992**

Age	Percentage
71	7.38
72	7.48
73	7.59
74	7.71
75	7.85
76	7.99
77	8.15
78	8.33
79	8.53
80	8.75
81	8.99
82	9.27
83	9.58
84	9.93
85	10.33
86	10.79
87	11.33
88	11.96
89	12.71
90	13.62
91	14.73
92	16.12
93	17.92
94	20.00
95	20.00
96	20.00
97	20.00
98	20.00
99	20.00
100+	20.00

each year to provide an annual income, although, if the taxpayer so desires, he or she may draw more than the minimum in any given year. Actually, if one draws too much early on, there may be a significant price to pay down the road.

Figure 5-4 shows how the minimum percentages work for RRIFs established after 1992.

For taxpayers younger than seventy-one, the required minimum percentage withdrawal each year is "one over ninety minus the taxpayer's age." Therefore, for a sixty-five-year-old individual who chooses to move his or her RRSP funds into a RRIF, the minimum withdrawal would be $1/(90-65) = 1/25 = 4\%$.

The Income Tax Act permits a retirement annuity to be commuted in whole or in part, at any time, in exchange for a lump sum. This measure is intended to alleviate hardships that might otherwise arise where an individual who has committed to an annuity now finds that his or her needs have changed. If more than the annuity amount is required, the ability to commute will provide an opportunity to obtain a lump-sum benefit.

The tax rules also allow you to base the term of an annuity or RRIF on the age of your spouse, if the spouse is younger. In the event that you were to die before your spouse, the benefits under any of the options might therefore be bequeathed to your spouse. Otherwise, the value of any remaining benefits must be included in income in the year in which you die.

It is important to note that the *rate of return on an RRIF is, in fact, flexible and is tied in with investment yields as they fluctuate both up and down.*

An RRIF owner is allowed to manage his or her own investments through directions to the trust or insurance company holding the funds, similar to the continuing provisions for self-administered RRSPs. There is a wide variety of qualified investments available, matching those allowed under RRSP investment rules. These include Canadian stocks, bonds, bank certificates, savings bonds, and mutual funds, as well as arm's-length investments in the shares of private Canadian corporations. In other words, *not only is the yield flexible, but so is the choice of investments.*

In some instances, individuals who retire early may want to take large amounts out of their RRIFs initially, and then take out decreased amounts once they start to receive Canada or Quebec pension benefits. Or they may want to slowly increase their withdrawals in circumstances where, for example, post-retirement plans include expensive travel. Presumably, at some future time, the RRIF could then be structured to provide for smaller withdrawals after, say, age seventy-eight or eighty, when anticipated travel and entertainment expenditures would decrease.

More Miscellaneous Rules Related to RRSPs

Note that direct transfers of lump sum amounts are permitted between most retirement savings plans on a tax-free basis. However, since 1988, individuals are no longer permitted to withdraw lump sum amounts from a plan during a year and subsequently contribute equivalent amounts to an RRSP within 60 days after the end of the year. Again, tax-deferred transfers must be made directly from one plan to another.

Although most superannuation and pension benefits do not qualify as earned income, there is a special provision that took effect in 1990 that will assist individuals reaching retirement in the next few years. Contributions to *spousal RRSPs* out of periodic (not lump sum) payments from a registered pension plan or deferred profit-sharing plan are permitted before 1995, up to annual limits of $6,000.

Registered Pension Plans

One of the most popular of the deferred compensation plans is the employer-sponsored registered pension plan. Essentially, a pension plan can be one of two kinds. It can be a "non-contributory" plan, in which the employer alone makes annual contributions on behalf of the participating employees; or it can be a "contributory" plan, in which both the employer and the employee make contributions.

Within the limits described later in this section, both employee and employer contributions are tax-deductible. The funds are placed in a trust and they are invested on behalf of the participants. As long as the trustees make qualified investments, the income generated on these contributions is not taxable. Thus, there is a compounding of both principal and income from year to year that builds up a lump sum that is ultimately used to provide retirement pension benefits.

Upon retirement, the amount accumulated on behalf of each particular employee is paid out, generally in the form of a life annuity, thereby providing funds towards future living expenses. Although the benefits received at that time are taxable, the employee is likely to be in a lower tax bracket after retirement than previously. As an additional tax incentive to participate in such a plan, there is the annual pension-income credit, which effectively makes the first $1,000 at least partially tax-free each year.

Defined Benefit Pension Plans Versus Money Purchase Pension Plans

There are essentially two kinds of pension plan programs. The first of these is called a Defined Benefit Plan. A defined benefit plan is one that undertakes to provide an employee with a certain percentage of his or her salary as a pension, depending on years of service. For example, the typical defined benefit pension formula might be: 1½%–2% per annum (to a maximum of thirty-five years, or 70%) multiplied by the average of the last (or best) three to five years' salary.

Thus, an employee whose average last (best) five years' salary was $40,000, and who worked for an employer for twenty years, might expect a pension of 40% (2% × 20 years) of $40,000, or $16,000 per year. In some instances, these pensions are indexed for inflation after retirement.

The major advantage of a defined benefit plan is the fact that a participant knows what he or she is likely to obtain from the program. If you retire after many years of service, a pension of up to, say 70% of your average final few years' earnings should be more than adequate to meet your post-retirement needs.

Nevertheless, from an employer's perspective, a defined benefit plan has a major drawback. A serious problem could surface if there is a severe bout of inflation at a point in time just before a large number of employees retire. It may then be that the particular program lacks adequate funding to provide the pensions that had been promised. So far, it appears that no major employers in Canada have run into the problem of having to "bail out" their pension programs, although the possibility is always there.

As an alternative to a defined benefit program, an employer can institute a "money purchase" plan. Under this kind of program, employer and (generally) employee contributions are invested annually at the best possible yields for as long as each participating employee is employed. Then, whatever has been accumulated to the credit of each particular individual is used to provide the best pension possible following that individual's retirement.

A money purchase plan has a drawback from an employee's standpoint, because the actual pension may become inadequate in times of heavy inflation. However, the same drawback works to the employer's advantage. This is because the employer is not at risk to provide a defined benefit for which adequate resources may be lacking.

Generally, defined plans are provided by government, public institutions, and certain large public corporations. For smaller businesses, it would appear that a defined benefit program is extremely risky to implement.

Employee Contributions to a Registered Pension Plan Beyond 1990

The basic rule for members of all pension plans starting 1991 is that *all* contributions in respect of post-1990 service will be tax-deductible as long as these amounts are required (as certified by a licensed actuary) to adequately fund a registered employer-sponsored plan. This rule will apply to both employer and employee contributions, regardless of whether they are made on a current or past service basis. For money purchase plans, the plan registration rules now limit total contributions made in the calendar year to 18% of the year's pensionable earnings, up to the following dollar amounts:

1991	$12,500	1994	$14,500
1992	12,500	1995	15,500
1993	13,500	1996	Indexed for increases in the average industrial wage

At this point, the government is not willing to commit to dollar limits beyond 1995.

In the case of a money purchase plan, whatever amount is not contributed by an employer, an employee may contribute and deduct personally – either to the pension itself or, as explained further on, to an RRSP.

A member of a defined benefit pension plan will receive information that will allow him or her to make additional contributions to a Registered Retirement Savings Plan on an annual basis. The maximum RRSP contribution will be reduced by a "pension adjustment," which is calculated based on the benefits that the specific pension plan is structured to provide. While calculations are complex, individuals will not have to be concerned with making them since Revenue Canada will advise everyone of the maximum contribution that can be made. One interesting byproduct of these rules is that individuals who belong to a pension plan for only part of a year will no longer be placed at a disadvantage when it comes to personal RRSPs.

Improved Minimum Standards for Private Pension Plans

Effective January 1, 1987, a number of important changes came into effect for pension plans under federal jurisdiction. The federal government anticipates that provincial governments and private employers will consider parallel reforms. Included among the key changes are the following:

1. Vested and locking in – under the old rules, an employee's rights to pension benefits only had to "vest" after ten years of service or at age forty-five. Under the new rules, an employee's right to pension benefits now becomes vested and locked in after only two years of participation. This ensures that workers who change jobs are able to save more effectively for retirement.

2. Improved portability – a big problem inherent in the old pension system was the fact that workers who changed jobs were often prevented from taking their pension entitlements with them to their new employments. As of January 1, 1987, a number of new options are available. An employee might choose to leave his or her pension entitlements with a former employer or may opt to transfer them to a new employer's pension plan with that employer's consent. Alternatively, there is a mechanism to permit transfers to a "locked in RRSP."

3. Employer contributions – in some pension plans, employers have historically contributed very little until employees had completed many years of service. This sometimes meant that workers who changed jobs ended up paying a significant portion of the cost of their own pensions. Under the new rules, employers are required to pay at least half the value of a pension earned when a worker changes jobs or retires.

4. Refunding provisions – the previous system of standards contained no rules for refunding employee contributions. Under the new rules, any unvested employee contributions must be returned to employees when they leave. Employers are also required to pay reasonable interest on employee contributions.

5. Eligibility for plan membership – under the old standards, in some instances full-time employees were prohibited from joining an employer pension and, as a general rule, part-time workers were never eligible. Effective January 1, 1987, pension plans are open to

all workers. Full-time workers must be eligible to join after two years of service while part-time workers attain eligibility if they earn more than 35% of the average industrial wage in each of two consecutive years.

6. Early retirement – some pensions did not provide for early retirement options. Under the new standards, pension plan members must be allowed to opt for early retirement ten years before normal retirement age.

7. Improving pensions for women – a number of pension reforms are of particular benefit to women. First, survivor benefits must amount to at least 75% of the full pension that was paid. Second, a surviving spouse is now entitled to the full value of a pension earned by a plan member who dies prior to retirement. Finally, survivor benefits may not be discontinued if a surviving spouse remarries. Pension reform now also permits the value of pension entitlements to be divided on marriage breakdown. Moreover, under identical circumstances, periodic benefits paid to women must be equal to those paid to men, even though women might be expected to live longer.

8. Inflation protection – the government would like to encourage pension plans to provide benefit increases to pensioners in order to maintain the purchasing power of pensions. The government admits, though, that a consensus on inflation protection standards has not been reached with the provinces and the private sector. Presumably, providing such protection could be extremely dangerous if inflation accelerates. It is expected that inflation protection will be limited primarily to very large employers and to the federal government itself, which can always print money to fund its own pension obligations if necessary!

9. Information disclosure – under the new standards, pension plans are now required to disclose information to participants about earned benefits and accumulated contributions each year.

Profit-Sharing Plans

Certain employers have rejected the registered pension plan route as a fringe benefit since it ties into fixed annual contributions regardless of profitability. Some of these have opted in favour of profit-sharing plans.

With profit-sharing plans, an employer's contributions depend on profits and are not restricted as to the amount that is deductible for tax purposes – as long as contributions are reasonable. Profit-sharing plans are also not subject to the severe investment restrictions of other (deferred) plans.

Profit-sharing plans do, however impose some important disadvantages. Employees are taxed immediately on employer contributions as well as on their share of a plan's income for the year.

Deferred Profit-Sharing Plans (DPSPs)

The Income Tax Act also provides for the registration of deferred profit-sharing plans. These plans are much like profit-sharing plans, since employer contributions are flexible, but they give employees the important advantage of not being taxed either as a result of these contributions or on the trust's annual income until benefits are actually received. In this respect, a deferred profit-sharing plan is much like a registered pension plan, except that *employees cannot make any contributions at all.*

Starting in 1991, deferred profit-sharing plan limits are 18% of earnings up to the following dollar limits:

1991	$6,250
1992	6,750
1993	7,250
1994	7,750
1995	Indexed

If an individual is a member of a DPSP and the employer contributes the maximum, the individual is still permitted to contribute up to an equivalent amount into a personal RRSP. For example, if an employer contributes $7,750 to a DPSP in 1996, and the individual contributes an equivalent amount to his RRSP, the total amount going toward building retirement savings will be $15,500.

It should be noted that a DPSP has two major advantages from an *employer's* standpoint when compared to a pension plan. Since a DPSP is a sharing of profits, little or no contributions need be made in years when business conditions are bad. In addition, the employer is not bound to guarantee a specific income for any employee that is tied into a percentage of some future salary, which could escalate sharply due to inflation.

Like the other deferred plans sanctioned by the Income Tax Act, there are strict investment controls for DPSPs and purchases of non-qualified investments or foreign investments (in excess of allowable limits) may result in penalties. After 1990, the ability to combine a corporate DPSP with a personal RRSP becomes extremely attractive.

Special Rules for Deferred Profit-Sharing Plans

Under the law before 1991, contributions or other amounts allocated to a beneficiary of a DPSP had to vest irrevocably in that beneficiary not later than five years after the date of allocation. This rule continues to apply for allocations made before 1991. For contributions to a DPSP in 1991 and subsequent years, a new rule requires immediate vesting for any employee who has belonged to the plan for two or more years. Any amount forfeited in the plan must be paid back to the employer of the beneficiary. Similar rules also apply to money purchase registered pension plans.

A DPSP may invest in the shares of the employer corporation. This is another benefit not available within the registered pension plan legislation. A proposal originally made in 1986 to limit investments by DPSPs in the shares of the employer to not more than one-half of a plan's assets has been dropped.

Special RRSP Rules for Members of
DPSPs and Money Purchase RPPs

Beginning in 1996, the money purchase limit will be indexed according to increases in average wages. You should note that increases in these limits come into effect *one year earlier* than those provided for RRSPs alone. An individual who belongs to either a DPSP or a money purchase RPP will be entitled to contribute to a personal RRSP based on the dollar maximums just noted minus an amount called the "pension adjustment" (PA). The PA for these individuals is simply the total of *all* employee *and* employer contributions made in the previous calendar year to all money purchase RPPs and DPSPs.

For example, assume that in 1993 an employer contributed $1,900 to a particular individual employee's money purchase RPP and the employee also contributed $1,700. Assume that the earned income of the employee in 1992 was $52,000. Thus, the maximum RRSP contribution for 1993 will be $9,360 (18% of $52,000). From this, the employee must also deduct his or her pension adjustment (PA) for the previous year (1992) of $3,600 (RPP contributions of $1,900 and $1,700). Therefore, the maximum allowable RRSP contribution in 1993 will be $5,760 ($9,360 – $3,600).

Special RRSP Rules for
Members of Defined Benefit Registered Pension Plans

For members of defined benefit RPPs, the total retirement savings limit is now also 18% of the previous year's earned income, to the dollar maximums that apply to members of money purchase plans, also minus a pension adjustment (PA). For members of defined benefit plans, however, the calculation of the PA is, as outlined previously, somewhat more complicated. It is based on a formula that is designed to reflect the value of accrued benefits to the employee under the RPP in respect of the previous year. Employers are now required to report PAs for each employee to Revenue Canada on the T4 slips every year. If an individual is entitled to benefits from the plans of more than one employer in the year, Revenue Canada will combine the PAs reported by each employer. Revenue Canada will use the reported PAs and tax return data to calculate and then advise all taxpayers (whether or not they belong to an RPP or DPSP) of their total RRSP contribution room. It appears that the current year limit plus the unused contribution room from previous years will be reported separately. It would also appear that taxpayers will not be notified each year until late in the calendar year. Therefore, anyone wishing to contribute to an RRSP earlier will have to estimate the maximum permissible RRSP contribution on his or her own. For those taxpayers who are members of DPSPs or money purchase plans, the calculation will be relatively simple. For anyone who is a member of a defined benefit pension plan, it may be necessary to get certain information from the administrators of the pension plan before the calculations can be made.

Your Own Pension Plan or Deferred
Profit-Sharing Plan (DPSP)

It is important for each individual to understand the pension plan or DPSP of his or her employer (if the employer does in fact have such a plan). Usually, there are various options available that are unique to each particular plan, and while I have discussed the general operation of pension programs, proper investment planning cannot be accomplished without an understanding of what the specific options are. For example, if your benefits are fixed at 2% for each year of service, you may not wish to make optional contributions – especially if you anticipate a lifelong career with the same employer.

However, if you are a member of a pension plan or DPSP and your total contributions are less than the allowable maximum, it would generally pay for you to make up the difference by contributing to a personal RRSP. In addition, if you are already involved in an employer-sponsored pension, you should be more inclined to use a spousal RRSP if you are married. This is so that you and your spouse can ultimately split post-retirement annuity incomes.

CHAPTER 6

A Tax-Shelter Update

Tax Shelters – A Brief Background

A tax shelter may result when a tax-deductible loss from a particular source is offset against other income. In Canada, there were three popular tax shelters in the 1970s: real estate investments, feature films, and oil and gas exploration ventures. Unfortunately, with changes in the tax rules and with the severe recession of 1982-84, many of these have disappeared.

In retrospect, it can be said that too many people placed shelter aspects ahead of investment considerations in the late 1970s. They forgot that a "tax loss" is not the same thing as a "tax shelter." An effective tax shelter only occurs when there are write-offs that produce losses for tax purposes, but where the *value* of the investment has not diminished and there has been no loss of cash. Just because a loss is deductible does not make it a tax shelter. Somebody in a 45% tax bracket who actually lays out one dollar is still out of pocket a minimum of fifty-five cents – even if the expenditure is deductible.

Several years ago, government programs to encourage research and development in high technology created a new tax shelter called the Scientific Research Tax Credit (SRTC). The SRTC was, however, short-lived. Certain loopholes were discovered and in 1985 the government decided that any incentives for research and development should go directly to those entities carrying on such activities and not to investors.

At the beginning of the 1980s, tax shelters sprang up in businesses providing recreational and other services through the use of yachts, recreational vehicles, hotels, nursing homes, and other similar property. Also in 1985, however, the income tax regulations were amended so that individuals are no longer allowed to shelter other income with losses created by depreciation from such property, even if it is used in a business that offers services combined with the use of the property itself.

These new rules do not apply if the investors are individuals who are *personally active* in the day-to-day operations of the business. In a case of a partnership, capital cost allowance (tax depreciation) is restricted unless the partners who are personally active are entitled to share in at least two-thirds of the income and/or loss of the partnership for the year. The new regulations became law for the 1986 tax year.

This leaves the Canadian public, figuratively speaking, naked in the tax shelter arena. Nevertheless, there are still some excellent opportunities. In this chapter, I will first introduce the most important tax shelter of all – the lifetime exemption from capital gains taxes on the first $100,000 of such profits ($500,000 for farmers and small-business owners). I will then move to a discussion of real estate, including your principal residence, because of its importance to most people. Finally, I will deal with a special kind of insurance policy called "universal life." The lifetime capital gains exemption is so important that a detailed discussion merits a separate chapter. Opportunities for adventurous planning are dealt with in Chapter Nine.

An Introduction to the Lifetime Capital Gains Tax Exemption

The lifetime capital gains tax exemption is the most encouraging tax change made in the last ten years, especially for small-business owners and entrepreneurs. It is a major initiative to encourage risk-taking and investment in both small and large businesses.

The exemption applies to a maximum of $100,000 on capital gains from most property and $500,000 with respect to qualified farm property and shares of small-business corporations. Three-quarters of capital gains in excess of the exemption limits are taxable after 1989.

After February 1992, the $100,000 capital gains exemption no longer applies to real estate, other than such property used as part of an active business.

Capital gains accrued to March 1, 1992 continue to be eligible for the capital gains exemption for real estate which is owned at the end of

February 1992. The eligible amount will be computed by simply prorating the gain over the period of ownership.

After 1987, the amount of capital gains eligible for the exemption is reduced by "cumulative net investment losses." In other words, if interest expense on money borrowed to acquire growth investments is claimed for tax purposes on an ongoing basis to create losses each year, these losses must effectively be "recaptured" in the year that capital property is sold at a profit. This last rule does not affect the total amount of exemption available to a person over his or her lifetime, but may retard the obtaining of benefits.

You should not that the rules are structured so that husbands and wives are *not* considered together. Therefore, for stock market and many other investments, it is possible for a husband and wife together to earn up to $200,000 of gains tax-free. In the case of a family business or farm, up to $1 million of tax-free growth can conceivably be realized through sales to third parties or be passed on between generations.

If an individual claims an exemption for a $500,000 gain on either qualified farm property or shares of a small-business corporation, or a combination of both, he or she is not eligible to claim up to a further $100,000 on other property.

The farm exemption applies to farm land and buildings, shares in farm corporations, and interests in family farm partnerships. Qualified property does not, however, include real estate unless it was owned by the taxpayer or the taxpayer's spouse or children for at least twenty-four months immediately before its disposition. Moreover, one of two other conditions must also be fulfilled. First, in at least two calendar years, *gross revenues* (for a fiscal period ended in the year) of the taxpayer or taxpayer's spouse or children, from the farming business in which the real estate was used, must have exceeded that person's *net income* from all other sources. Alternatively, it must be shown that throughout any twenty-four-month period, the property was used by a family farm partnership, or a family farm corporation, owned by the taxpayer or the taxpayer's spouse or children in the course of carrying on a farming business in Canada.

In the case of a small-business corporation, the exemption only applies if the shares were not held by anyone other than the taxpayer or family members throughout the immediately preceding twenty-four-month period. A small-business corporation is generally defined as a Canadian-controlled private company that uses all or substantially all of its assets in active business carried on primarily in Canada. Also included are Canadian private holding companies whose assets are shares in operating companies, which themselves qualify as small-business corporations.

The special principal residence capital gains exemption, which has been available to Canadians since 1972 and which will be dealt with later in this chapter, is not affected by the capital gains exemption rules.

The capital gains exemption represents a great opportunity for a more aggressive investment policy than before. In other words, your potential rate of return can be considerably higher, making it more advantageous to engage in risk activity.

Throughout the remainder of this book, reference will be made to capital gains and the exemption where appropriate. For small business, which is covered in Chapters Twelve to Fifteen, there is now a larger than ever incentive to split ownership between husbands and wives.

Tax Shelters in the Real Estate Industry – An Era Ended

The income tax rules for real estate investment have changed dramatically over the last ten years, virtually eliminating real estate as a tax shelter. In the "good old days," investors in rental or commercial developments were permitted to obtain an immediate write-off of "soft costs" incurred prior to the completion of any construction project. These expenditures included items such as legal and accounting fees, costs of obtaining financing, interest expense during construction, and property taxes related to real property. Immediate write-offs for soft costs by investors are no longer permitted.

In the past, the total of these "first-time write-offs" often amounted to as much as 20% or 25% of the value of any construction project, and the tax savings served to greatly subsidize the amount of net cash required to purchase property. Under the new rules, such costs must be added to the capital cost of land and building. The amounts that are added to the building (i.e., "capitalized") will then be written off at the same depreciation rate as the building itself – 4% a year. The need to capitalize these costs will also ensure that these amounts will be recaptured when the building is sold if, in fact, the property does not depreciate.

Real Estate As an Investment

The drastic steps taken by the federal government in the last few years to reduce inflation removed many tax incentives and caught most

Canadians by surprise. High interest rates throughout much of the 1980s made real estate a difficult choice as an investment in many parts of the country. Now, however, we have a very different picture. Interest rates have decreased by almost half and if rents start to go up, the scene may soon change again for the better.

In 1980, when I wrote the first edition of this book, I suggested that you could borrow money at 13% (then the current rate) to acquire property even if at the start you received no rental return on your money. Given an after-tax cost of only around 7% (assuming deductibility of interest), I suggested that increases in the market value of property would more than offset this cost. This approach may again be valid and we will examine a case study, which will show you in detail what I mean. Specifically, you will see that you do not need a substantial amount of cash in order to enter the real estate market. As long as you have borrowing power and can subsidize a negative cash flow out of excess earnings from your job, business, or profession, real estate might be just the right investment for you. The name of the game is leverage – making investments using other people's money. If interest rates stay down and/or the Canadian dollar is devalued over the next couple of years, there may soon be a quick revival of investor interest in real estate – even within the Toronto area where the market has been somewhat "cold" over the past couple of years.

The important thing to realize is that investment interest expense continues to be tax-deductible – even in cases where the related investments are not "profitable" on an ongoing basis. For many Canadians, therefore, the cost of borrowing money for investment translates to only a little more than fifty cents on the dollar. On the other hand, if you make a capital gain on eventual sale, the government will not take more than one-third of your profit.

A Real Estate Case Study

To illustrate the concept of examining real estate primarily as an investment, here is a specific study. While relevant interest and tax rates may have changed a bit, the method of analysis is still valid. You will see that a "bad" investment can become a "good" opportunity when you take into account leverage and interest deductibility.

Several years ago, a group of friends came to me and asked if I wished to join in a small real estate venture. The idea behind this "partnership" was for each of us to put up $10,000 or $15,000 and to try to find properties that would carry themselves out of rental revenues with minimal downpayments. I liked the idea and so I agreed to participate.

Several weeks later, a real estate agent brought me a listing describing a small apartment building for sale in one of the nicer sections of Calgary. My friends had inspected this property and were impressed by its excellent condition and the fact that it was fully rented. I was asked to review the numbers. The first thing I did was prepare the schedule which appears in Figure 6-1.

What I wanted to do was determine the probable cash flow from the property before mortgage repayments. In my projections, I used a 3% vacancy allowance. Of course, a vacancy factor varies from time to time and place to place and the 3% is for illustration only – it should not be constructed as being reasonable in all circumstances.

Figure 6–1 **Projected Statement of Income and Expenses for Proposed Apartment Building Investment**

Gross rents projected on an annual basis		$70,000
Less: 3% vacancy factor		2,100
		$67,900
Less: Expenses		
Taxes	5,000	
Insurance and heating	3,000	
Light and power	1,500	
Garbage	700	
Janitor	2,200	
Management fee	3,400	
Maintenance and supplies	2,400	18,200
Cash flow before mortgage		$49,700

My next step was to calculate how much financing the property could carry. There was an existing first mortgage of $282,000 which had recently been placed on the building at $10\frac{3}{4}\%$. I determined the cash flow after first mortgage as follows:

Cash flow before mortgage	$49,700
First mortgage $282,000 at 10 ¾ % — annual payments from amortization tables	32,400
Cash flow after first mortgage	$17,300

The next question was how much capital one should invest in order to earn $17,300. To answer it, I reasoned that either my friends and I had investment capital or we did not have the funds necessary to acquire the property. At that time, if we had cash, we could have invested in second mortgages at a 13% rate of return. Alternatively, we could have pooled our borrowing power to obtain a second mortgage at that same 13% rate. In either event, money was "worth" 13% at that time.

I consulted my mortgage tables and I then determined that a cash flow of $17,300 would provide a 13% yield on an investment of $130,000. In other words, if we invested our own money, $17,300 would provide a 13% rate of return to *us* while, on the other hand, if we borrowed $130,000 instead, the property could absorb this debt and still break even. I therefore computed the value of the property as a whole to be $412,000, being the sum of first- and second-mortgage financing ($282,000 + $130,000).

The asking price was $589,000, and I told my friends to forget about this property as an investment since it was greatly overpriced. However a few weeks later, I was informed that the property had, in fact, been sold for $567,000. My friends were somewhat upset and suggested rather drily that I review my calculations. I checked my figures and found that I had made no arithmetic errors. Being somewhat curious as to the buyer's motives, I went on to do some additional analysis. I first concluded that whoever had bought this property had overpaid by $155,000.

Actual selling price	$567,000
Break-even price	412,000
Excess cost	$155,000

I then reasoned that the purchaser must either have had funds of his own or substantial "borrowing power." If he had capital, I concluded that he was willing to invest $155,000 at a zero rate of return instead of the 13% that he could otherwise have obtained in second mortgages. Conversely, if he borrowed the additional funds at 13%, my tables told me that the annual cash-flow loss would be $20,500. My first inclination was to doubt the sanity of the purchaser. He was either giving up $20,500 a year that he himself could otherwise have earned, or he was willing to pay *out* this amount each year to a lending institution.

However, I decided to carry the calculations a little further. In the first years of ownership, whenever a rental property produces a cash-flow loss because of financing, most of that loss (as much as 99%) is as a result of interest expense. Accordingly, the loss is deductible. This loss *cannot* be made *larger* through depreciation, but in my example, the *after-tax* cash-flow loss would be considerably less than $20,500. In fact, if I assumed an investor in the 45% bracket, the *after-tax* cash-flow loss became only $20,500 × 55%, or $11,275.

Against this loss, I would then have to balance a projected appreciation in value. Suppose real estate in Calgary was expected to appreciate by 8% a year. Eight percent of $567,000 is $45,000. Even after taking off (for simplicity) a 30% provision for real estate commission costs and taxes on the gain, there might still be an anticipated after-tax appreciation after only one year of $31,500. If you compare the after-tax cash-flow loss of $11,275 against $31,500 of (probable) appreciation, the investment starts to appear more and more attractive. The only problem, however, is that the cash-flow loss is *definite* while the appreciation in value is *speculative*.

The Risk Factor

A good friend of mine has what he calls a "greater fool theory" with respect to real estate, and recent events have proven it. In the late 1980s, real estate became overpriced in many places in Ontario because everyone appeared willing to lay out substantial amounts of money, figuring that there would always be a "greater fool" somewhere who would automatically overpay an *extra* 10%-15% less than one year later! As long as there was no recession, everyone made money. However, when hard times arrived, many of those who were left holding overpriced properties found themselves in financial difficulties.

You should never pay too much for property unless you can accept the risk of a potential loss. Ironically, real estate investments tend to favour those who have made money in the past. If you are wealthy, you can afford to subsidize a property that is losing money and still hang on until market conditions improve. As long as there is no sacrifice in your standard of living, then the investment might be worth the gamble. However, if you buy property subject to heavy debt and you are relying on capital appreciation in order to "bail out" quickly, then you are treading on dangerous ground.

I would be remiss if I didn't admit that the case study in the previous section is somewhat oversimplified. Anyone with a degree of sophistication when it comes to real estate analysis would not begin to chart a property over only a one-year term. Usually, five-year projections are made and the sophisticated analyst brings back all future cash flows or deficiencies (including after-tax profits on eventual sale) to a present value for purposes of his or her calculations.

If you are contemplating a specific real estate investment, you should deal with advisers who are capable of assisting in the preparation of these more technical calculations. Of course, keep in mind that the further you go from the present time in your projections, the more likelihood there is of significant errors entering into the picture.

Looking Down the Road

The current restrictions on soft-cost write-offs eliminate real estate construction projects as a tax shelter for most Canadians. On the other hand, in the next year or two, if rents increase, you may find that even middle-class investors will be able to re-enter the real estate market without having to resort to tax incentives. Only time will tell. As long as interest expense on money borrowed for investments remains tax-deductible, the opportunity to use leverage is certainly attractive.

The trick is to watch closely, since the real estate market never stands still. At the right time, a person who jumps in can do quite well. You must never forget, however, that real estate is an *illiquid* investment. It cannot be sold on the open market at a moment's notice in the same way as a publicly traded stock or bond. Nevertheless, if you approach the early 1990s in the same way as I do – as being a period of "ups and downs" – you should begin to look at real estate as a relatively short-term investment. If interest rates drop further and if the economy in many parts of Canada begins to rebound, you may want to consider buying. However, if high interest rates are then reintroduced, take whatever profit you can and get out before the next "bust."

Other Tax Changes

A discussion of real estate could not be complete without a brief review of some of the other tax changes which have come about in the last few years.

Capital Cost Allowance – First-Year Rate

The government has made several modifications to the capital-cost-allowance system, which allows business and investors to deduct depreciation costs. The law continues to prohibit investors from creating or increasing rental losses through capital cost allowance. In addition, tax depreciation on assets acquired is limited in the first year to *one-half of the normal rate of write-off otherwise provided.*

Anyone who acquires a "multiple unit residential building" (MURB) after June 17, 1987, is not allowed to create or increase rental losses by deducting depreciation against other income. After 1993, existing MURB owners who have acquired such property before June 18, 1987, will also be prohibited from creating or increasing such losses.

Effective 1988, the rate of Capital Cost Allowance on buildings acquired by Canadians was decreased from 5% to 4%. Starting in 1990, depreciation write-offs for tax purposes only begin in the year that the assets are "put into use." In other words, it is no longer possible to depreciate construction projects in process or fixed assets acquired within the last few days of a tax year.

Demolition of Buildings

The opportunity to claim a full tax write-off (terminal loss) on the demolition of a building has also been eliminated. The rules essentially restrict the deduction for tax purposes to three-quarters of the loss, as if this were a capital loss instead of a business loss. The reason for this change is that, in prior years, buyers of real estate who were acquiring property primarily for the value of the land used the old rules to pass on tax benefits to sellers. A seller would demolish the building before the sale and use the (fully tax-deductible) terminal loss on the building to offset the capital gain on the land. To show his gratitude, the seller would then give the buyer a better price.

Instalment Sales

One area in which caution must be exercised pertains to instalment sales. If you sell property and you do not receive the full proceeds, you are required to report your entire profit over three years (if the profit is fully taxable as ordinary income) or five years (where the profit is taxed as a capital gain), even if you are paid over a long-term period. These rules make it difficult to structure long-term payouts without tax penalties.

There is, however, an exception for farmers and small-business owners who choose to sell their holdings to their children. In these cases, ten-year instalment sales are permitted.

Your Principal Residence

In general, the benefits of a real estate investment hinge on the deductibility of mortgage interest. Of course, when it comes to your own home, such interest is not deductible. Even so, a principle residence remains a good investment because a gain on sale is not subject to capital gains tax – quite independent from the lifetime exemption rules discussed earlier in this chapter. Besides, once you are faced with the choice between non-deductible mortgage payments and non-deductible rent, I feel that you are better off as an owner. In the long run *you* gain from any appreciation.

Is a Second Home a Good Investment?

Until several years ago, husbands and wives could arrange a double capital gains exemption on two principal residences. This provision has however been repealed. Now, only one family residence will qualify for tax exemption.

The major difference between a "primary" principal residence and a "secondary" principal residence is the question of need. When it comes to a primary home, we all need shelter to come out of the rain and snow. A country home or cottage is an entirely different situation. One doesn't usually "need" a second residence.

If your lifestyle is such that you would personally make use of a cottage for a substantial portion of the year, then, by all means, if you can afford it, go ahead and buy. Under these circumstances, if you are willing to use after-tax dollars to subsidize the ownership, this is a choice that only you can make. Figure 6-2 shows how much capital growth you actually require just to break even, assuming you are in a 45% tax bracket and borrow money at 12% to invest in a second home in cases where a 33% (45% × 75%) capital gains tax applies.

Figure 6–2   **Capital Growth Required to Break Even in a Second Home If the Gain Is Taxable**

Cost of borrowing (non-deductible)	12.00%
Annual capital growth required to break even before taxes	17.91%
Less: 33% capital gains tax ($^3/_4$ of gain × 45% tax bracket)	5.91%
Annual capital growth required to break even after taxes	12.00%

If you are interested in recreational property for only a few weeks each year, you might be better off channelling your investment into a property that is purchased primarily for rental purposes and is only used personally on occasion. This will allow you to *deduct your interest expense* even if the property shows a "loss" for tax purposes.

If you and your spouse own two homes, there are a couple of other tax-planning opportunities that are worth noting. First, the property not designated as a principal residence should probably be held by the family member (husband or wife) who is likely to be in a lower income-tax bracket at the time that the property is sold. The purpose, of course, is to pay the least capital gains tax on sale. The person who holds the second property should not necessarily be the one who is in the lower bracket today. For example, if a husband is fifty years old while his wife is thirty-five, and both are working, it is probable that the husband will retire well in advance of his wife. Under those circumstances, the couple should consider structuring the ownership of the second property in the husband's name. Then, if the property is sold subsequent to his retirement, the tax may be substantially less than if the wife were to sell it in a year while she was still working.

A second area of potential planning is to acquire a second home initially in the name of a family member who has no principal residence and is in a low tax bracket. If that family member occupies the property from time to time, he or she could designate it as a principal residence and make a tax-free gift of the sales proceeds back to you upon ultimate sale. Alternatively, if that person dies and directs the property back to you under his or her will, there will be no taxes arising at the time of death (because of the capital gains exemption for a principal residence), and you will then recognize a new tax cost for the house at its then-current fair market value. This is ideal planning in cases where an affluent couple who can afford two principal residences have parents who are apartment dwellers but who would spend time with their children in a country house during the course of the year. Of course, the children would have to trust the parents to bequeath the second property back to them and not to remaining brothers and sisters! You should note, however, that an unmarried dependent child under the age of eighteen is not permitted to own a principal residence for tax purposes. In any event, these are matters to be explored together with your accountants and lawyers.

Life Insurance Policies As Tax Shelters

All insurance policies other than pure term insurance offer an investment component in addition to the coverage. Under traditional arrangements, an insurance company takes the portion of the premium that is not required to maintain the yearly life insurance coverage (the total premium minus the "risk" premium) and invests these dollars to provide additional benefits for the policyholder. The policyholder's actual return takes into account:

- the investment earnings of the insurance company,
- the life insurance company's actual operating results, and
- any changes in mortality rates.

Customarily, however, there is no clear-cut disclosure of policy costs (such as commissions and administration fees), premiums applicable to the life insurance coverage itself, and the portion of the premium that is invested. Since policy "dividends" basically depend on the three factors mentioned above, insurance proposals invariably specify that the investment yield is "not guaranteed." As a result, many consumers have lost confidence in such insurance products over the years, primarily because they fail to understand all these concepts. The popular wisdom is to buy pure term insurance and invest the difference *elsewhere*.

In the last decade, however, a new insurance product has been developed and is becoming much more widely marketed across North America. Although each insurance company involved in selling this product has adopted its own unique description, the most common name for the concept is "universal life." While the different insurance companies have all introduced their own special "bells and whistles," I will describe what a universal life policy is and why it should be considered by Canadian investors.

Basically, universal life means flexible premiums and flexible coverage. The policyholder starts out with his or her own estimate of how much insurance he or she needs. The policyholder then makes a premium deposit that first covers the provincial premium tax, as well as actual insurance costs and client fees. The actual insurance charges are based on the cost of maintaining the required insurance coverage at a rate based on the equivalent cost of a yearly renewable term policy. However, the key point is that *extra* premiums over and above the insurance element (in accordance with a government-approved formula) can *also* be deposited with the particular insurance company at the same time. These funds can then earn interest *on a tax-sheltered basis* – as long as the policy qualifies as "an exempt policy" under specified income-tax guidelines.

What makes the universal life concept somewhat unique is that the investment element is clearly spelled out under the terms of the contract.

In addition, investors are usually offered a choice between a short-term interest account, which ties in to the prevailing interest rate as it fluctuates daily, and a guaranteed interest cash-value account, which enables investors to earn a fixed rate of return for between one and ten years. The net result is similar to the option of buying term insurance and investing the difference with, say, a bank or trust company.

The first major benefit, however, of a universal life program is that the investment income within the policy *compounds on a tax-deferred basis,* again, as long as the amount of insurance coverage is sufficient for the contract to retain its status as an "exempt" policy. This advantage becomes rather startling over a period of time. If we assume, for example, that interest rates stabilize for many years at a 9% level, it becomes a matter of comparing an accumulation at this rate against an after-tax rate otherwise available through a bank or trust company of only around 5% (for a policyholder in the 45% tax bracket).

In one case study that was prepared for me recently, the difference exceeded $165,000 after a twenty-five-year period on a policy with a first-year coverage of $200,000.

Under most of these universal life programs, a policyholder is entitled to increase or decrease the amount of his or her coverage on a frequent basis, usually annually. In some cases, coverage is adjusted automatically for changes in the Consumer Price Index. In other cases, medical evidence of insurability is required to increase coverage. Of course, if additional coverage is taken, the payment necessary to maintain the yearly renewable term-insurance element increases accordingly. But this, in turn, also increases the amount of *additional* funds that can be deposited into the interest-bearing account maintained by the insurance company for the policyholder, to earn additional tax-deferred interest income.

There are several other benefits of a universal life plan. For example, once the cash account has built up over several years, it then becomes possible for the policyholder to maintain his or her coverage in whole or in part by simply allowing the insurance company to draw funds out of the investment account to pay annual premiums. This enables the policyholder to *pay premiums out of income that was tax-sheltered.* Note the contrast to other types of insurance policies, where premium payments are always made with after-tax income. The benefits of a universal life arrangement become more pronounced as the cost of the yearly renewable term element becomes more expensive as the insured gets older.

There are two further benefits that should also be considered. First, setting a premium level within acceptable government guidelines and knowing exactly how much money is going into the investment account represents a good forced savings plan for most Canadians. This is especially true if arrangements are made with the insurance company to have payments deducted from the policyholder's bank account on a monthly basis.

Finally, and perhaps most attractive of all, is the opportunity to transform the tax deferral into an *outright tax savings.* This would apply in cases where the policyholder is prepared to leave his or her funds with the insurance company until death. At that time, a universal life policy is structured to pay off the amount of coverage still in force *plus* the cash value build-up. The *full* amount is then returned to the policyholder or the estate completely tax-free.

A universal life program is suitable not only for individuals concerned with personal estate planning, but also in circumstances where insurance is required under a buy-sell (business continuation) program. If the insurance is held by a corporation, the cash accumulation can be used not only to provide for the buy-out of a shareholder at the time of death but can also be made available to fund an alternative buy-out in the event of a shareholder's retirement.

Today, it is virtually impossible for anyone to predict with any degree of certainty what interest and inflation rates will be in the future. A major advantage of a universal life product is therefore the opportunity to adjust the amount of insurance and savings portion on a regular basis. Presumably, if an individual's income increases over time, he or she can afford to make additional payments and can compound the cash value accordingly.

You should note, however, that a universal life contract should be treated as a long-range program. In other words, although coverage and premium payments are flexible, there must be a commitment to maintain the policy on an ongoing basis. This is because in the first few years the investment yield, while competitive, is still eroded by policy charges, including agents' commissions. It may take three or four years before the policyholder truly starts to benefit more from a universal life arrangement than by buying term insurance and investing the difference elsewhere. However, once that initial phase-in period expires, the benefits of universal life compare quite favourably with other investment alternatives.

CHAPTER 7

Maximize Your
Investment Yields

Planning Around Earned Income

The first step to maximizing investment yields is what I call "planning around earned income." In all probability, your earned income by itself is sufficient to put you into a fairly high tax bracket. You may find that it is no longer feasible for you to put off paying taxes on some of this income through a deferred compensation program because of the tax changes highlighted in Chapter Four, and that your employer is not willing to accommodate you with a significant range of fringe benefits. You may also find that incorporating your own activities as a consultant (as outlined in Chapter Eleven) is just not possible.

If you find yourself in this position, you should at least direct your efforts towards effective tax planning for investments. My concept is very simple: from a tax point of view, the last thing anyone with a high *earned* income needs is investment income. If you are already in a tax bracket greater than 40% because of your salary or business income, then almost one-half of your investment yield will immediately be eroded by large amounts of additional income taxes. How, then, do you go about planning effectively?

Pay Off Your Home Mortgage

If you are typical of most Canadians, the first major step in proper planning is to discharge your home mortgage as quickly as possible. Assume for purposes of illustration that you have a mortgage of $50,000 on your home at an interest rate of 11%. Assume, as well, that you *also* have $50,000 in cash, which you have recently inherited. Your mortgage costs you $5,500 a year in interest, and this amount is not deductible. If, however, you take your $50,000 inheritance and invest it at the same interest rate of 11%, you will receive $5,500 of interest income. On the surface, there is an offsetting income and outflow. However, the $5,500 received is fully taxable. If you are in a 40% tax bracket, you will only keep $3,300 on an after-tax basis. There is certainly very little merit in retaining $3,300 while paying out $5,500.

In fact, if your mortgage payable is at 11% and you are in a 40% tax bracket, you must earn over 18% as a pre-tax return on investment capital to make it worthwhile to carry the mortgage on your home. If anyone can show me how to earn a guaranteed 18% per annum on my money *with no risk,* I would appreciate a telephone call (collect) or a letter!

Thus, I recommend that a home mortgage be paid off as fast as possible. In the hypothetical case above, you should use the inherited capital of $50,000 immediately to discharge your debt. The only exception might be if you are one of the very few people with a low-interest "locked in" mortgage that dates back to the pre-inflation era.

Amortization

To amortize a loan is to extinguish it by means of payments over a period of time so that eventually the debt is reduced to zero. The most common amortization programs involve repayment schedules calling for identical monthly payments over the term of the borrowing, with each payment consisting of a combination of both principal and interest. Initially, most of the payments are used to pay interest. However, as the principal amount of the debt increases, more and more of the payments are used to reduce the capital amount.

This is shown in Figure 7-1, which illustrates a $10,000 loan at 11% interest compounded semiannually over twenty-five years.

Initially, each payment is almost all interest. Over the years, however, each instalment will contain less interest and more principal. This is because the borrower only pays interest on the outstanding principal balance of the loan at the time each payment is made.

If interest rates rise, the only possible way to keep monthly mortgage payments down is to lengthen the term over which the loan is amortized.

Figure 7–1 **25-Year $10,000 Loan at 11%, with Interest Compounded Semiannually, Monthly Payment – $96.26**

Year	Payments Made *$96.12 × 12*	*Interest*	*Principal*
1	$1,155	$1,075	$ 80
5	1,155	1,025	130
10	1,155	935	220
15	1,155	785	370
20	1,155	515	640
25	1,155	65	1,090

As you will see, there may be some benefits, but there are also severe pitfalls.

For example, what if the twenty-five-year term on the above $10,000 loan were extended to thirty, thirty-five, or forty years? While the monthly payments would decline, the borrower is faced not only with a much longer payout period, but also with a *significant additional debt*. This is illustrated in Figure 7-2.

Figure 7–2 **Amortization of $10,000 at 11% Over Various Periods**

$10,000 at 11%	*25 Years*	*30 Years*	*35 Years*	*40 Years*
Monthly payment	$ 96.26	$ 93.40	$ 91.80	$ 90.89
Annual cost	1,155.12	1,120.80	1,101.60	1,090.68
Total cost	28,878.00	33,624.00	38,556.00	43,627.20
Total interest paid	18,878.00	23,624.00	28,556.00	33,627.20

Monthly payment over 25 years	$ 96.26
Monthly payment over 40 years	90.89
Difference	$ 5.37

Total interest over 40 years	$33,627.20
Total interest over 25 years	18,878.00
Difference	$14,749.20

The results of our analysis are somewhat mind-boggling. By spreading the debt over forty years instead of twenty-five years, there is a monthly saving of only $5.37 in the required monthly mortgage payments. However, the borrower must not only bind himself or herself to payments over an additional fifteen years, but is actually *increasing the total debt* by $14,749.20!

Mortgage-Acceleration Savings

While extending your debt obligation can, in the long run, be extremely costly, paying down your mortgage from time to time by making extra payments may be one of the best methods available to force yourself to save money. This is especially important planning for a principal residence, where the interest is non-deductible. Most mortgage contracts today will allow a borrower to repay at least 10% of the original amount of the debt each year as a special principal repayment.

Figure 7-3 shows the principal balance outstanding on a loan of $10,000 at the end of each year for twenty-five years where the interest rate is 11%. At the end of year one, the principal balance outstanding is $9,920, while at the end of year eight it is $9,000. Therefore, if the borrower were to repay $1,000 on the first anniversary of the mortgage, he or she would thus be eliminating almost *one-third* of the *total* annual payments that would otherwise be required. In other words, if the monthly payments stay the same (which they would) and the borrower makes *no further* special payments against principal, the debt would be completely extinguished only seventeen years later. Given a special payment of $1,000 at the end of the first year, he or she would then only owe $8,800 at the end of year two, $8,580 after year three, and so forth. Of course, if additional principal payments were made at the end of the second year (and subsequently), the debt would be eliminated that much more quickly.

Figure 7–3 **Balance Outstanding on a 25-Year Loan of $10,000 at 11% (Rounded to Nearest $10), Monthly Payment – $96.26**

End of Year	Amount	End of Year	Amount	End of Year	Amount
1	$9,920	10	$8,580	19	$5,090
2	9,820	11	8,340	20	4,450
3	9,720	12	8,070	21	3,740
4	9,610	13	7,770	22	2,950
5	9,480	14	7,430	23	2,070
6	9,330	15	7,060	24	1,090
7	9,180	16	6,640	25	0
8	9,000	17	6,180		
9	8,800	18	5,660		

Perhaps the best opportunity a family has to pay down a mortgage is when a wife has been home for several years looking after young children and then rejoins the labour force. At this point, the family comes to a very important crossroad. It could choose to use the extra income to buy a new car, or treat itself to a vacation trip. However, if husband and wife can simply exercise a bit of restraint for *one year only* and apply the first $10,000 that the wife earns (after taxes) against their mortgage, they will have made a tremendous advance towards the security of owning a fully paid home. On a $100,000 mortgage at 11%, you have seen how it takes eight years for $10,000 of debt to be extinguished in the absence of mortgage-acceleration payments. I hope that the message is clear.

The Mortgage Term

You must always be careful never to confuse the *amortization* of a loan with its *term*. If you are told that a mortgage is to be amortized over twenty-five years, you must not assume that it has a twenty-five-year term. The term of a mortgage is the period of time that is given to the borrower before the lender can demand the principal balance owing on the loan. At one time, lenders did in fact make loans for long periods of time, such as twenty-five years, at fixed rates of interest. Today, however, mortgage terms rarely exceed five years. Thus, although the amortization schedule may reflect the payments necessary to discharge a debt over twenty-five years, the borrower, in most cases, must still repay the principal balance at the end of five years. Of course, the lender will usually renew the mortgage – at current prevailing rates. (Today, three-year, one-year, and even six-month term mortgages are becoming more and more common.)

Again, examine the schedule in Figure 7-3. If payments of $96.26 are made monthly over twenty-five years, a loan of $10,000 at 11% would be extinguished. However, here is the problem. At the end of five years, the lender will want his or her money and, on a twenty-five year loan, you will still owe $9,480. To repay the loan you would probably have to commit yourself to another mortgage and borrow almost $9,500. Assume that the new mortgage is for a further five-year period at the same rate and also with payments calculated to amortize over a twenty-five year period. At the end of the second five-year period, your outstanding balance would be around $9,000. When you have to repay this loan, you can repeat the process.

Each new five-year term will result in smaller monthly payments because the principal amount at the start of each succeeding term will be less. However, instead of amortizing the loan down to zero over twenty-five years, it may take *over one hundred years to discharge the loan completely. There is only one way a twenty-five-year mortgage can be paid off in full over twenty-five years. The principal balance owing each time a mortgage is renewed must be amortized for a period that is not longer than the remaining number of years in the original amortization.*

Borrowing Money from Private Sources

With today's high cost of residential housing, more and more young people are finding it difficult to acquire their homes without some sort of family subsidy. Perhaps you may be fortunate to have a "rich relative" who would be willing to lend you money. First of all, your relative would probably be earning slightly less on his or her capital if it is in term deposits than you would have to pay if you were to approach a lending institution. Perhaps your benefactor might be persuaded to pass this difference on to you. In other words, if he or she is receiving 8% interest on a term deposit, he or she may be willing to accept a similar rate on a private loan secured by your residence. Moreover, your relative may also be willing to allow you to pay interest only until your income increases sufficiently for you to start discharging principal. In many cases, a private lender is quite content with an interest yield on capital only. The lender does not necessarily *want* to receive blended payments of capital and interest. There is the satisfaction of keeping his or her capital intact and not having to worry about reinvesting small payments of principal, which you would otherwise pay from time to time.

Sometimes, people will take advantage of the fact that interest income is taxable while the corresponding expense is not deductible when funds are borrowed for personal purposes. For example, if an individual in a 40% bracket is earning interest at 8%, he or she is not even netting 5% after taxes. That same individual might be willing to lend money to a friend or relative at only 6% or 7% to assist the latter in buying a house, provided the interest is paid in cash. Often, the borrower won't object to such an arrangement because he or she will pay a substantially lower rate and the payments cannot be deducted anyway. Thus, the borrower pays substantially less than the prevailing mortgage rate, while the lender ends up keeping more than what he or she otherwise would have retained, had "conventional" taxable interest been received.

Because any practice involving undeclared income is fraudulent, you are cautioned to stay away from such an arrangement. However, I have seen cases where mortgage loans are made at *no interest* but where the borrower makes an annual (non-compulsory) gift each year to the lender that is (coincidentally) equal to 6%–7% of the original loan. This procedure is acceptable. You should note that gifts made are not deductible and gifts received are not taxable.

After Burning the Mortgage . . .

Once your home is paid for, you have some room to manoeuvre. If you find an appealing investment, you may *then* borrow the capital that you need against your paid-up home. If you borrow *specifically for the purpose of making investments,* your interest expense becomes tax-deductible.

Note that there is no shortcut to be taken. If you use an inheritance or your savings for investment purposes without having first paid off the mortgage on your home, you will *not* be permitted to argue that you *could have* paid off the mortgage in the first place and then borrowed for investment capital. In tax cases that have come before the courts, the judges have insisted on a proper "tracking." If you take a shortcut, be prepared to suffer tax penalties.

Investment Losses – New Rules

While borrowing money on a tax-deductible basis in order to make investments is certainly quite attractive, there are, however, some new rules that have recently been implemented as part of former finance minister Wilson's tax reform. After 1987, net taxable capital gains eligible for the lifetime $100,000 exemption are reduced by investment losses deducted by a taxpayer in computing income for tax purposes. The adjustment for investment losses is made on a cumulative basis.

For purposes of these rules, an individual's cumulative net investment loss at the end of any year is the amount by which that individual's investment expenses for that year and prior years (beginning after 1987) exceed his or her investment income. The investment expenses that have to be considered include deductions such as interest on money borrowed to earn interest, dividends, or other income from property, and carrying charges for investments in partnerships and co-ownerships.

The application of this new rule can be illustrated with a simple example. Assume your only investment involves borrowing $10,000 on January 1, 1993, to purchase one hundred shares of a public company and that the annual interest expense on your loan is $1,000 and the shares pay no dividends. Then assume that you sell the shares at the end of 1994 and make a capital gain of $12,000, of which $9,000 is a taxable capital gain (three-quarters of $12,000). In these circumstances, the maximum capital gains exemption that you will be allowed to claim in 1994 would be $7,000. That is, $9,000 of taxable capital gains, less your cumulative net investment loss at the end of 1994 of $2,000 (two years of interest expense). In other words, if you take advantage of an on-going deduction for interest expense on borrowed money, your deduction will be at least partially recaptured in the year that your investments are sold. Nevertheless, the opportunity to get on-going tax deductions in exchange for capital growth is still well worth considering.

Transactions with Family Members

Once your home mortgage has been paid off, the next step in effective planning is to try to split investment income with family members. The idea is to take advantage of other persons in the family who are in lower tax brackets than yourself.

While this section will consider transactions both with a spouse and with children, you should note that the Income Tax Act has historically differentiated between a spouse and anyone else. Consequently, any references to a taxpayer's "children" can be interpreted as broadly as you wish. A "child" can therefore mean a grandchild, niece, nephew, brother, sister, or even close friend. The same tax rules also apply to transactions with your parents.

It should be noted that, effective 1993, the Income Tax Act now treats common-law spouses as if they were married. In this book, therefore, a reference to a spouse also includes a spouse under a common-law relationship.

Husbands and Wives

One of the many differences between the Canadian tax system and that of the United States is that Canada taxes a husband and wife separately, whereas the United States permits the filing of joint tax returns. Since Canada treats husbands and wives as separate taxpayers, the Income Tax Act is therefore somewhat concerned with the potential that might exist for income splitting between spouses. Tax rates for individuals are graduated. Accordingly, the tax on a single taxable income of, for example, $55,000 would be significantly higher than the tax otherwise payable on two taxable incomes of $27,500.

In order to prevent splitting of investment income, there is a tax rule that states that where a taxpayer transfers property to a spouse, or to a person who subsequently becomes a spouse, the income generated by the transferred property reverts back to the transferor. In addition, the rules also provide that if the transferee disposes of the property and substitutes something else, the income on the substituted property *also* reverts back to the transferor. These "income-attribution rules" apply as long as the transferor is alive, resident in Canada, and the transferee is his or her spouse.

Note, however, that an actual gift of cash does not have any tax consequences at the time the gift is made. This is the case no matter whether the recipient is a spouse *or* anyone else. The donor does not get a tax deduction, nor is the recipient taxed. While at first glance this may be surprising, the rationale is apparent if you stop to examine the nature of cash. Cash is simply income on which taxes have already been paid.

For example, if you are male and you give your wife $100,000, the gift itself will not have any tax implications. However, if she invests the money at 10%, the interest income of $10,000 will be taxable in your hands notwithstanding the fact that your wife received the actual funds. Moreover, if your wife takes "her" capital of $100,000 and acquires shares in a public company, receiving a dividend of, say, $7,000 in a subsequent year, then you will be taxed on that dividend as well. In this case, the public company shares would be considered "substituted property."

There is, however, an interesting omission in the tax rules that apply to transfers between spouses. The courts have held, for example, that the income-attribution rules only apply to income generated from the transferred property itself (or from substituted property). The rules have no bearing, however, on what is referred to as "second-generation," or compound income. Thus, if your wife were to take the $10,000 of interest earned in the first year and invest this sum separately, deriving additional interest of $1,000 in the second year, this latter amount will be taxed in her hands and not in yours.

Of course, if we put the dollars into proper perspective, it becomes evident that in spite of the "second-generation-income" advantages, a gift between husband and wife will not result in significant savings. Even if you are in a top tax bracket of 45%, and your wife is not otherwise taxable at all, the most you can save out of having made the gift of $100,000 at the beginning of the first year is 55% of $1,000, or $550, at the end of the second year. Certainly, the tax saving is not material when compared to the initial gift.

Expanding on the Rules

Historically, the attribution rules applied whenever property was either given or sold to a spouse. For many years, therefore, it was recommended tax planning to split income between spouses by simply making *loans* of investment capital. Such loans would generally not be interest bearing and would usually be repayable on demand. The after-tax income that was built up by the spouse in the lower tax bracket was then used for various purposes such as the repayment of a home mortgage or just to provide funds for further investments.

Unfortunately, former finance minister Wilson chose in 1985 to put an end to such planning. Income attribution with respect to transfers of property to a spouse (or a minor) was extended to apply to loans outstanding on May 22, 1985, or made after that date. The new rules apply to direct transactions as well as to trust arrangements accomplished by any means whatsoever.

The Demise of Family Investment Corporations

Perhaps most surprisingly, Mr. Wilson also ultimately chose to put an end to the use of investment corporations for the purposes of splitting income between spouses and minors. For transactions entered into after November 21, 1985, involving investment corporations, dividends are attributed back to the high-bracket family member to the extent that the investment capital is attributable to him or her. Accordingly, such arrangements can no longer be recommended. Fortunately, however, the legislation is not retroactive, and investment corporations that were previously formed in which the growth and income-producing shares are held by a low-tax-bracket spouse and/or a trust for minor children may still be used.

The actual rules attributing income out of investment corporations set up or receiving property after November 21, 1985, are quite complex, although there are some major points that are rather straightforward. First, there is no attribution out of investment income of a corporation until dividends are actually paid, and no attribution in excess of the amount of dividends paid. Secondly, if a high-tax-bracket individual makes a loan to an investment corporation and the loan is subsequently repaid, the repayment of the loan freezes the maximum amount that can be attributed back to him or her. Finally, if interest is charged by the high-bracket family member on the loan at a prescribed rate, which varies quarterly, there is no attribution of income at all.

The surprise in this extension of the rules stems from the fact that corporate earned investment income is already subject to fairly high taxes. It appears that the government was willing to add a significant amount of complexity to make sure that there is no leakage in any taxes through family income-splitting arrangements.

You should again note that the government's attack on investment corporations used by family members is not retroactive. Arrangements entered into before November 21, 1985, are allowed to stand undisturbed. Moreover, and perhaps even more importantly, the special attribution rules do not apply to corporations formed for the purpose of earning active business income. In other words, if a proprietorship is incorporated and the taxpayer carrying on business sets up the company so as to involve a spouse and/or minor children in the shareholdings of the business corporation, no attribution will apply.

An active business corporation, however, is defined as one where substantially all of the assets are used in carrying on an active business. In an Interpretation Bulletin, Revenue Canada defines "substantially all" as meaning 90% of the assets or better. A holding company whose shares are held by family members also qualifies for tax relief, provided substantially all of its assets are either directly active business assets or shares and loans to corporations which qualify as small-business corporations.

It would appear that if family members are involved in a small-business corporation at a relatively early stage and the corporation is successful, there is no restriction against the corporation eventually taking surplus earnings and making passive investments. As long as this is done after the fact, it appears that the investment income could then be allocated among family members. However, caution will have to be exercised. Chapter Thirteen expands on this important area of tax planning.

Other Changes in the Rules

There are other changes to the income-attribution rules as well. As I mentioned, before 1985, income attribution always applied on transactions involving gifts and sales. Now a sale for fair-market-value consideration no longer triggers income attribution between husbands and wives. The new exemption from attribution is available for transfers of property if, at the time of the transfer, the fair market value of the transferred property does not exceed the fair market value of the consideration received by the transferor and the transferor did not take advantage of any of the tax roll-over provisions.

To qualify for the exemption, fair-market-value consideration must be received at the time of the transfer. Where the transferor receives indebtedness, there is an exemption for income attribution on a year-to-year basis, provided that interest is charged on the indebtedness at a rate no less than either the prescribed rate of interest, or at the rate that would have been agreed upon between arm's-length parties under similar circumstances at the time the indebtedness was incurred. In such a case, the exemption from attribution is only available if the interest payable on the indebtedness in respect of that year and each preceding year has been paid no later than thirty days after the end of each year. As in the past, any attribution ceases in the event that spouses separate or get divorced.

The Principal Residence – A New Opportunity for Planning

There is perhaps a new opportunity for tax planning for husbands and wives that did not previously surface. In most cases husbands and wives have joint and undivided interests in their principal residences. Often, one of the spouses is in a much higher tax bracket than the other and has also accumulated investment capital. In the past, the high-bracket spouse would have made a loan to the low-bracket spouse in order to achieve income splitting. It may now be possible for the high-bracket spouse to buy the low-bracket spouse's interest in the principal residence for a fair-market-value consideration. Under these circumstances, the low-bracket spouse may then be able to take the money received and make investments, reporting the investment income perhaps without fear of attribution. Whether in fact this will work remains to be seen.

As an illustration, let us examine the case of a husband who is an executive or business owner and a wife who is a homemaker. Previously the tax authorities would never have been concerned about the fact that the principal residence would be held jointly. This is because a capital gain on ultimate sale is tax-free in any event. However, in this example, if all the equity in the house had come from the income-earning husband's efforts, there is a possibility that a sale by the wife to the husband of her interest in the house for fair-market-value consideration would not solve any problems for purposes of avoiding income attribution. This is because the authorities could deem that the wife's equity was really a prior gift to her from her husband.

On the other hand, there has always been a tacit understanding that a wife not employed outside the household is entitled to a half-interest in the family's principal residence in exchange for her efforts as a home-maker. Whether or not Revenue Canada is prepared to challenge this concept remains to be seen. Nevertheless, what appears to be clear is the fact that in planning, one should structure arrangements wherever possible so as to hold income-producing assets in the name of the spouse in the lower bracket. Non-income-bearing property would then be held by the higher-income spouse.

For example, assume that a husband earns $60,000 while his wife earns $20,000. It now becomes exceedingly important for the wife to try to retain as much of her income as possible for investment purposes. All living expenses should therefore be paid for by the husband out of his salary in this example.

Anti-Avoidance Rules

Additional rules have been incorporated into the Income Tax Act to ensure that the attribution rules cannot easily be circumvented. One concept that had been suggested was that a low-bracket spouse could borrow money for investment and then sell the investments to a high-income spouse who has the available cash to acquire these holdings. The low-bracket spouse would then repay the loan, leaving the high-bracket spouse with investments on which the income would then be attributed back to the low-income spouse. Unfortunately, the government twigged to this potential loophole and there is an anti-avoidance provision to cover it. This is considered an artificial transaction and any opportunities to use this reverse attribution have been blocked.

Another important rule guards against avoidance through the use of intermediaries. For example, in the absence of this rule, an individual might lend or transfer property to another person and that person might in turn lend the capital or transfer the property to or for the benefit of the original transferor's spouse. One tax advantage that the anti-avoidance rules block is the opportunity that might otherwise exist to have an individual deposit money with a financial institution at a low rate of return on the condition that the institution would lend an equivalent amount of money also at a low rate to the individual's spouse.

Fortunately, the regulations involving income attribution do not materially affect owner-managers and members of their families. There is still ample opportunity to pay reasonable salaries to family members. Loan-guarantee fees can be paid where applicable and, by involving family members as shareholders in an active business company, income splitting through dividends can still be accomplished.

Redirecting Inheritances

In some cases there may be opportunities for adventurous tax planning where an individual's capital would otherwise be derived from an inheritance. Specifically, an individual in a high tax bracket who anticipates receiving a significant inheritance could ask his or her benefactors to redirect the inheritance to a low-income spouse.

For example, assume that James Jones is an executive with a large Canadian corporation and earns $150,000 a year. Mr. Jones has elderly parents who are reasonably well off and who may be expected to leave him approximately $250,000 in investments. Assuming Mrs. Jones is a homemaker with no income, Mr. Jones could simply ask his parents to redraft their wills leaving the inheritance to his wife instead. Thus, the investment income ultimately derived from the receipt of that inheritance would be taxed in her hands and not his.

Of course, I must suggest extreme caution before you actually embark on such planning, not so much from a tax stand-point but having regard to various other circumstances. For example, what if Mr. and Mrs. Jones split up? Presumably, if a divorce or separation occurs after the inheritance is received, the assets represented would constitute family property which might have to be split equally between them, no matter who had actually received the money. To that extent there may not be a whole lot of risk involved in the suggested plan. On the other hand, you would have to consider the rules in your particular province pertaining to marriage breakdown. If a divorce occurs while Mr. Jones's parents are still alive, the tax plan could be undone by having Mr. Jones request from his parents that they amend their wills if they would no longer find it expedient to treat a former daughter-in-law as a beneficiary. However, a danger might arise in a situation where the parents are still alive but are not capable of changing their wills because of mental or physical infirmity.

It should be possible to circumvent any problems here by simply having the wills of the parents properly drawn in the first place. The bequest to the daughter-in-law could be made contingent on her still living with

Mr. Jones at the time the parents die and within the sixty days following. A further clause in the will could provide that in the event that this condition is not met, the inheritance would revert back to Mr. Jones.

In short, while the redirection of potential inheritances may make sense as a tax plan, it would be incumbent on the individuals involved to assess the potential pitfalls. If there are any strains in the marriage, clearly such an arrangement should be avoided.

Transfers of Capital Property between Spouses

Having dealt with the income generated from property transferred by one spouse to the other, we now need to consider some important capital gains implications of such a transaction. If you transfer capital (growth) property such as stocks (in both public and private companies), corporate bonds, or real estate to a spouse, the gift is deemed ordinarily to have taken place at the transferor's tax cost. In other words, no matter what the current value of that property is, no capital gain or loss is recognized at that time.

However, when the transferee subsequently sells the property, the capital gain or capital loss reverts back to the transferor. The computation of this gain or loss is based on the transferor's original cost for tax purposes. Basically, you accomplish absolutely nothing in the way of reallocating capital gains or losses by making gifts of capital properties between spouses. There is a full capital-attribution rule whenever the gain or loss is ultimately realized on a sale to a third party. This can be illustrated by an example in which:

- the cost of capital property (e.g., land) to the husband is $10,000.
- the fair market value at date of gift to the wife is $20,000.
- the property is subsequently sold by the wife for $70,000.

Regardless of the fact that the fair market value of the property is $20,000, the husband will be deemed to have disposed of it at his cost of $10,000. However, when his wife subsequently sells the property, the entire capital gain of $60,000 will revert to the husband.

(A taxpayer is permitted to transfer capital property to a spouse at fair market value without receiving any consideration under certain circumstances. While the recipient will benefit from any future growth in value, the transferor will pay taxes on accrued gains at the time of transfer. This election is, however, generally only of use where there is a division of property in preparation for a separation or divorce. This is discussed in the next chapter.)

At the time of former finance minister Wilson's 1985 tax changes, it was unclear whether the new income-attribution rules between a husband and wife would apply to capital gains as well as ordinary income. It is clear now that Mr. Wilson chose the hard-line approach. This means that if a low-bracket spouse borrows money at a low rate or zero rate of interest for the purpose of making growth investments, the eventual capital gains will be attributed back to the lender spouse. This is over and above any income generated by the investments on an ongoing basis.

You should note that capital attribution only applies on transactions between a husband and wife. In the case of transactions with other persons, there is no capital attribution, although attribution of ongoing income will often come into play.

Transactions with Persons Other Than Spouses

There are other significant provisions in the Income Tax Act that are also designed to prevent income splitting. Whenever a taxpayer transfers property to a minor, the income from the transferred property reverts back to the transferor until the minor reaches the age of eighteen. This provision is designed to prevent anyone from splitting income with his or her children or grandchildren while they are still below the age of majority and then making use of the income generated from the property for the taxpayer's own advantage.

In passing, I raise the somewhat rhetorical question of whether or not it would really be advisable to make large gifts to children under the age of eighteen, regardless of the tax consequences. Even if there were no income-attribution rules, would you really want your children to have sizeable investment capital of their own at the age of eighteen?

Even before the recent tax changes, you could not circumvent the rules by making loans to children or grandchildren when the recipients are under eighteen. The restriction stems from legal problems. A child under the age of eighteen has no legal power to contract anywhere in Canada. When something cannot be done under common law, the courts have held that it cannot be accomplished for tax purposes either.

There are, nevertheless, some opportunities to split income with minor children that you should consider. For example, if you are carrying on business (either incorporated or unincorporated) there is no legal restriction against paying salary to a minor child. This is as long as the child is truly rendering services in exchange for pay. This planning will be discussed in more detail in Chapter Thirteen.

The Registered Education Savings Plan

A Registered Education Savings Plan is a trust that you may set up for the benefit of your children or grandchildren to defer tax on investment income. The purpose of the program is to provide funding for college and university education. Although the contributor must invest tax-paid money, income earned on funds within a Registered Education Savings Plan can accumulate free from tax until paid over as ordinary income in the hands of children or grandchildren for educational purposes. At any time, the original investment can be withdrawn tax-free by the contributor.

There can be a disadvantage if a Registered Education Savings Plan program is set up for the benefit of one child only and that child does not continue his or her education beyond the high school level. The income earned in such circumstances could be forfeited. On the other hand, if a discretionary trust arrangement is entered into for the benefit of any or all of the children (or grandchildren) of the contributor, it is then possible to obtain the economic advantages of the program as long as at least one of the contingent beneficiaries continues his or her education.

A Registered Education Savings Plan must have at least 150 subscribers. Maximum contributions to a Registered Education Savings Plan are limited to $1,500 per year for each beneficiary and Registered Education Savings Plan payouts may only be made to full-time students for plans entered into after February 20, 1990. Contributions on behalf of any one beneficiary may only be made for up to twenty-one years. Assuming the $1,500 annual maximum limit is maintained without indexation, this will result in a lifetime maximum contribution limit of $31,500 per beneficiary. The maximum period in which income may accumulate on a tax-deferred basis is limited to twenty-six years. This therefore permits payments to be completed by the time most students are finished with their post-secondary educations. To ensure that no one attempts to unduly defer investment income, a 1% per month tax on contributions in excess of $1,500 a year is imposed as a penalty on individuals who overpay into Registered Education Savings Plans. A contributor may avoid the tax on excess contributions by having these amounts withdrawn before the end of the month following the one in which the excess amount rose.

While the income from a Registered Education Savings Plan is taxable when distributed to beneficiaries, you should note that each beneficiary is likely to be in a low tax bracket at that time and, as well, can use the tuition fee tax credit as an offset against any taxes payable. This program is targeted to individuals who have tax-paid capital and who intend eventually to subsidize their children's post-secondary education.

The opportunity to compound investment income without ongoing taxes for an extended period of time and to use these funds to provide support for your dependants is something that certainly merits closest attention. This is especially true in light of the recent restrictions imposed on loan arrangements to spouses which I discussed previously.

Transfers to Adults Other Than One's Spouse

Note that it is permissible to transfer (non-capital) property such as cash by way of *gift* to someone other than a spouse who is over the age of eighteen and, if the transferee is in a lower tax bracket, a tax advantage could result. However, the transferor must always be concerned that the transferee, who now has title to the property, might not adhere to the wishes of the transferor as to either the investment of the capital or the disposition of the income. As such, substantial inter-vivos gifts made solely for the purpose of income splitting are not generally suggested as a practical vehicle for tax planning.

Loans to Older Children

Until recently, if children (or grandchildren) were eighteen or over, it was extremely advantageous to split income by making loans. However, without any fanfare, the government introduced some new provisions in 1988 designed to block many of the tax advantages of making loans to adults other than one's spouse. These changes nullify income-splitting benefits where it "may reasonably be considered that one of the main reasons for a loan was to reduce or avoid tax" by causing the income to be taxed in the hands of a low-bracket individual instead.

These new rules only apply in cases when low-interest and interest-free loans are made between individuals. If so desired, a taxpayer may circumvent attribution by actually transferring ownership of an income-earning investment by way of gift or sale. There is also no attribution if a loan is made and the recipient invests to earn capital gains instead of ongoing interest or dividends. Moreover, loans made to allow the recipient to invest in a business will not trigger attribution, nor will those bearing interest at "the prescribed rate."

It is questionable how far Revenue Canada will go to administer these new anti-avoidance provisions. If a loan is made to assist a child eighteen or older to pay tuition fees out of income earned, can this be construed as a tax avoidance scheme? What about a loan to a handicapped elderly parent?

Even if Revenue Canada decided to audit all college students with investment income of $5,000 or more, there is little exposure. In the worst case, a parent might have to pay taxes on income that would have been taxable anyway plus a (small) interest charge.

Modest Gifts to Older Children

In spite of the relatively new loan restrictions, it may still be possible to obtain a significant tax advantage by making modest gifts to older children to assist them in paying for things such as university education. The next example, Figure 7-4, depicts a typical situation where a parent, by making a $60,000 gift to a child, could save up to $2,390 using 1993 tax credits and rates.

This saving, which results from capitalizing on the child's lack of income, is certainly significant in comparison to a total investment income of $6,000. Multiply this benefit by the number of years that the child would attend university, and there is a substantial advantage.

Family Planning

If a person had planned a family so that one child would be finishing university just as the next one is starting, you can see that the benefits of the above plan could be compounded. As one child graduated, the parent could ask that the money be returned, and the funds would then be available to gift to the next child. Of course, if several children were in university at the same time, then a parent would need more money in the first place to compound the advantages.

Transfers of Capital Property to Children and Others

With respect to capital gains, as opposed to the cash transactions just discussed, there continues to be a significant difference between transfers made to a spouse and transfers made to anyone else. A transfer of capital

Figure 7–4 **Example of Tax Savings Resulting from a Gift
to an Older Child**

Assumptions

1. Parent has $60,000 of investment capital, bearing interest at 10%. Parent is in the 45% tax bracket.

2. Parent has a child over age 18 attending university. The child has no income and the parent uses the after-tax investment income to pay tuition fees ($600) and to provide support.

Alternative 1: No gift to adult child.

Interest income to parent (10% × $60,000)	$6,000	
Less: Income taxes thereon (45%)	2,700	
Net interest income		$3,300
Add: Combined federal and provincial tax savings from		
Tuition credit (25% × $600)	$ 150*	
Education credit (assume 8 months × $20)	160*	310
Net cash flow		$3,610
Cash flow utilized:		
To pay tuition		$ 600
To pay expenses		3,010
Net cash flow		$3,610

Alternative 2: A $60,000 gift is made by the parent to the child. A term deposit is purchased by the child.

Child's tax position:	
Interest income (10% × $60,000) = Taxable income	$6,000
Calculation of federal tax 17% × $6,000	$1,020
Less: Basic Personal Credit (estimated)	*1,100
Net federal tax payable	Nil
Net provincial tax payable is also	Nil
Cash flow utilized:	
To pay tuition	$ 600
To pay expenses	5,400
Net cash flow	$6,000
Advantage of gift ($6,000 – $3,610)	$2,390

* The tuition fee and education credits would be transferred to the parent. This would result in additional tax savings of $310. These credits are transferable to a supporting individual whenever the student does not need them to reduce his or her own taxes payable to nil.

property to anyone else must take place for tax purposes at *fair market value*. Figure 7-5 shows how this is the case whether the property is sold or given.

Figure 7–5 **Example of Capital Property Transfer to Child**

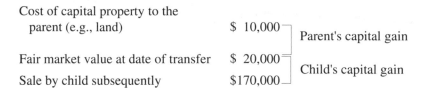

Cost of capital property to the parent (e.g., land)	$ 10,000	⎤ Parent's capital gain
Fair market value at date of transfer	$ 20,000	⎡
Sale by child subsequently	$170,000	⎦ Child's capital gain

As indicated in the example, there is a tax trade-off. Where the parent's land has a cost of $10,000 and a fair market value of $20,000, giving or selling that property will result in an immediate capital gain. The advantage of the transaction, however, is that the child receives the benefits of future growth.

In order to spread the capital gain over several years, the proceeds of a sale can still be deferred, but the rules generally require the vendor to pay tax over three to five years. A ten-year instalment sale is, however, permitted for farms and small businesses transferred from parents to children.

In some cases, it may be possible to reduce the impact of the tax restrictions. Suppose the parent in the example just illustrated sold only a few acres of his or her land at a time, over twenty years. This would create an effect similar to that of a long-term instalment sale.

General Tax Planning for Capital Gains

Planning for capital gains is largely a factor of the extent to which any individual has already used up his or her lifetime exemption. Note, however, that if there is no disposition of property, there is no capital gain to be reported. One of the most popular methods that sophisticated investors use to postpone gains is simply *not selling*, but *borrowing* instead against increases in values of investments in order to build up their holdings. Borrowing with a pledge of property as collateral has no implications for tax purposes.

The ability to borrow is also useful since you can often borrow dollar for dollar against full increases in value. This is better than selling property and having your reinvestment potential eroded by taxes payable. If you own real estate, such as vacant land, and are considering a sale, another good tax-planning technique might be to rent out the property instead. Consider the following situation, where an annual pre-tax cash flow of $6,963 would result if a property were sold and the after-tax dollars were invested to yield 10%:

Cost of property	$ 10,000
Anticipated selling price	100,000
Capital gain on disposal	90,000
Taxable capital gain ($^3/_4$)	67,500
Taxes at 45% (assuming no capital gains exemption)	30,375
Cash available to reinvest ($100,000 – $30,375)	69,625
Available pre-tax return at assumed rate of 10% (per annum)	6,963

As an alternative, a purchaser who is willing to pay $100,000 might be willing to pay a rental of, say, $15,000 per annum under a long-term lease. The agreement could also incorporate an option for the purchaser to buy the property at *today's fair market value* in twenty-five years.

From the vendor's position, however, an annual rental of $15,000 per year provides him or her with a substantially larger cash flow than if he or she were to reinvest the after-tax proceeds of sale ($15,000 versus $6,963). The vendor is also guaranteed to get the agreed-upon purchase price in any event at the end of twenty-five years.

Planning for Capital Gains on Personal Residences

As mentioned previously, a special tax exemption applies to a gain on the sale of a principal residence. A principal residence is an accommodation owned by a taxpayer (either alone or jointly), which is ordinarily inhabited by him or her, a spouse or a former spouse, or a dependent child at any time during the year – as long as the taxpayer designates the property as his principal residence. As discussed in Chapter Six, a family owning two residences may designate only one of them as a principal residence for any given year.

The accommodation can take any form such as a house, apartment, farm, condominium, or even a share in a cooperative housing corporation. A principal residence also includes not only the building, but the land on which it is situated, up to a limit of one acre. For any additional land to be treated as part of the principal residence, the owner must establish that it is "necessary to the use and enjoyment of the housing unit as a residence."

So far, there have been a few tax cases on the topic of excess land, and it would appear relatively certain that if you live in a community where the minimum lot size is, say, five acres, the extra land would fall under the exemption as well.

Technically, your capital gain must be calculated in the same way as gains on other assets. However, there is a formula exempting a portion of the gain based on the number of years during which the property was designated as a principal residence as a proportion of the total number of years of ownership.

Since your entire gain is normally exempt, Revenue Canada officials do not require any designation of property as a principal residence to be filed from year to year. It is only when property is disposed of and where a *taxable* gain results, that a designation must be filed with your tax return for that year.

There are actually rules that will allow an individual to have up to *two* sales of principal residences in the same taxation year. Thus, if an individual moves from Montreal to Toronto, and then on to Vancouver, all in the same year, it is possible for the disposition of both the Montreal house and the Toronto house to be tax-free. (Actually, there is no requirement that these houses be situated in different cities.)

A Word of Caution to Habitual Renovators

From time to time, there are newspaper and magazine articles about people who have a rather interesting hobby. They buy older homes, move into them, fix them up, and resell them at a profit. If someone undertakes such a venture only sporadically, he or she can still expect to qualify for the principal-residence exemption for the gain on sale. However, if an individual develops the habit of buying, fixing, and selling a different house each year, Revenue Canada officials will consider these transactions to be a business. *As such, the entire gain could become taxable.* There have been a number of tax assessments of which I am personally aware that resulted from investigations initiated from information in newspaper articles. Thus, anyone who practises this rather interesting hobby should either maintain a low profile or be prepared for the possible adverse tax consequences that may result from human-interest stories.

Changing the Use of a Principal Residence

To accommodate people who are subject to temporary transfers, the Income Tax Act permits a taxpayer to move out of a home and still designate the property as his or her principal residence for up to four years. In order to make this election, the individual must remain resident in Canada and must not designate some other property as a principal residence during that period. If the designated property is rented out during that time, capital cost allowances may not be claimed to reduce rental income.

There is an extension to this rule, which permits a principal-residence designation to continue beyond four years in cases where the individual (or a spouse) is transferred by an employer and later reoccupies the home. This is provided that reoccupation occurs no later than one year following the year in which employment with that employer terminates.

These rules are designed to provide tax relief where a property is first a principal residence and then later becomes a rental property. Before 1985, no similar alleviating provisions existed for a reverse situation. If a property started off as a rental property and *then* became a principal residence, the owner had a problem. The rules of the Act provided that at the time there was a change of use, there was a deemed disposition of the rental property at current fair market value. *This triggered recaptured depreciation and capital gains even though there was no change in ownership.* The taxes payable had to be paid without any corresponding inflow of cash. The only consolation, of course, was that *future* growth in the value of the property was exempt from tax under the principal-residence rules.

Fortunately, the rental property conversion problem no longer exists. The tax rules were amended in 1985 so that no capital gain need be calculated until ultimate disposition on property originally acquired as a rental property and later converted into a principal residence. However, if you would like to obtain such relief, you are not permitted to claim capital cost allowance (depreciation for tax purposes) after 1984. If you own a rental property and you are contemplating moving in, any prior years' capital cost allowance will be subject to recaptured depreciation at the time you change the property's use. However, the postponement of being forced to realize a capital gain should provide you with a tremendous benefit.

Whenever an individual occupies part of a property and rents out the other part, the "housing unit" will consist of the portion occupied, and the rental portion is subject to capital gains treatment when a disposition takes place. If a housing unit is used for non-residential purposes, such as where a doctor carries on a practice using part of the home, only that portion occupied by the owner as a housing unit is eligible to be treated as a principal residence. Any gain on disposal of the non-residential portion will be subject to normal tax calculation.

At some point in time, most Canadians must make a decision about whether to buy a home or to rent. Certainly, there are many factors that must be taken into account. However, in defence of home ownership, it should always be considered that a personal residence is the only major asset on which profits can be realized without a part being caught up in the tax collector's net, if your lifetime capital gains limit has been reached.

CHAPTER 8

Tax Planning for Separation and Divorce

My purpose in this chapter is to deal with four specific topics:

- the tax consequences of alimony and lump-sum settlements to both the recipient and the payer;
- transfers of property from one spouse to the other in contemplation of separation and divorce at the time of marriage breakdown;
- allowable personal credit claims for the two parties both in the year that a divorce or separation takes place and subsequently; and
- some general tax tips governing the receipt or payment of alimony.

The Tax Treatment of Alimony

Under the Canadian income-tax rules, alimony and separation allowances are tax-deductible to the payer in the year that these amounts are paid and they are included in computing income of the payer's spouse or former spouse in that same year. However, for this tax treatment to apply, five specific requirements must be met:

1. The amounts must be paid as alimony or as an allowance for the maintenance of the spouse or former spouse, children of the marriage, or both.
2. The spouses must be living apart at the time each payment is made and throughout the remainder of the year pursuant to a divorce, judicial separation, or written separation agreement.

3. The amounts must be paid pursuant to a decree, order, or judgement of a court, *or* pursuant to a written agreement between the parties.
4. Each payment must be one of a series of payments payable on a periodic basis.
5. The amounts must be paid to or for the benefit of the spouse or former spouse (as explained in the next section).

While the rules may appear, at first glance, to be quite straightforward, there are many important technical points and grey areas that require clarification. Let's therefore go back to the five conditions that I just outlined and deal with them one by one.

Alimony is an "Allowance"

First, let's explore the concept of alimony paid as an allowance for the maintenance of a spouse or former spouse. The tax authorities consider an allowance to be a sum of money determined in advance by a court or by the parties themselves, as being the required, recurring payment to be made by the payer in order to maintain the payee and/or the children. To be deductible, the use of the allowance must be at the complete discretion of the recipient, who must not be required to account for it.

In some instances, however, the Income Tax Act and the administrative practice of Revenue Canada do permit a payer to deduct payments made to a third party on behalf of a spouse or former spouse. These include medical expenses, educational fees, home-heating costs, mortgage payments, and utility bills. Of course, if they are deductible on the one side, they are taxable in the hands of the beneficiary for whom these payments are made.

In order for third-party payments to qualify as alimony or separation allowances, it must be very clear that there is an agreement between the parties and that these payments have been deducted from the amount otherwise payable to the beneficiary spouse, with the express concurrence of that spouse. Alternatively, the amount must be paid to a court or an agency of the court pursuant to a court order. The only exception is any expense that represents either the purchase price of a house or mortgage payments, where the principal and interest amounts exceed 20% of the original principal balance owing on the mortgage. Such payments are considered as lump-sum and will not be deductible to the payer nor taxable to the recipient.

You should note that the Revenue authorities do consider an amount subject to adjustment in accordance with the Consumer Price Index or a similar formula, or any other indexed series of payments, to qualify as an allowance. This is the case even though the exact future amounts payable are not specified in the order or agreement.

As I explained, the allowance must be for the purpose of maintaining the spouse or former spouse or the children of the marriage or both. Under the income-tax rules, payments made to someone who was previously a common-law spouse qualify as alimony as long as they are made pursuant to a provincial court order. However, maintenance payments are not deductible to the payer if they are made on behalf of children who are not children of the marriage. For example, payments made to support children from a former spouse's previous marriage would not be deductible by another husband or former husband unless these children had been legally adopted.

Spouses Living Apart

Now let's turn to the second criterion, the rule that the spouses or former spouses must be living apart at the time each payment is made and throughout the remainder of the year pursuant to a divorce, judicial separation, or written separation agreement. The concept of living apart is extremely important. The government is naturally concerned about income-splitting arrangements between a husband and wife that are artificial. For example, in the absence of special rules, consider the following. Assume that you are a man who is earning $40,000 a year while your wife has no income and is at home looking after your children. It would pay you to get divorced or enter into a legal separation arrangement under which you would agree to pay your wife an alimony of $20,000 a year. This way, when the smoke clears, you would pay tax on $20,000, and she would pay tax on $20,000, and you would be able to take advantage of the low tax bracket twice. Of course, if you continue to live together, this arrangement is clearly a sham. Therefore, the Income Tax Act guards against this potential abuse by imposing the requirement that the parties live apart.

One key factor, as well, is the concept of living apart not only at the time each particular payment is made but throughout the balance of the year. In other words, if a couple reconciles, either legally or merely by mutual consent, late in a given year, this will have the effect of negating all alimony and separation allowance payments made previously during that particular year, as far as taxes are concerned. In other words, the payer will not get a deduction for the payments and the recipient will not be taxed for them.

Remember my reference to a divorce, judicial separation, or written separation agreement. Generally, payments made pursuant to a divorce or judicial separation become merely a question of fact. However, many court battles have been fought over the years on the subject of *written* separation agreements. At one time, support payments made before the date of a court order or written separation agreement were not deductible by a payer nor were they included in calculating the recipient's income. Recently, however, the government changed the rules for payments made before a court order or written agreement, where the deductible and taxable treatment would have applied if these payments were made after that date. Payments are now deductible to the payer and included in the income of the recipient, if the order or agreement *eventually* entered into so provides and the amounts were paid in the year the order or agreement was made *or* in the immediately preceding year.

Thus, if a couple separates in mid-1993 and a written agreement or court order is not obtained until late 1994, the payer will still be able to deduct any 1993 and 1994 support payments in full, provided that these are referred to in the eventual agreement or court order.

Again, I cannot stress how important it is to have a written separation agreement in place on time in the absence of a court order or judicial decree. To cite some cases, the tax courts have held that payments pursuant to an oral agreement do not constitute alimony for tax purposes. In addition, an agreement between the lawyers representing both parties has been held not to be a proper written agreement between the parties themselves. Also, evidence of cancelled cheques issued by the payer and endorsed by the payee did not alone constitute a valid written agreement. In simple language, you must be careful. You've got to dot your proverbial i's and cross your proverbial t's.

Alimony is a Series of Payments

Let's now deal with the concept of a series of payments payable on a periodic basis. The concept of periodic payments is another one of those vastly contentious areas and has been the subject of many courtroom battles. Periodic payments are interpreted as payments that are made periodically; recurring at fixed times, not at variable periods; not at the discretion of one or more individuals, but from some prior obligation.

The big bone of contention is evaluating payments as periodic on the one hand or lump-sum settlements on the other. A lump-sum settlement is not deductible to the payer nor is it taxable to the recipient. Let's look at some of the potential pitfalls in dealing with Revenue Canada. First, if an individual makes a lump-sum payment to a spouse or former spouse in place of several periodic payments not yet due, but imposed in future under a court order or agreement, this lump-sum payment will not qualify as the equivalent of periodic payments. Also, where an amount is paid for a period prior to an order or agreement, and the order or agreement requires that the payment be made after the date of such order or agreement, this amount will also fail to qualify because it was not payable on a periodic basis.

The only tax relief that is apparently offered is in cases where a lump sum can be identified as being on account of periodic payments due after the date of a court order or agreement but which had fallen in arrears. In such a case, the lump sum will generally be considered as "qualifying periodic payments."

But, again, you must be careful. There was an interesting tax case that was heard by the courts a few years ago. A woman received a lump sum of $6,000 in settlement of $12,000 for which her former husband was in arrears under a separation agreement. When Revenue Canada attempted to tax her on this amount, she took the position that this was merely a lump-sum payment in settlement of a legal action and was not taxable to her. The court agreed because the amount was not paid under the original order for support. We can assume that the payer did not get a corresponding deduction.

Even in cases where lump-sum payments of arrears are considered income when received, you should note it is certainly conceivable that the tax bite to the recipient will be significantly higher than if payments had been spread out over several years.

Then again, be aware that you have some flexibility. A lot depends on how a court order or separation agreement is drafted. For example, the parties may agree that a specified amount of money is to be paid in total. Settlement may then be made wholly or in part by means of regular periodic payments over a specific length of time. Generally, if the agreement or order states that these payments are an allowance for the support and maintenance of the spouse or former spouse and/or the children, as long as each regular payment is consistent with that purpose and the payments are spread over an extended period, they will be treated as alimony or maintenance.

You should also note that periodic allowances would still qualify as such even if they are paid only through part of each year. For example, assume that an agreement states that the children will reside with the wife for ten months of the year and with the husband for the remaining two months. Thus, if the monthly allowance for the maintenance of the children is payable by the husband only during those months that the children live with their mother, the tax treatment as alimony will not be disqualified. The husband in my example will be able to claim a deduction and the wife will be taxable even though, for two months out of the year when the children are residing with the payer, no such allowance is actually paid.

You should be aware that where payments continue to be made after the death of the payee, they are not deductible by the payer whether they are made to the payee's estate, to the children directly, or to anyone else. However, if the payer is not permitted a deduction as alimony or maintenance, he or she might still be entitled to a personal credit for the child or children. Also, if custody of the child or children reverts back to the payer, he or she may, under certain circumstances, be eligible to claim child-care expenses as well.

As I mentioned earlier, there have been literally dozens of tax cases that have come before the courts over the years dealing with the question of whether or not payments should be treated as alimony or separation allowances. Let me just refer to a few recent cases to emphasize how careful you must be in seeking the proper advice and in structuring your planning in an appropriate manner.

In one recent case, a separation agreement called for three payments spaced a year apart. The payer was not permitted to claim a deduction, since the three-year payout was not considered to be periodic.

In another case, a husband made extra payments to help out his former wife and children in circumstances where these payments were not required under the existing separation agreement. He was not permitted to claim any deduction for these gratuitous amounts.

To summarize, therefore, there are several important planning steps that must always be considered. First, be aware of the tax consequences of any payments made before a written separation agreement is signed by both parties or a judicial order is brought down by a court. Unless an agreement is formalized by the end of the following year, the payer will not get a deduction nor will the recipient be required to take these amounts into income.

Second, payments that are in excess of the amounts called for under the agreement or order will not be treated as alimony or separation allowances.

Third, lump-sum settlements in lieu of financial commitments for alimony or support are not deductible to the payer or taxable to the recipient.

Fourth, be very careful in trying to determine the tax consequences of payments that vary from time to time, such as educational expenses, camp fees, or medical costs. In spite of recent changes to the law, it would be much more prudent for anyone seeking a deduction to make the ordinary payments high enough to cover these more sporadic costs.

One further point that should be noted governs the benefits that you can derive from this chapter. While my orientation has been towards structuring the types of arrangements that will provide tax deductibility to the payer, keep in mind that if you are someone who is *receiving* money or is *about to receive* a financial settlement of some kind, it may be in your interest to have the arrangement structured so that you need *not* pay taxes on all or part of that which you will receive. It is just as important for the potential recipient of funds or benefits to know the tax consequences as it is incumbent on the payer to know where he or she stands. For example, if you are given the choice between receiving a lump-sum settlement of $10,000 or alimony for one year only of $1,000 a month, you cannot make an intelligent choice unless you carefully assess your after-tax position.

Property Transfers in Contemplation of Divorce or Separation

Before looking at property transfers between husbands and wives in contemplation of separation or divorce, it is important for you to review the general rules that apply whenever property is transferred between husbands and wives, which I discussed in Chapter Seven.

If property has been given by one spouse to the other, general income-attribution rules do not apply when the spouses are living apart and are separated pursuant to an order of a court or a written separation agreement. This is an *automatic* exception to the general rule and it means that income attribution will cease at the time of separation. Taxes on this income will be paid by the recipient of the gift, not by the person giving it. Of course, a formal divorce negates income attribution as well. But there is one catch. The problem arises where individuals who are separated cease to live apart within twelve months from the date on which they entered into a written separation agreement. A quick reconciliation will have the effect of bringing back the income-attribution rules *retroactively.* Presumably, both parties would be required to file amended tax returns to reinstate the general income-attribution rule.

It is interesting to note that the retroactive adjustment only applies if a separation evidenced by a written agreement between the two parties is terminated. There is no retroactive adjustment if the spouses cease to live apart within twelve months after a separation order is granted by a court.

So far, I think that these rules are relatively simple to apply. In fact, there is really no specific tax planning involved. It appears only proper that attribution should cease in situations in which one spouse is receiving income from property transferred by the other spouse and the transferor no longer lives with the recipient.

What are more complicated, however, are situations under which capital or growth property is transferred between spouses either before, during, or after a separation. Good examples of growth property include real estate, shares in both public and private companies, and even corporate bonds, which tend to fluctuate in value, as well as investments in precious metals such as gold and silver.

Again, as I explained in Chapter Seven, the general thrust of the Income Tax Act is to guard against attempts made to split income artificially, and the general rule is quite straightforward. Whenever a taxpayer transfers growth property to a spouse, the transfer is deemed to take place at the transferor's cost for tax purposes. In the case of depreciable property such as a building, the transfer is deemed to occur at cost minus the accumulated depreciation claimed for tax purposes in prior periods. In order words, under this general rule, the transfer does not give rise to any income in the hands of the transferor at the time the property changes hands. However, the Income Tax Act then goes on to state that when the recipient eventually disposes of the acquired property, the entire capital gain or capital loss and, in the case of property such as a building, recaptured depreciation revert back to the transferor. In the final analysis, it is as if the transfer had never been made. No tax advantage is achieved.

There are a number of important exceptions to this particular rule, which apply in situations where marriages break down. For example, if a transfer of growth property takes place pursuant to a written separation agreement or in accordance with a court order governing a separation, the transferor may elect to have the property deemed sold to his estranged spouse at fair market value. Presumably, such an election is made by simply reporting the disposition on the personal tax return as if it were a sale at fair market value. This will trigger capital gains and/or recaptured depreciation in the year the transfer is made. Then, if the property is subsequently sold by the recipient spouse, any *additional* capital gain and/or recaptured depreciation will be the responsibility of the person who received the property. This is provided that *both* spouses together file a written agreement with their income-tax returns for the year during which the separation took place.

Even if capital or growth property had been transferred from one spouse to the other before a separation ever occurred, and the recipient spouse continues to hold that property at the time of separation and afterwards, the attribution of capital gains to the transferor can be prevented, if that same joint election is filed in the year that a separation takes place. If this is the case, the spouse who sells the property becomes responsible for both capital gains as well as, in the case of depreciable property, recaptured depreciation.

Without question, the foregoing rules are somewhat complicated and you might be asking yourself, what do they really mean? Actually, these provisions are relatively new and have only been part of the Income Tax Act for a few years. The impact of these rules can be best be illustrated by means of a simple "real life" example.

Back in the early 1970s, a friend of mine and his wife separated. Under the terms of their separation, he transferred to her a real estate investment that he had held in his own name. My friend and his wife were separated for about a year before they decided to go through with a divorce. Then my friend's wife got some good advice. The advice was to sell the real estate before the divorce went through so that her husband would be stuck with both the recaptured depreciation and the capital gain. This is because no election to transfer at fair market value was available at that time and there was only the very simple rule that stated that attribution of income *and* capital gains applied as long as a couple was legally married.

My friend came to me and asked whether he had any recourse, but I was unable to help him with his tax problem. I pointed out, however, that had his wife waited until after the divorce, she would have been stuck with the entire tax bite, even the tax on recaptured depreciation for the period before she actually owned the property.

In a nutshell, the recent changes make it possible for a husband and wife to effectively settle up their accounts at the time that a separation takes place. You might ask why a husband might be willing to elect to transfer property to his wife or vice versa at fair market value in the year of separation if it means prematurely triggering taxes payable. If you stop to think for a moment, however, the answer does become clear.

Under the general matrimonial provisions of most provinces, property held by husbands and wives is presumed to be divided equally at the time that a marriage is dissolved. Generally, if assets are held primarily in the name of the husband, a reasonable proportion is thus transferred to the wife anyway. Of course, if assets are to be allocated in equal proportions, it only stands to reason that *liabilities* should be allocated in this manner as well.

In other words, it should be possible to calculate and isolate the taxes payable as a result of any property transfer. Half of the taxes then become the responsibility of the recipient of the property. Assume, for example, that a husband holds $200,000 in term deposits in addition to a real estate investment. Half of the term deposits and all of the real estate are to be transferred to his wife. The taxes payable as a result of the real estate transfer are, let's say, $30,000. Instead of transferring the real estate investment as well as half the term deposits, the amount of term deposits transferred should be reduced to take into account the tax liability. He would give her half of $170,000 instead of half of $200,000.

For many middle-income and upper-income individuals, this particular set of rules is perhaps the most important set of provisions governing marriage breakdown. Failure to understand them can result in extreme penalties. Also, it seems fairly obvious that if someone gets bad or inadequate advice from his or her own advisers, that there is legal recourse against these advisers.

For example, assume that a husband transfers growth property to his wife in contemplation of divorce and there is no election made to deem the transfer to take place at fair market value. The wife then sells the property during the term of the separation but before the divorce goes through and the husband gets stuck with the entire income-tax liability. If his advisers had failed to tell him about this potential problem, I would suggest that he could take legal action.

On the other hand, what happens if the wife delays and sells the property only after the divorce goes through? Under these circumstances, she must cope with the entire tax bite. In this case, I think she would have recourse against *her* advisers for not having informed her about the available elections that could have been filed. You can see that this whole matter is a potentially explosive situation.

You should note, however, that the preceding problems do not arise when an interest in the family home is transferred from one spouse to another. This is because of the general income-tax exemption from capital gains on the disposition of a principal residence. As I explained, however, you must use caution in dealing with other real estate holdings. This includes vacation property that does not qualify as a principal residence.

Personal Credits in the Year of Marriage Breakdown and Subsequently

Let us now deal with the topic of personal credits and the rules that apply to the break-up of a husband-wife family unit. First of all, if, in the year that a separation takes place, a husband pays alimony or maintenance support to his wife, he has the choice of either claiming a deduction for the alimony or maintenance actually paid or the standard personal credit otherwise available with respect to the dependent spouse. In 1993, the federal tax credit for a spouse is approximately $940, although it is reduced by 17% of the spouse's net income in excess of around $560.

So, what do you do? Clearly, if you separate in 1993 and the tax savings from your deductible alimony and/or maintenance in 1993 exceeds the available spousal tax credit, by all means, claim your actual payments. On the other hand, if you separate late in the year and before that time your spouse had no income or very little income, you may be better off claiming the spousal credit. You should note that this is the choice of the payer and does not involve the recipient of alimony or maintenance at all. What the payer does will also have no impact on the recipient's tax position.

After the year in which a divorce or separation occurs, a payer is only entitled to deduct alimony or maintenance payments.

If you were separated and you reconcile in a given year, your spouse's income for the whole year must be considered in determining your married credit. In addition, as I mentioned earlier, you are not permitted to deduct any separation allowances, even for the period before you were reconciled.

In some cases, both parents may claim credits for the same children in the year of separation or divorce but not in the years following. For example, if one spouse was supporting the family before a marriage breakdown and the children become dependent on the other spouse for the remainder of the year, both parents may claim credits. However, if the parent having custody of the children claims the "equivalent-to-married credit" for a particular child, the other parent may not make any claim whatsoever for that same child.

The Equivalent-to-Married Credit

If you are divorced or separated and support a relative related to you by blood, marriage, or adoption, who lives with you and is wholly dependent on you, you may be eligible for this special credit. The reason that it is called an equivalent-to-married credit is because the dollar value is the same as a credit for a spouse. In addition, the same net income limitations apply. In other words, you may claim as much as $940 in 1993 as a credit provided that your dependent relative did not have a net income over $560.

The most common situation for such a credit is that of a divorced woman who is living with her dependent children. She may claim one of the children as equivalent to a spouse instead of the ordinary credit for a child. If you claim a child as equivalent to married, you must still take family allowances received for that child into income.

You should note that no tax credit is given for dependants aged over eighteen except for those who are infirm. Instead, there is a tuition fee credit for students that is transferrable to a supporting individual in cases where the student does not require the credit to reduce his or her own taxes to nil.

If an individual pays maintenance allowances for a particular child, he or she may not use that child as a dependant. Also, as I mentioned earlier, if a spouse or former spouse to whom alimony or maintenance is paid dies, the payer may not continue to deduct support payments paid directly to the children or to someone else on the children's behalf. However, depending on the circumstances, the children might then be treated as dependants, with perhaps one of them qualifying for the equivalent-to-married credit.

General Tax Tips Concerning Alimony

Before concluding this chapter, I want to acquaint you with a few general tax tips governing the receipt or payment of alimony. First, from a recipient's point of view it is always important to budget for taxes that will eventually fall due. This is especially serious if the recipient of alimony also has other income, for example, from employment.

Assume that a woman is working part-time and is earning $15,000 a year. On top of that she receives alimony or support from a former husband. The fact that her employment income is in the $15,000 range puts her into approximately a 25% income-tax bracket. This means that the alimony will be subject to taxes of at least 25% from the first dollar. Of course, if the alimony is large, the effective tax could conceivably be somewhat higher. Failure to budget for this tax cost can be rather stressful when it comes time to file a tax return the following April.

If you are in the position of receiving alimony or maintenance payments over and above other income, it would be well worth your while to sit down and calculate your eventual tax exposure at the beginning of each year. Then, it becomes important for you to save the necessary dollars to pay your tax liability. One way that this might be accomplished, at least to some extent, is through a forced-savings program. For example, perhaps you go to your employer and ask him or her to increase the taxes withheld at source against your regular salary. One way to do this is to have taxes deducted as if you were single, not taking into account your potential claim for your children, including the equivalent-to-married credit that might otherwise be available. In this manner, part of your tax liability arising from the receipt of alimony or maintenance can be settled through additional tax payments on your employment income throughout the year.

It is important for *anyone* who receives alimony and/or maintenance to recognize that this income is treated as "earned income" for tax purposes. The significance is that it therefore qualifies for a potential transfer to a Registered Retirement Savings Plan (RRSP), as explained in Chapter Five. The opportunity to shelter to least part of alimony or maintenance income within an RRSP is something that should be explored.

If you are employed and are therefore subject to tax deductions at source, you may have a potential cash-flow problem if you *pay* large amounts of alimony. This is because the benefits of a tax deduction are not usually received until you file and receive a tax refund. However, to cope with this timing problem, the Income Tax Act gives you the right to have your deductions at source reduced, as long as you certify that failure to allow a tax reduction will present an "undue hardship."

Finally, let me turn once again to the topic that I started this chapter with, the subject of comparing alimony or maintenance to lump-sum payments. I suggested that, in general, a payer would like to have the payments classified as alimony or maintenance in order to obtain a deduction while a recipient might prefer to receive lump sums. Of course, there is always the possibility that the payer is, for one reason or another, in a lower tax bracket than the recipient. For example, what if the payer has substantial tax write-offs or a deductible loss from a business? Under these circumstances, the payer might be well advised to structure a financial settlement with a spouse or former spouse as a lump-sum payment, *especially if the payer can get a discount off the amount otherwise payable.*

One potential opportunity is for the payer to turn over all or most of the proceeds from the sale of the family home or for the payer to surrender his or her equity in the home for a reduced consideration. As I explained earlier, a transfer of an interest in a family home from one spouse to the other does not carry with it any of the income-tax implications that I dealt with in the section of this chapter concerning property transfers.

Marriage breakdown tends to be a contentious issue, to say the least! While I have tried to highlight tax strategies that may fit certain situations, I strongly recommend that you seek professional advice before implementing any specific tax-planning steps should you be confronted with this issue.

CHAPTER 9

The Capital Gains
Exemption, Canadian Dividends,
and the Alternative Minimum Tax

In this chapter, I will take an in-depth look at the lifetime capital gains exemption. I will also review the taxation of dividend income received by an individual, along with the alternative minimum tax which took effect beginning in 1986.

The Capital Gains Exemption

As I explained in Chapter Seven, the lifetime capital gains exemption is certainly the most encouraging tax concession to be granted by government in many years. On most property, the exemption is set at $100,000. For farmers and small business owners, an *extra* $400,000 is also available. As mentioned in Chapter Six, the capital gains exemption for a principal residence is not affected by this other incentive, although capital gains on investment real estate acquired after February 1992 (other than as part of an active business) no longer qualifies.

You should note that the capital gains exemption does have one potential drawback. It appears that the exemption may act as a disincentive for individuals to invest in public-company shares through their RRSPs. Even before the exemption was introduced in 1985, a major deterrent to such investments was the fact that dividend accumulations within an RRSP were ultimately transformed into other income and no dividend tax credit could therefore be claimed by the planholder. Moreover, the tax-free portion of capital growth was transformed into taxable income. Now that full capital growth is taxable within an RRSP while exempted within the $100,000 limit when investments are held outside an RRSP, it appears that many Canadians may resist the lure of the market or mutual funds as RRSP investments.

On the other hand, I assume that the government hopes that, outside of RRSPs, taxpayers will be inclined towards growth investments because of the incentive of not having to pay tax on fairly substantial gains.

Special Planning for Major Shareholders of Profitable Businesses

It has been said that as a result of the capital gains exemption, holding investments through a corporation may now prove to be unattractive for some Canadians. This is because if a corporation sells capital property at a profit, its gains will not qualify for the exemption. (The exemption is only available to individuals.) It appears, however, that business owners whose incorporated businesses generate profits not required for expansion can arrange their affairs quite easily to have their proverbial cake while eating it too.

Specifically, assume that a Canadian-controlled private corporation earns $100,000 of profits before taxes and after paying a normal management salary of, say, $70,000 to you, the owner-manager. If these profits are not needed for business expansion, and are drawn out by way of bonus, you as owner-manager would be able to reinvest only around $55,000 after your personal tax bite. This is because your ordinary salary is more than enough to place you into a 45% tax bracket. On the other hand, if corporate taxes are paid instead, 80 cents on the dollar may be reinvested. If you prefer to keep your investments separate from your active business, a holding company could be used to own the shares of the operating company and the operating company could pay a dividend out of these surplus funds to the holding company. This is discussed in more detail in Chapter Fifteen.

The key is that it is certainly preferable to have $80,000 rather than only $55,000 in spite of the loss of a potential capital gains exemption down the road. With proper planning, however, you can obtain the use of the larger amount of corporate retained earnings while *still* qualifying for a capital gains exemption. There is nothing that would prevent you, as the shareholder in my example, from borrowing the corporation's funds in order to make your investments personally. If the after-tax dollars are retained by the operating company, a loan of $80,000 could be made for personal investments. This is a substantial improvement over having only $55,000 to invest after personal taxes.

Of course, you would have to be careful insofar as timing is concerned. A loan to a shareholder for personal purposes cannot remain outstanding on two successive year-end balance sheets of the corporation without having the loan retroactively included in the shareholder's income. However, with proper planning, it may be possible to use the corporation's funds for up to literally two years less one day. As long as the loan is repaid on time, no adverse tax implications need arise. You would also have to avoid repaying the loan and then immediately borrowing the money back. If this were done, such an arrangement would constitute a series of loans and repayments, which under the provisions of the Income Tax Act is equivalent to not having repaid the loan at all.

The question arises as to how such an investment loan is to be repaid. There are several possibilities. If the investments acquired with the proceeds of the loan have been sold at a profit to third parties before the deadline, the repayment of the loan in cash would be straightforward. If the securities are still held for further growth and they have already appreciated in value, they could be transferred to the corporation itself. If the difference between the fair market value and the cost of the investment is within the shareholder-manager's capital gains exemption limit, one would simply arrange a sale at fair market value, crediting the shareholder's loan with the cost and setting up a loan *payable* to the shareholder equal to the profit. If the shareholder's gain exceeds the exemption available at that time, one could use a Section 85 rollover. Section 85 rollovers are beyond the scope of this particular book, but professional tax advisers are quite familiar with them.

The only problem that may arise is in situations where the investments have dropped in value. First, you would probably have to sell the securities at arm's length in order to trigger a capital loss. This is because a loss on a transfer of capital property to a controlled corporation is automatically deemed nil. Further, even if the securities are sold at arm's length, a capital loss can only be utilized to the extent that you realize subsequent capital gains. What about the shortfall? The difference between the entire amount of the loan and the amount repaid must then be treated either as a bonus or as a dividend. In the final analysis, this may trigger taxes totalling 45% of the deficiency. However, the key point is that any shareholder-manager is certainly going to be no worse off than had he or she taken a bonus or dividend for the full amount of the profit made by the corporation in the first place in order to make investments personally. In other words, why pay the tax immediately if the tax can either be deferred or, if the securities appreciate, be avoided completely?

The only matter that remains is the question of imputed interest. No doubt such a loan by a corporation to a shareholder-manager would trigger a taxable benefit of interest calculated at the prescribed rate adjusted quarterly. *However, the same amount that is added to income should then qualify as a tax-deductible carrying charge. In other words, the taxable benefit would be cancelled out.*

In short, you may then get the best of both worlds, the opportunity to build up investment capital using eighty-cent corporate dollars after the small-business deduction, while also being permitted to make investments that would be eligible for the capital gains exemption personally.

The Reverse Estate Freeze

Another offshoot of the lifetime capital gains exemption is a concept that I like to call the reverse estate freeze. It appears that the exemption opens an area for tax planning that has never before existed in Canada. The concept of the reverse estate freeze involves making use of parents and grandparents of modest means as vehicles to hold growth property for children or grandchildren who are considerably wealthier.

In other words, investment holdings may now be structured so that these parents and grandparents make capital gains that would otherwise be realized by their children or grandchildren. The parents or grandparents would obtain tax shelter through their own capital gains exemptions, which they otherwise would not require since they would not otherwise have investments of their own. Then the idea would be to pass on either appreciated property (to the extent it has not been sold to third parties) or an increased capital base after gains have already been realized, by way of gift or bequest down to the children or grandchildren. In the case of appreciated property, the recipients would acquire it at a "stepped-up" cost base and this would shelter their future capital gains from taxes as well.

The reason such a program has never before been viable, even before 1972 when there were no taxes on capital gains, is that, in those days, one had to deal with federal estate and gift taxes. Moreover, most provinces had legislation for provincial succession duties. Thus, tax planning tended towards reducing an elderly person's estate, not increasing it.

We may be witnessing a brand new era in Canadian tax planning. Of course, we will have to wait and see whether or not this kind of planning will, in fact, be blocked sometime in the future. In the meantime, here is an example involving an investment such as public-company shares, with which I will explain more clearly the type of planning that may become popular.

Assume that Mr. X is an upper-income executive or entrepreneur. Before 1993, he made no capital gains and incurred no losses. He is a fairly astute stock-market player, however, and let's assume that by March 31, 1993, he has sold capital property and has triggered cumulative capital gains for the year of $100,000. He realizes that $25,000, representing the tax-free quarter of the capital gain, is free and clear and that the other $75,000 may be sheltered by using the lifetime exemption. However, his cumulative exemption is now completely exhausted.

Mr. X would like to take $100,000 and buy shares in a certain company listed on the Toronto Stock Exchange. He is fairly sure that, before the year end, these shares could be sold for double, or $200,000. Mr. X happens to be single but he has a widowed mother who is living on her Old Age Security as well as a modest pension from her late husband's former employer. Mr. X can simply take his $100,000 investment capital and make a non-interest-bearing demand loan to his mother. The investment would then be made by Mr. X's mother. Sure enough, the investment appreciates and he instructs her to sell the securities on December 15, 1993, for $200,000. The $100,000 capital gain is then fully sheltered, one-quarter by way of the ordinary exclusion from tax and the other three-quarters through the special exemption. Mr. X's mother then simply repays the $100,000 loan and makes a *gift* of the $100,000 profit on which no tax consequences result to either herself or her son. Thus, Mr. X effectively realizes $200,000 of capital gains in calendar year 1993 totally tax-free.

An even more astounding example of a reverse estate freeze pertains to a family farm situation where, as I mentioned, a much larger $500,000 capital gains lifetime exemption is available and where the opportunity also exists to "roll down" an interest in such property to a child or grandchild at the transferor's adjusted cost base. Of course, if a rollover is used, income taxes are only deferred as opposed to forgiven, since the recipient acquires the property at the adjusted cost base of the transferor.

Here's how the system can be beaten. Assume that Mr. A owns a farm either incorporated or unincorporated with a cost for tax purposes of zero (to keep the example simple) and a fair market value of $1 million. He is a widower and the entire farm is in his name. Mr. A, who is fifty-five years of age, would like to pass the farm to his son, Mr. B, who is thirty-two. Mr. A also has a father, Mr. C, who is seventy-eight years old and who is retired. It would be advantageous if son B could acquire the entire property at an adjusted cost base of $1 million so that if he wishes to sell it, he can do so without attracting any tax. Here is how this may be accomplished. Father A sells or gifts a half-interest in the farm to grandfather C for $500,000. Since the original cost of this interest in the farm was zero, father A triggers a half-million-dollar capital gain which is, of course, sheltered by the exemption. Grandfather C receives the property at the "stepped-up" cost of $500,000 and retains it. Father A then rolls over the other half-interest in his farm to son B, who acquires this interest at a cost for tax purposes of zero under the ordinary farm rollover provisions. Son B then either sells or gifts his newly acquired half-interest to his grandfather C at its fair market value of $500,000. Again, son B's capital gain is sheltered by means of the special exemption. Grandfather C now owns the entire farm property with a fair market value of $1 million and a cost for tax equal to that same amount. Son B continues to farm and can be compensated for his efforts.

Ultimately grandfather C dies, with the farm now worth $1.5 million. Presumably, several years have elapsed since the original transactions. Grandfather C's executors then transfer the farm to grandson B at its fair market value of $1.5 million. Grandfather C's capital gain of $500,000 is also sheltered by the exemption. Son B now owns a farm with a fair market value of $1.5 million and an equivalent cost for tax. Thus, by interposing grandfather between father and son, it becomes possible to escape capital gains taxes on an extra half-million dollars. This would not otherwise be possible if father and son had simply transacted directly.

The opportunities to escape taxes are, as I mentioned, astounding. Assume that father A, instead of being a widower, had a wife who owned a half-interest in the farm property. Assume, in addition, that grandmother is still alive. Clearly, with a little bit more paperwork, an extra million dollars of growth could pass to grandson B on a tax-free basis via his mother and grandmother. One must really question whether this is what former finance minister Michael Wilson had in mind when he introduced his legislation!

Let's return for a moment to the earlier example where a successful stock-market player uses his widowed mother to make capital gains on his behalf. If we re-examine this example, you can see that the opportunities are even better. Assume Mr. X is forty-two years old and that his mother is age seventy-two. Statistically, he will outlive her by about thirty years. Since the lifetime capital gains exemption is available at any time, *the key point is to try to use the older generation's available exemption as quickly as possible and retain the younger generation's exemption for use later on.*

In the example that I discussed previously, I assumed that Mr. X had already made capital gains in 1993 and had used up his available exemption. Let's backtrack and assume that Mr. X had not used up any of his exemption at all but was only now starting to make stock-market investments. He would be better off lending the money that he has to invest to his mother and letting her make the investments on his behalf. Then, once mother's lifetime capital gains exemption is used up, Mr. X could begin to make investments in his own name and also take advantage of the exemption rules.

In a case where a husband and wife both have elderly parents of modest means, it is thus conceivable that up to $600,000 of total capital gains exemptions may be enjoyed as long as the husband and wife have no siblings who want to get into the act by using their parents' exemptions as well.

Let's go one step further. Assume that husband and wife own all the shares of a very profitable Canadian-controlled private corporation which is earning $200,000 a year after management salaries. They now decide to start another business and their children are too young to be made shareholders in the corporation. Clearly, if husband and wife together own the shares of the new company, the new business will be "associated" for tax purposes with the old one. Since the first business is using the full benefits of the small-business tax rate, taxes at roughly 40% would apply from the first dollar of corporate profits made by the new entity. (The concept of "associated companies" is covered in more detail in Chapter Thirteen.) On the other hand, if the shares are held by the elderly parents, there is no reason for the two companies to be deemed associated. The small-business tax rates would therefore apply to both.

Let's assume the new business prospers and does well. Ultimately, the shares become worth $1 million. If the parents are still alive, at that point they could gift these shares at fair market value either to their children or to their grandchildren. The recipients would pick up the shares at a "stepped-up" cost for tax purposes. Of course, if the husband and wife acquire the shares, the companies would become associated from that point in time. However, there would be no penalty taxes relating to prior profits. Alternatively, if the grandparents die, the shares can be passed on either to the husband and wife or to their children, and the same tax consequences would result.

In other words, the capital gains exemption lends itself to the formulation of multiple corporations which might not be associated for tax purposes and which could get a small-business tax rate advantage as well as a capital gains advantage.

Another similar opportunity for aggressive planning arises if an individual is likely to make substantial capital gains over and above the exemption limit and has another relative, such as a brother or sister, who would not ordinarily realize capital gains of his or her own. As long as that person is eighteen or over, a loan can be made on a non-interest-bearing basis, and the other person can make the investments instead. When the investments are sold, the loan could then be repaid and a gift made equal to the profit. Of course, the gift does not have to be equal to the entire profit. It might be more reasonable if only a portion of the profit, say 90% of it, were gifted back to the person who provided the capital in the first place. Essentially, the remaining 10% could be construed as an accommodation fee for having "sold" one's capital gains exemption to a brother, sister, or other relative.

You should note, though, that the reverse estate freeze does have one potential drawback not related to tax. Where property is transferred to others, one may not be guaranteed that the same property, or the profits therefrom, will eventually be gifted or bequeathed back to where the original transferor desires. What if, in my farming example, the grandfather gifts the farm to *another* child or grandchild? Then again, if we assume that, in most estate-planning situations, family relationships are reasonably good and stable, there may not be a substantial risk involved. It appears that each case has to be looked at on its own merits. All the same, this is clearly an interesting opportunity for tax planning.

Capital Gains Over and Above the Lifetime Exemption

The proportion of a capital gain or loss required to be included in computing an individual's taxable capital gain or allowable capital loss is three-quarters beginning in 1990. Figure 9-1 reflects the impact of *combined* federal and provincial taxes on capital gains for individuals in the highest personal tax bracket on the assumption that the provincial rate is 50% of the federal tax. While the exemption for gains above $100,000 disappears, it is still possible for such an individual to retain at least two-thirds of capital gains realized.

Figure 9-1 also shows the comparison of corporate capital gains retention. Essentially, if the exemption is ignored, it doesn't make any difference whether a capital gain is realized by an individual or through his corporation. As I mentioned earlier in this chapter, in cases where one controls a Canadian-controlled private corporation which is eligible for the small business tax rate, an advantage might be obtainable if the corporation earns profits taxed at only around 20% and such profits are not required for business expansion. It will thus be possible to reinvest eighty cents on the dollar in capital property investments. As an alternative, if profits are distributed to high tax bracket individuals for personal investments, the tax bite may be as high as around 45% combined federal and provincial tax. This would mean that only fifty-five cents out of each dollar of bonus or salary could be reinvested in growth property. The bias for investing may therefore shift to corporations and away from personal investing in such cases.

Figure 9–1   **The Tax Consequences of a Capital Gain**
             Ignoring the $100,000 Cumulative Lifetime Exemption

Individual

1. Capital gain	$100
2. % included in income	75%
3. Amount included in income	$75
4. Top federal tax bracket ($60,000+)	29%
5. Provincial tax at 50%	14.5%
6. Top marginal combined rate of tax	43.5%
7. Tax on capital gain (line 3 × line 6)	$32.63
8. Net retention on capital gain	$67.37

Corporation

1. Capital gain	$100
2. % included in income	75%
3. Amount included in income	$75
4. Federal tax rate	28%
5. Provincial tax rate (estimated)	14%
6. Combined tax rate	42%
7. Tax on capital gain (line 3 × line 6)	$31.50
8. Net retention on capital gain	$68.50

Interest Versus Dividend Income

Having exhausted the topic of capital gains, let us now look at the tax implications of receiving either interest income or dividend income in Canada. There are two distinct comparisons that should be made:

1. the relative yields of both interest-bearing and dividend-bearing investments, and
2. the effectiveness of both kinds of investments in counterbalancing the impact of inflation.

As of late 1992, it would not be unreasonable for an investor to expect a return of about 7% where funds are placed to earn interest. On the other hand, if you invest in Canadian public-company common stock, you might encounter difficulty in finding investments that pay dividends of more than 3%. On the surface, therefore, there would be a 4% differential in yield between interest-bearing securities – such as term deposits, mortgages, or Canada Savings Bonds – and many Canadian public-stock investments.

Although an investment in term deposits, mortgages, or bonds may produce what appears to be a superior yield, most people are aware that part of the advantage is offset by the decreasing value of the dollar, which accompanies the inflationary process even in times when inflation is low. Nevertheless, being somewhat security-conscious, many still feel that a 4% spread in yields is too large to warrant an investment in the stock market. It is recognized that over the long term, stock-market investments could appreciate and these may provide a reasonable hedge against inflation, but there is still the "downside" risk of potential declines in value.

Unfortunately, many Canadians lack sufficient information when it comes to making proper investment decisions. Much of the problem stems from exposure to our American neighbours. In the United States, there is no difference between the receipt of interest and the receipt of dividends by an individual; both are taxed at regular personal rates. In Canada, however, there is a very important distinction between these two kinds of income. Dividends are subject to a "gross-up and credit treatment," while interest income is simply taxed at ordinary marginal rates. A comparison of after-tax retention for individuals in various tax brackets can only be made after one understands how Canadian dividends received by an individual are taxed.

The Taxation of Canadian Dividends Received by an Individual

When an individual receives a Canadian dividend, the dividend is included in the taxpayer's income. In addition, he or she is then required to include in income a *further* 25% of the amount actually received. This extra 25% is called "one-quarter gross-up."

The grossed-up dividend (125% of the actual dividend) is then taxed at the individual's marginal rate for the year. Initially, this appears to create a penalty situation where more than what was actually received is taxed. However, in arriving at the individual's taxes payable, there is a dividend tax credit that is *equal* to the 25% gross-up. (The federal dividend tax credit is approximately 75% of the gross-up, while a provincial dividend tax credit covers the balance.)

Figure 9-2 illustrates how $100 of Canadian dividends is taxed when received by individuals in various tax brackets.

Figure 9–2   **Schedule of Tax Payable on $100 Canadian Dividend**

	$30,000	$60,000	$60,000+
Taxable income level	$30,000	$60,000	$60,000+
Individual's marginal tax bracket	25%	40%	45%
Cash dividend	$100	$100	$100
25% gross-up	25	25	25
Additional taxable income	$125	$125	$125
Tax in marginal bracket	$ 31	$ 50	$ 56
Dividend tax credit (combined federal and provincial)	25	25	25
Net tax payable	$ 6	$ 25	$ 31

If you examine the schedule, it becomes apparent that the tax treatment of dividends does not result in a penalty to the shareholder who receives them. Although the shareholder initially pays tax on an amount greater than what is actually received, the dividend tax credit *more than compensates* for this inequity. If, for example, you are in a 25% tax bracket and you receive $100 of additional income from any other source *except* Canadian dividends, you would expect to pay $25 on the incremental income. However, on a Canadian dividend, the tax is only $6. Similarly, an individual in the 40% bracket only pays $25 on a $100 dividend, while someone in a 45% bracket pays only $31.

The favourable tax treatment of dividends from Canadian companies takes into account the fact that a dividend is a distribution out of profits on which *a corporation has previously paid tax.* The dividend tax credit is intended to compensate the individual shareholder for at least a portion of the corporate tax previously paid.

Tax-Free Dividends of Up to $22,000

The gross-up and credit system has a very interesting by-product, which is a major factor in tax planning for certain Canadian investors. Specifically, up to $22,000 of Canadian dividends can be received by an individual *totally tax-free* as long as he or she has *no other income.* This is illustrated in Figure 9-3, which uses average tax rates applicable across Canada.

The example in Figure 9-3 shows a dividend of $22,000 that is grossed-up by an extra $5,500. However, after applying the personal tax credit, the federal tax otherwise payable is completely offset by a federal dividend tax credit. The net effect is to reduce federal taxes to nil. If there is no federal tax to pay, there is also no provincial income tax.

Remember that the concept of tax-free dividends only applies where an individual has no other income. If the individual in our example has an *extra* $1,000 from *any source whatsoever,* the taxable income would become $28,500 instead of $27,500. In this case, since the individual is in a 25% combined federal and provincial tax bracket, the extra $1,000 of income would attract $250 of taxes. There would be no further dividend tax credits available to offset this additional burden.

Thus, if you receive dividends as well as other income, the other income "floats to the top" and gets taxed at your marginal bracket with no

Figure 9–3 **"Tax-Free" Dividends**

Cash dividends from Canadian corporations	$22,000
25% gross-up	5,500
Net income	$27,500
Federal tax on net income at 17%	$ 4,675
Less: Basic personal tax credit in 1993 (estimated)	(1,100)
Federal dividend tax credit (13.33% × $27,500)	(3,665)
Federal tax after credits	Nil
Provincial tax is therefore	Nil

relief. If you have substantial other income, you should be aware that the tax advantages of Canadian dividends are reduced considerably. You should also note that there is no direct relationship between dividends and other income. Therefore, you could *not* receive, for example, $12,000 of salary and a further (tax-free) $10,000 of dividends. The interaction of various dividend and other income mixes must be determined on a trial-and-error basis with the aid of your own accountant in your particular province.

Comparing Interest to Dividends

Now that you understand the tax treatment of Canadian dividends, you should take a few minutes and examine Figure 9-4. As the comparison shows, the after-tax retention on dividends for taxpayers in *all* brackets is one and one-quarter times as high as the corresponding retention on interest. Thus, for anyone who is taxable, a 6% dividend is comparable to interest at 7.5%. Similarly, the yield on a 5% dividend will be as much as the yield on 6.25% interest, after tax. Therefore, the difference between earning interest at, say, 9% or dividends at 5% is really only a difference of 2.75 percentage points (9% minus 6.25%). In addition, the 2.75% difference is really a further *pre-tax* difference. For a taxpayer in a 45% bracket, when the additional 2.75% interest is taxed, it translates to just a little over 1.5% after tax.

Figure 9–4   **A Comparison of After-Tax Retention, Canadian Dividends Versus Interest Income**

	25%	40%	45%
Individual's marginal tax bracket	25%	40%	45%
Alternative 1: $100 Canadian dividends			
Cash dividend	$100	$100	$100
One-quarter gross-up	25	25	25
Taxable income	$125	$125	$125
Tax in marginal bracket	$ 31	$ 50	$ 56
Combined federal and provincial dividend tax credit	25	25	25
Net tax	$ 6	$ 25	$ 31
Net retention (cash dividend minus tax)	$ 94	$ 75	$ 69
Alternative 2: $100 Canadian interest			
$100 interest	$100	$100	$100
Tax in marginal bracket	25	39	43
Net retention	$ 75	$ 61	$ 57
Ratio of Dividends: Interest	1.25:1	1.25:1	1.25:1

Let's put this into proper perspective using sample numbers. Assume you have $20,000 to invest and have a choice between a term deposit paying 9% interest or a Canadian blue-chip stock paying a dividend of 5%. If you opt for the share investment, then, as explained, you must be prepared to sacrifice 1.5% of $20,000, or $300 per annum. Then you must ask, what are my chances of the stock appreciating by at least an amount offsetting my $300 loss? Of course, there is some risk involved. The securities could decline in value because of poor market performance overall or because you just happened to pick the wrong stock. On the other hand, if you invest $20,000 in interest-bearing investments, you can be *sure* that your $20,000 capital will only be worth about $19,000 at the end of one year given anticipated inflation rates!

I must stress that the foregoing example is only valid where an individual is taxable in the first place. If you are in a 45% tax bracket, there just doesn't seem to be much value in earning 5% *net* interest income when the inflation rate is also 5%. On the other hand, I have no criticism if your fifteen-year-old son invests his summer earnings in a term deposit. The reason is that your son presumably hasn't reached the point where his income is taxable. If that is the case, a 9% *gross* return on a term deposit is the same as his *net* return. For him to invest in dividend-bearing securities would, in fact, involve a difference in yield of about 4%.

I also would not be too upset if your eighty-year-old grandmother had her life savings invested in term deposits. Even if her income is taxable, she would be much more concerned with the security element of having money available at any time than she is about the devaluation of the dollar.

Finally, I am not averse to interest-bearing investments when they are held by pension plans, Registered Retirement Savings Plans, or deferred profit-sharing plans. *As long as the investment income is tax-sheltered, the after-tax yield and the pre-tax yield are one and the same.* I would not, however, recommend an interest-bearing investment for anyone whose income is taxable unless the after-tax yield was at least equal to the annual inflation factor.

The Alternative Minimum Tax

In December 1985, the government tabled a motion to implement a minimum personal income tax which took effect January 1, 1986. The impact of the minimum tax is to ensure that virtually every Canadian individual pays at least a minimum tax of approximately 25% of his or her adjusted

Figure 9–5 **Alternative Minimum Tax Computation**

Part 1

Net income for regular tax _____

Add: Losses (oil & gas exploration/films) _____
MURB rental losses created by CCA _____
Excluded one-quarter of capital gains _____
Registered pension contributions _____
RRSP contributions _____
Gains on disposition of Canadian cultural property _____
One-half of bonus interest on CSBs _____
Forward averaging withdrawal _____ _____

Net income plus additions _____

Less: Gross-up on Canadian dividends _____
Capital gains deduction claimed _____
Alternative minimum tax exemption $40,000
Unemployment insurance, old age
security and other repayments payable _____
Non-capital losses of other years _____
Capital losses of other years _____ _____

Alternative minimum tax taxable income ═══════

Part 2

Alternative minimum tax taxable income _____

Federal tax at 17% of AMT taxable income _____
Less: CPP/UIC contributions tax credit _____
Charitable donation tax credit _____
Personal tax credits
(self-dependents) _____
Medical expense tax credit _____
Tuition credit _____
Education credit _____ _____
Net federal tax on AMT taxable income _____
Add: provincial tax at _____% _____

Total tax on alternative minimum tax taxable income ═══════

"Regular" federal and provincial tax before surtax ═══════
Greater of alternative minimum tax and
"regular" tax _____
Add: Federal surtax _____
Add: Provincial flat tax and provincial surtax _____
Less: Miscellaneous federal credits _____
Miscellaneous provincial credits _____

Net income taxes payable ═══════

taxable income. This percentage is arrived at by taking a federal tax rate of 17% and assuming a provincial add-on of around 50% of the federal tax otherwise payable. The schedule in Figure 9-5 summarizes how the alternative minimum tax works. Essentially the minimum tax requires certain items otherwise deducted in arriving at regular net income to be added back. The major items are losses arising from oil and gas or mining exploration and development tax write-offs, losses created by claiming capital cost allowance on MURBS or films, registered pension plan contributions, and Registered Retirement Savings Plan contributions. Moreover, the excluded portion (one quarter) of capital gains must be added back.

There are several other items that must be considered that are not really worthy of much comment, such as gains on the disposition of Canadian Cultural Property and one-half of bonus interest on Canada Savings Bonds. From the adjusted net income, one would then subtract the lifetime capital gains exemption utilized in the current year, the gross-up on Canadian dividends, losses carried over, as well as a basic $40,000 exemption. The $40,000 amount ensures that most Canadians are not actually subject to the minimum tax calculations.

Once the taxable income for the Alternative Minimum Tax is calculated, the federal tax at 17% is computed, and after some adjustments and a provincial tax add-on, this amount is compared to the regular tax after any dividend tax credit. The individual's income taxes payable are whichever is the greater of the Alternative Minimum Tax and the regular tax, less special tax credits (such as the investment tax credit, foreign tax credit, and so on).

You should note that capital gains on principal residences are not subject to the minimum tax. Also, most people will not be affected by the minimum tax if they have earned income (such as salary, business income, or professional income) that forces them into reasonably high tax brackets. The tax in excess of 25% which is payable on the earned income will effectively shelter a reasonable amount of capital gains, pensions, or RRSP contributions. However, even if one is not ultimately affected by having to pay more tax, there is nevertheless the problem of record keeping.

Note that there is still a major loophole which is not closed by the minimum tax legislation. It is possible to reduce net income for *both* regular tax and minimum tax by borrowing money for investment and writing off interest expense in anticipation of future capital appreciation.

On balance, however, the government has tried to create a fair system.

As such, in order to recognize fluctuating incomes and tax liabilities for individuals, *the amount by which the minimum tax exceeds the regular tax for any year may be carried forward to offset regular tax payable over the following seven years, to the extent that the regular tax payable exceeds the minimum tax in these later years.*

When he introduced his legislation former finance minister Michael Wilson gave the opinion that, as a result of this carry-forward mechanism, the value of tax incentive deductions and credits would not be eliminated by the minimum tax. At the same time, he said, the minimum tax ensures that these incentives cannot be used alone or in combination to reduce tax below an acceptable level, that is, 25% in any year.

Although conceptually Mr. Wilson's "generosity" can be appreciated, the complexity of the reporting cannot be ignored. What he did was to introduce a brand-new mini-Income Tax Act that will certainly affect the lives of many middle-income and upper-income individuals. After all, unless the forms are completed, you cannot know for certain whether or not you are subject to the minimum tax rules.

From a planning perspective, it would appear that if you earn the majority of your income from employment, business, or professional sources, and you also have investments, you are best off realizing your capital gains over an extended period of time instead of realizing these gains within a short period. The reason is that over an extended period, the tax otherwise payable under the minimum tax rules would be offset by the regular tax payable on your other earnings.

In other cases, actual numbers to optimize planning will have to be worked out using trial and error and with reference to the actual combined federal and provincial tax rates on a province-by-province basis. In any event, it seems clear that your entire tax position must be reviewed from year to year in order to determine exposure under the minimum tax rules.

CHAPTER 10

Tax and Investment Planning for the Retirement Years

This chapter outlines specific strategies to help you assure yourself of a comfortable retirement, regardless of the age at which you choose to retire.

To determine whether you are ready for retirement, you must be able to answer yes to four specific questions:

1. Am I in a financial position to maintain a standard of living that is adequate for my needs and those of my spouse?
2. Am I mentally prepared to move away from the environment of a structured working day to the unstructured life that follows retirement?
3. Will I be able to use my time in an effective manner so that I will get satisfaction from what I do and avoid boredom and depression?
4. Are my goals and objectives compatible with those of my spouse?

This chapter is restricted to dealing with the first question, ensuring a successful retirement from a financial and investment standpoint. It examines inflation and life expectancy; how the government assists retired Canadians through pension programs; the importance of a Registered Retirement Savings Plan as a means of providing retirement capital; income splitting between husbands and wives; effective money management and how to evaluate various investment alternatives; and finally, tying up the loose ends through proper estate-planning techniques. Some of these topics are dealt with in greater detail in other chapters of this book as well.

Understanding Inflation

Perhaps the biggest problem facing people close to retirement age is the spectre of renewed inflation. At the time this is being written, in late-1992, the Canadian inflation rate is exceptionally low, but no one knows what the future will bring. All too often, however, the impact of the Consumer Price Index on our lives is blown way out of proportion. In my opinion, inflation is not nearly as deadly an enemy as you might think.

Let's consider for a few moments how inflation works. If we look back at 1981-82, a period of *high* inflation, the numbers will prove that you need not be too concerned with inflation – as long as you have planned properly. At this point, you may want to take a look at Figure 10-1. It shows the changes in the Consumer Price Index from April 1981 to April 1982, at a time when the inflation index was in double digits.

Figure 10–1   **Major Components of the Consumer Price Index**

	% Change April 1982 from April 1981		Statistics Canada Weighting %		Weighted Changes (Column 1 × Column 2)
Housing	13.8	×	35.4	=	4.9
Food	6.1	×	21.1	=	1.3
Transportation	16.3	×	16.2	=	2.6
Clothing	6.0	×	9.6	=	0.6
Recreation, reading, and education	8.7	×	8.6	=	0.7
Tobacco and alcohol	15.7	×	5.4	=	0.8
Health and personal care	10.3	×	3.7	=	0.4
All items			100.0		11.3

Here's how the Consumer Price Index works. There are seven items that are included in the statistical computations. The categories are housing; food; transportation; clothing; recreation, reading, and education; tobacco and alcohol; and health and personal care. Statistics Canada measures the percentage changes in the cost of a basket of goods and services from the end of one month in comparison to the same month in the previous year. Then, a percentage increase is calculated. For example, the food index would take into account the price of a loaf of bread a year ago compared to the price today. As you can see from Figure 10-1, in all cases prices rose between April 1981 and April 1982 by between 6% and 16%.

Then, Statistics Canada applies a weighting formula. The formula takes into account the fact that all of us tend to spend more of our disposable incomes on certain components rather than others. On average, our biggest expenditure is for housing, 35.4 cents out of each dollar. Then come food; transportation; clothing; recreation, reading, and education; followed by tobacco and alcohol (almost double what we spend on health and personal care). If we then take the actual percentage increases multiplied by the weighted averages, we get figures that, when added up, give us changes in the Consumer Price Index.

If you now stop to look at the third column in Figure 10-1, you can see that *at a time when inflation was in double digits,* only two items in the entire Consumer Price Index were meaningful. They are housing and transportation; at that time, 7.5% out of the 11.3% total increase.

There is one important lesson that you must learn from this. Specifically, *as long as you can stabilize your own housing and transportation costs, you really don't have to be particularly concerned about how consumer prices move.* No matter who you are, no matter how aggressive or non-aggressive in your investment policies, there are two things that you must target for by the time you retire. First, you must have your house paid for by that time. If you choose to continue to live in that home, you will still be subject to annual increases in your taxes and utilities, but these probably won't go up by more than a few hundred dollars a year. Alternatively, if you choose to sell your house, the fact that it's paid for will provide you with capital. If you take that money and invest it conservatively, taking advantage of some of the income-splitting techniques with which I deal in this book, you should be able to generate sufficient investment income to pay your rent.

The second point is that by the time you retire, you must target to have a late-model car fully paid for. In fact, if your family consists of a husband and wife, you might consider two late-model cars both fully paid for. Then, if you have to, you can probably keep those same vehicles serviceable for much of the remainder of your lifetimes. Again, you may not be able to "fix" your entire transportation costs. After all, insurance, gasoline, and even licence fees are subject to change, but a good portion of your transportation costs will be stabilized. Actually, depending on your lifestyle and where you reside, you may find that you don't want or need a car subsequent to retirement. If you have had two cars previously, you may find that one car now suffices.

What I'm really trying to show you is that, as I mentioned before, general changes in the Consumer Price Index can be quite misleading. The CPI is an overall calculation, but each family's individual inflation factor is somewhat different.

Consider as well some of the other components of the Consumer Price Index. Food, for example. Obviously, the cost of feeding a family of two is significantly less than the cost of feeding a family that is supporting children. Tobacco and alcohol is another interesting category. Take another look at Figure 10-1. At the time that inflation was 11.3%, the consumer price increase attributable to tobacco and alcohol alone was almost 1%. If you and your spouse didn't smoke or drink, this would have reduced your family's susceptibility to inflation. And the list goes on. It costs less to provide clothing to a family of two than it does to clothe a large family with growing children. Also, by the time you retire, you should not be paying education costs and, if necessary, you can tailor your recreation expenditures to fall within your means.

So, the first concrete plan that I suggest to you in dealing with retirement is to control your housing and transportation costs as much as you can. Then inflation need not be seen as a mortal enemy.

Understanding Life Expectancies

That's the good news. What's the bad news? Well, the bad news, if you can call it that, is that you will probably live a lot longer than you expect. Most people are hung up on the fact that men ordinarily live to age seventy-two, while women live perhaps three years longer. This is true. These are the overall statistics for life expectancy. However, the older you get, the longer you can expect to live in total. Take a look at Figure 10-2, which is an extract from the Standard Canadian Life Expectancy Table.

You can see that if you're sixty-five years old, you have a life expectancy of seventy-nine if you are male, and eighty-two and a half if you are female. At age seventy, you can expect to live to eighty-one if you are male, and eighty-four if you are female. This is fairly easy to explain. Picture a room filled with people all seventy years of age, all reasonably healthy at this point. On average, they will live more than another decade.

Figure 10–2 **Mortality Table – Male and Female Life Tables
– Expectations of Life in Years**

Age	Male	Female	Age	Male	Female	Age	Male	Female
60	16.95	21.39	70	10.90	13.85	80	6.41	7.88
61	16.27	20.58	71	10.38	13.17	81	6.05	7.39
62	15.61	19.79	72	9.88	12.51	82	5.70	6.93
63	14.96	19.01	73	9.39	11.86	83	5.36	6.48
64	14.33	18.25	74	8.92	11.24	84	5.04	6.06
65	13.72	17.47	75	8.47	10.63	85	4.74	5.67
66	13.12	16.72	76	8.02	10.03			
67	12.54	15.98	77	7.60	9.46			
68	11.98	15.26	78	7.19	8.91			
69	11.43	14.55	79	6.79	8.38			

In other words, the fact that a person is seventy years old does not necessarily mean that he or she will die within two years.

So, whatever you accumulate by the time you retire has to be sufficient to meet your needs for an extended period of time. This means that over and above paying for your house and car, you have the responsibility of setting aside some additional capital.

What Can I Expect from Government?

Before we look at what *you* have to do, let's see what you can reasonably expect from the government. At age sixty-five, you become eligible for the Old Age pension, which at the beginning of 1993 is just over $350 a month. In addition, if you have worked in Canada since 1966, you should be eligible for the maximum Canada Pension Plan, which is a further

Figure 10–3 **What Can I Expect from the Government?**

Reasonable expectation in today's dollars:
Husband and wife both over age 65 – only husband had been working
Old Age Security 2 × $350 = $ 700
Canada Pension Plan 1 × $650 =   650
                                      $ 1,350   per month
                                      $16,200   per annum

Note: A single person who had been working before retirement could expect $350 a month in old age pension as well as $650 a month from the Canada Pension Plan. This amounts to $1,000 a month or $12,000 annually.

$650 a month in round figures. Figure 10-3 provides a calculation of what a husband and wife can reasonably expect to receive today if both of them are age sixty-five or over and only one of the two had been working before retirement. You can see that the pension-income level is in excess of $16,000 a year for a couple. This does not take into account potential income under the Guaranteed Supplement, which I will ignore for purposes of this chapter. After all, if you take reasonable steps to plan for your retirement, you shouldn't need the Supplement nor be eligible to receive it.

You should also note that if your other income exceeds around $52,000 a year, you may have to repay all or part of your Old Age Security (not Canada Pension) benefits. But, if you have such high income, you probably won't miss the required repayment.

One of the decisions that you may have to make is whether or not to apply for the Canada Pension Plan at age sixty-five. You don't have to apply at that age, but if you don't continue to earn pensionable income, it is certainly in your interest to do so. If you continue to be employed or to carry on an unincorporated business, it may be better for you to delay your application and continue paying premiums until age seventy, in order to increase your monthly pension. One reason to do this would be if you had very low earnings in earlier years, which could be replaced by higher earnings after age sixty-five. If you're unsure what to do, I suggest that you visit the nearest Canada Pension Plan office and ask for some assistance. In fact, a visit to that office can be well worth your time so that you may check that you have made sufficient contributions so that your spouse will qualify for survivor's benefits in the event of your death. A detailed analysis of the Canada Pension Program as well as the Old Age Security Program is beyond the scope of this book, although my key point is that a couple can probably rely on an income in excess of $16,000 a year, which will be indexed for inflation, while a single individual might receive around $12,000.

There are various other tax-related considerations that come into play at age sixty-five. For example, provincial health and hospital-insurance premiums are generally reduced or even eliminated. You get an additional personal tax credit (in 1993) of around $900 that you may claim on your income-tax return. This is also indexed annually. Thus, between husband and wife, the additional tax credits over and above basic personal credits are an extra $1,800. You also become eligible for the annual pension-income credit, which I dealt with in Chapter Five when I discussed Registered Retirement Savings Plans and employment-related pensions. Finally, you are exempt from the requirement to pay Unemployment Insurance premiums if you continue to work.

To summarize what I have said so far, I have suggested that you target to have your house and car (or cars) fully paid for by the time you retire. In addition, you may comfortably rely on the Canadian government to provide you with an annual income of between $12,000 and $16,200, depending on whether you are single or married.

After these factors are considered, saving sufficient capital to meet the remainder of your living expenses and provide a little bit of luxury is not an insurmountable task. For many people contemplating retirement, there are benefits from a pension-plan program resulting from prior employment. In some instances – for example, if you were a government employee – your employment-related pension may even be indexed. Some pension-plan programs are geared to provide up to 70% of your final year's income while in full-time employment. About half of pension plans provide a widow's pension, which is usually at least 50% of what the deceased spouse was getting.

Whether or not a pension will be paid to the surviving spouse may depend on whether the contributor dies before or after retirement. Some private plans only provide for a return of contributions if the contributor dies before retirement. Or they may guarantee payment of a pension for a specified number of years, if he or she dies after the pension begins to be paid. As I explained in Chapter Five, if you are eligible for an employer pension plan, you owe it yourself to learn about your entitlements and options.

The Registered Retirement Savings Plan (RRSP)

For many people, however, the cornerstone of a successful retirement is the Registered Retirement Savings Plan program. For a complete discussion, I again refer you back to Chapter Five.

You should be aware that, in addition to regular RRSP contributions, you are also permitted to make special transfers of certain lump sums received at the time of retirement and subsequently. If, for example, you get a payment in recognition of long service, perhaps comprising accumulated sick leave and vacation pay not taken during your term of office, or if you receive payment from your former employer for loss of office (in other words, because you have been asked to take early retirement), these payments will be eligible for special transfers into an RRSP. The maximum amount is $2,000 for each year of service while you were also covered by an employer-sponsored pension or deferred profit-sharing plan, and $3,500 for each year of service before 1989 while not covered by such a program.

One key point is that you are not required to draw money out of your RRSP until age seventy-one. Thus, if you find that, at age sixty-five, your other income is sufficient to meet your post-retirement needs for several years, you can leave your RRSP funds alone to earn income on a tax-sheltered basis. At age seventy-one, you would start to draw an annuity, which could be used to provide income for yourself and your spouse for the remainder of your lives.

You have probably been subjected to a tremendous amount of advertising over the years on the subject of RRSPs. You are probably conscious of the fact that if someone starts saving at age thirty-five, there is no reason, given reasonable investment returns, that such an individual shouldn't have a million dollars in his or her RRSP by the time he or she retires.

However, for many people, to start saving in an RRSP at such a young age is quite difficult. Also, the contribution levels used to be a lot lower than they are today. What if you have never invested in a Registered Retirement Savings Plan and you are only five or six years away from retirement? It still isn't too late to start, especially if you now no longer have any dependent children. Assuming you are earning $30,000 a year or more and that you can command a reasonable interest rate, you should be able to save at least $50,000 by the time you retire. This will certainly be enough to give you an annual income of between $5,000 to $7,000 a year, which, when added on to the amounts you can expect to receive from government programs, can be of substantial benefit.

Many people, in fact, cannot start to put aside significant RRSP funds until their mid- or late fifties. This is because their disposable incomes are tied up in paying off home mortgages and in providing education and living costs for their children. Once the family unit is down to two people, the goal of saving money can be a lot easier to achieve. If you use the RRSP, take advantage of spousal programs and try to double up on the pension-income credit that I discussed in Chapter Five.

Other Tax-Planning Techniques

Let's now take a look at some more tax-planning techniques. There is a good chance that, if you are serious in your desire to build a comfortable retirement, you will already have some capital saved, over and above money in an RRSP and a house and car that are paid for. You could conceivably sell your house and invest your money to produce an income large enough to cover your rent as well as many of your other living expenses. For some people, the sale of a house can be very attractive, since the capital gain on the disposition of a principal residence is tax-free under Canadian law. However, maximizing investment yields then becomes an extremely important concept. What I would suggest is that you arrange to split your investment income with your spouse. Always try to take advantage of the low tax brackets twice. I have discussed this in Chapter Seven.

Effective Money Management

Let's now discuss money management. In general, I suggest that anyone approaching the retirement years take steps to avoid substantial business or investment risks. This is unless you have enough assets that a loss of capital won't affect your position. One area in which I suggest extreme caution is in conjunction with bank guarantees. I personally saw a number of situations several years ago in which parents approaching retirement age guaranteed the bank indebtedness of their children who were involved in businesses. When the businesses failed as a result of the recession of the early 1980s, the parents were forced to make good on their guarantees – in one or two cases, at a cost of their entire accumulated savings. Sometimes it may be tough to say no, but you may have no choice.

Generally, most people approaching their retirement years want their assets to stay as liquid as possible. Consequently, most monies are kept in investments such as term deposits or Canada Savings Bonds. There are, however, a couple of alternatives that you may want to consider and I'll discuss these in the next few pages. Before I do, though, I suggest that you avoid a common mistake and that is keeping too much money in your personal chequing account. Usually chequing accounts do not bear any interest at all or, if they do, the interest rate is negligible. Keep your chequing accounts only as high as you have to in order to cover whatever payments you are required to make from time to time. Keep the balance of your funds in a daily-interest account until needed. Then you can make transfers to your chequing account to cover amounts that you have to pay out.

Another important point is always to be aware of what your tax bracket is. This will tell you how much the government will take away from basic income over and above pensions or RRSPs. For example, if your taxable income from pension sources is say, $11,000, you are already in a 25% income-tax bracket. This means that if you earn interest income, the government will take away twenty-five cents out of each additional dollar. So, if you are earning, say, 7% interest on a term deposit or Canada Savings Bond, you should realize that your net yield is only about 5%.

You will also find that an understanding of tax brackets is useful if you wish to assess the impact of holding down a part-time job subsequent to retirement. For example, let's assume that you are reasonably well off and have investment and pension income that puts you into a 40% bracket, with a taxable income of around $30,000. If you take a part-time job that pays you $6 an hour, you will really only be earning 60% of that, or $3.60 – in other words, a net amount considerably lower than the minimum wage. If you are thinking of taking the job in order to keep busy or because the job has some appeal to you, by all means go ahead, but if it's purely a financial decision, the high tax cost that already comes into play at your taxable income bracket should be taken into account.

The Pros and Cons of Annuities

A big decision that you may have to make is whether or not you want to live on income only or whether you are also willing to dip into your capital. A lot depends on whether or not your income is adequate to support your lifestyle and your own personal circumstances. For example, what if you don't have any children or other beneficiaries to whom you wish to leave an eventual estate? After all, you know the old saying, "You can't take it with you."

If you are willing to spend capital, the big question is how much can you use up each year so that you don't run out of money during your lifetime. You could solve this problem quite easily if you knew exactly how long you were going to live, but most of us just don't know. Fortunately, your solution might simply be to purchase an annuity from an insurance company, which deals with the problem of uncertain lifespans by pooling many lives together in its calculations of how much it can afford to pay out in exchange for lump sums of money received. There are a number of annuity options that are available. One thing to consider is your health. If your health is bad, you may get a better deal than if your health is good!

This is because if you have a shorter life expectancy than average, the issuing company might give you a greater annual income for the same purchase price.

You should explore the types of annuities that are available to you. First, there is the ordinary life annuity, which pays you an agreed sum at stated intervals for the rest of your life. Upon death, all obligations to make these payments cease. An ordinary life annuity is not usually too popular because people are concerned that they might die prematurely. So, unless you have an iron constitution and are pretty sure that you won't get hit by a bus, an ordinary life annuity should not generally be considered unless you have no spouse and absolutely no heirs whatsoever.

A second option is a joint-and-last survivor annuity for you and your spouse. This means that payments could continue until the last of husband and wife dies. You could build in a guaranteed-term option as well. For example, if both you and your spouse die prematurely, the payments could be structured to continue for the remainder of the guaranteed period.

Another option is a term-certain annuity, which will pay you money for the rest of your life or for a specified number of years. Term-certain annuities of fifteen or even up to twenty years are not uncommon. The advantage of such an arrangement is that, if you were to die prematurely, the payments would continue for the rest of the guaranteed period. Trust companies as well as insurance companies provide these kinds of annuities.

Finally, there is the concept of an escalating annuity, under which the payments increase annually. At the start of the payout period, the amount that you would receive would be lower than from a regular annuity but the payments would become greater within a few years. The purpose of such an annuity is to compensate for the impact of inflation and the fact that as time goes on, you may require a greater income flow to meet your living expenses.

What about the Stock Market?

So far, in dealing with investment yields, I have concentrated on interest income. I would like to provide a few thoughts, however, on the stock market as a potential consideration. Usually, one tends to think of the stock market as involving risk, and I am not suggesting that you may want to use your savings subsequent to retirement in order to speculate. However, there are a number of Canadian blue-chip stocks that bear fairly substantial dividends. Some of these are common shares but most are preferred shares.

The interesting thing about a Canadian dividend is that it qualifies for a dividend tax credit, a concept that is unique to Canada. This has been discussed in Chapter Nine. You should recall that, if you are in a taxable position, no matter what bracket you are in, the yield on a Canadian dividend is one and a quarter times the equivalent yield from interest. In other words, if a stock bears a dividend of 6%, on an after-tax basis that is equivalent to interest at 7.5%. Similarly, an 8% dividend will provide you with the same after-tax dollars as if you were earning interest at 10%. I strongly suggest that, if you have a reasonably large amount of investment capital, you discuss the market with a qualified investment counsellor at your convenience.

Life Insurance Considerations

Another topic that must be considered is life insurance. If you are like most Canadians, you have at least some coverage. If you have permanent insurance as opposed to a term policy, you should try to ensure that your coverage is paid up by the time you retire. I wouldn't like to see anyone in a position where he or she is bound to pay premiums after the earned-income years are ended. If you have a whole life policy, the chances are that it has a cash surrender value. The cash surrender value can be drawn out and used to pay premiums or to buy additional paid-up insurance, it can be turned into an annuity, or it can be used as security for a loan.

In some instances, if you draw the cash surrender value out, you will be taxed. Also, if you surrender your policy, your coverage ceases. On the other hand, you may be able to borrow against a policy under very favourable conditions. If you have life insurance, especially policies with cash surrender values, you can see that it is necessary to make an important decision. This should only be done after careful consideration and with a full understanding of all the options. Once you make your decision, it is possibly irrevocable. By all means, speak to your own insurance agent, but I also suggest that you get some independent advice as well from an accountant, lawyer, or other financial adviser.

Effective Estate-Planning Techniques

Finally, consider your estate planning. This topic is covered in detail in Chapter Sixteen. If you are married, your concern should be directed not only to your own retirement, but also to the financial needs of your spouse. If you have a large estate, no doubt you will be somewhat concerned about passing assets on to your children, or maybe even grandchildren, at as inexpensive a tax cost as possible. Again, I counsel you to sit down and discuss estate planning with your own advisers.

Fortunately, the tax rules relating to husbands and wives are quite generous. Very simply, under Canadian tax law an entire estate can pass from husband to wife or wife to husband without triggering any adverse income-tax implications whatsoever. In other words, you don't have to pay any taxes on the transmission of an estate until the last of husband and wife dies. This is unless you want to trigger taxes earlier by passing certain assets on to other beneficiaries.

In some cases, you may not want to pass assets directly to your spouse but might instead prefer to use a trust. This would apply if you want to direct the ultimate disposition of your property so that it passes on to the beneficiaries that *you* so intend. A good example of when a trust will is appropriate is if you (or your spouse) are in your second marriage and either of you has adult children by previous marriages. You may want to ensure that your spouse is protected but, in the final analysis, you may want to take steps to guarantee that your assets pass to your children and not necessarily to those of your spouse. Again, family circumstances are always different and your accountant and lawyer are there to advise you.

I recommend that before you retire, you make calculations of the projected income from your assets both in your lifetime and in the event of your death. In other words, even if you and your spouse could live together comfortably at present, the big question often is whether your spouse could maintain a good lifestyle if you die first. For example, when you die, your Old Age Security pension will no longer be paid. Your spouse, on the other hand, will continue to receive any pensions that he or she may be entitled to by virtue of being age sixty-five or over. Payments from the Canada Pension may be substantially different as well and, as I already mentioned, the provisions with respect to private employment-related pensions vary dramatically, depending on circumstances. In some instances, there is a substantial reduction if a former employee dies, and in other cases, there is even a complete discontinuance. Sometimes, ongoing payments will only be made as long as the surviving spouse does not remarry.

Effective 1987, the Pension Benefit Standards Act has been amended to alter existing pension legislation significantly. The new rules provide increased portability, transferability at the time of a job change, and several measures designed to improve pensions for women. Specifically, survivor pensions will no longer be terminated if the survivor remarries, and the value of pension credits and pensions already being paid will be split equally between spouses upon marriage breakdown. While welcome change continues to be made, I suggest that you still be conservative in dealing with the question of maintaining your spouse's lifestyle after your death.

Perhaps to some extent, life insurance will balance against potential income reductions in these circumstances. If you maintain an insurance policy that pays off at the time of death, keep in mind that the full proceeds are tax-free. The investment yield from your insurance can certainly be used by your spouse to offset reductions in income from other sources.

Normally, when you die, the fair market value of any RRSP would be included as part of your income in the year of death. However, if you had bequeathed your RRSP to your spouse, he or she could roll it into another RRSP and delay payment of taxes until money was actually received. In order to have such a "rollover," however, it's extremely important for you to have a proper will.

Making a Will

It appears that at least half of all Canadians who die in any given year don't have wills. Believe me that the problems and expenses caused by not having a will can be astronomical. I cannot stress how important it is for you and your spouse to have up-to-date wills.

In preparing your will, keep in mind that circumstances change from time to time. For example, what if you sell your home? Instead of having real estate as perhaps your major asset, you might now have cash. Make sure that your dependent family members are well provided for. In some instances, if there are more than enough assets to maintain your spouse adequately, I think you should consider bequests to your children at the time of your death and not necessarily when the last of husband and wife dies. In my opinion, it is possible to overprotect a spouse and that is almost as bad as underprotecting. Why make children wait until they are in their fifties or sixties to inherit property? This is often the case if one of the spouses lives into his or her late seventies or eighties.

In putting your affairs in order, make sure all your documentation is easily accessible. For example, your birth certificate, social insurance number, prior years' tax returns, marriage certificate, description of all securities that you own and their locations, and a list of safety deposit boxes, key numbers, and where they are, should all be easy to find. Your insurance policies should also be readily accessible as well as your current will. If you have made prior wills, I suggest that you destroy them so that there is no confusion.

Summary

If you plan properly for your retirement, you will find that a tremendous load will be lifted from your shoulders – the necessity of scrounging to earn money to pay your living expenses will be gone. You will find that, perhaps for the first time, your income will be permanent and not dependent on keeping a job. Pension income and income from investments will come in without any further requirement to work or perform. You will be able to spend your days in a manner that you desire and your money will continue to roll in. The work of the past will provide the income of the future, leaving you free to enjoy the rest of your life.

CHAPTER 11

Incorporating Your Earnings – The Ultimate Solution?

Advantages of Personal-Service Companies

By definition, a personal-service corporation is a company that earns fees or commission income. Generally, the income arises as a direct result of the activities of one or a few individuals. Personal-service corporations set up in the past include:

1. Professional corporations (in certain provinces only) for doctors, dentists, lawyers, and accountants;
2. Management companies for professionals; and
3. Corporations for athletes, entertainers, executives, commissioned salespeople, and business consultants.

Personal-service companies can be used for tax-planning purposes in a variety of situations. Perhaps their most common application is for professionals and other individuals who are in a position to contract their services through the use of a corporation. In most provinces, only *individuals* can lawfully carry on certain activities, such as the practise of law, medicine, dentistry, or public accountancy. The exceptions are in the provinces of Alberta, British Columbia, and New Brunswick, which allow taxpayers in the professions the right to incorporate in full. Effective 1990, lawyers practising in Ontario may also incorporate their professional activities. In other provinces, professionals can incorporate part of their practices through the use of a management company.

182

The advantages of personal-service corporations stem from the fact that "active business income" of a Canadian-controlled private company qualifies for a small-business tax rate of around 20% on the first $200,000 of profits each year (the actual rate varies from province to province). Although any profits over $200,000 are taxed at approximately 40%, it is unlikely that the profits of most service companies in any given year (after salaries are paid out) would be in excess of $200,000 in any event. Thus, the high rate of tax is not really applicable.

Management companies have also been used by taxpayers in an attempt to transform what was previously employment income into income from a business.

To summarize the advantages of management companies (where they have been successful in avoiding the attack of Revenue Canada):

- They provide the ability to split income between members of one's family – as long as salaries paid are for services rendered and are reasonable in the circumstances. Income splitting by way of dividends is also available.
- They create the existence of a new taxpayer (the corporation itself), which may qualify for a low rate of tax of approximately 20% on business income. After-tax dollars retained by the company can then be invested on behalf of its "owners."
- As retained earnings accumulate, depending on how the management company is set up as to shareholdings, estate freezing and income splitting can both be achieved.
- A management or service company earning business income may be subject to much more liberal deductions for expenses than would an individual's employment income. The corporation could pay for such costs as conventions, business-promotion expenses, and owning and/or operating an automobile.

At one time, one of the major reasons for incorporation was the inability of a taxpayer carrying on an unincorporated business to pay a salary to a spouse. In 1980, however, this restriction was eliminated and such salaries now constitute valid deductions for tax purposes. Of course, the remuneration will have to be included in the spouse's income and the payments must be reasonable in relation to services rendered. The spouse paying the salary must also be carrying on a bona fide *business* activity.

Professionals and others who employ spouses in their businesses may find that the advantages of incorporation are reduced considerably. It will be useful to incorporate only where profits are in excess of their families' spending requirements and where the corporate rate is to be preferred relative to higher personal marginal tax rates, or if there is an advantage in paying dividends. These matters will all be discussed in the next three chapters, which include tax-planning techniques for any Canadian private corporation, large or small.

Employees Versus Independent Contractors

The question of whether a person is employed or self-employed often arises in connection with the deductibility of expenses. It is important because self-employed persons are allowed to deduct all reasonable expenses incurred for the purpose of gaining or producing income, except capital outlays, while employees are more strictly limited to expenses that rarely go beyond such items such as union dues, and, in certain cases, unreimbursed travel expenses.

Whether or not an individual is employed or self–employed is also of major concern for purposes of unemployment insurance. A self-employed person is not covered under the unemployment insurance program and is not required to make payments to that fund, while most employees are eligible for coverage but must make contributions.

The meaning of the word "employee" is not defined in law. It therefore becomes necessary to refer to common law tests to determine the legal relationship. What is the most appropriate test is not completely clear, and no single test is, in itself, decisive in determining whether an individual is an employee or an independent contractor. Accordingly, the facts of each particular case are crucial, no matter what test is being applied.

The following tests have evolved through court cases:

1. Control – is there a "master/servant" relationship?
2. Integration – to what extent or degree does the individual form part of the payer's operations and/or organization?
3. Economic reality – is the individual actually in business, or does he or she work for someone else?
4. Specific result – is the individual required to perform general work or only to accomplish a specific job?

The material that follows will review the four tests in detail in order to provide some useful guidelines for situations that are unclear.

The Control Test

Perhaps the most important factor in distinguishing between an employee and an independent contractor is the nature and degree of control exercised by the payer over the payee. The control test determines whether one person is in a position to order not only *what* is to be done but *how* it is to be done. Where such control exists, the relationship has generally been regarded by the courts as that of an employer and employee.

The following four traditional characteristics of a "master/servant" relationship are covered under the control test:

1. Selection – the master retains the power to select the servant.
2. Dismissal – the master has the right to suspend or dismiss the servant.
3. Method of work – the master has the right to control the method in which the job is carried out.
4. Remuneration – the master sets the payment scale for wages or other remuneration to the servant.

Many years ago, the control test was regarded as the sole conclusive test. It is still important but is no longer appropriate as the only consideration. The shortcomings of the control test become evident in circumstances where it is difficult for the payer to exercise substantial control over the manner in which the work is performed. For example, the courts have found this test to be quite inflexible in determining the employment versus self-employment issue for professionals and highly skilled tradespeople.

The Integration Test

The integration test examines the extent or degree to which an individual forms a component part of the payer's operations and organization. Where the payer hires an individual and the work of that individual forms an integral part of the payer's business, then the hired individual is generally considered an employee. The integration test encompasses three characteristics:

1. Integration – is the work integrated and done as part of the business of the payer or is it simply an accessory to the payer's business?
2. Part and parcel – is the individual who is receiving payment an integral part of the organization that pays him or her?

3. Ordinary man – would the ordinary person view the relationship as one of employer and employee?

The Economic Reality Test

The economic reality test requires an analysis and assessment of the entire relationship between the parties in order to determine whether a particular individual is carrying on business for personal gain or for someone else. Such an assessment of the relationship involves five criteria:

1. Control – how much control is exercised by the payer over the work and the manner in which it is done?
2. Risk – does the payee bear any risk of loss with respect to his or her activity, and to what extent does the payee have an opportunity for profit?
3. Financial investment – does the payee have an ownership of machinery and equipment and is the investment substantial?
4. Lasting relationship – is there a permanent relationship between payer and payee?
5. Diversity – is the payee permitted to provide similar services to other parties and is the payee actively involved in searching out other business opportunities?

Where the recipient of remuneration receives direction from the payer, supplies no capital, takes no financial risks, has no liability, has formed a lasting relationship, and does not have the opportunity to render services to others, it is generally held that he or she is an employee.

The Specific Result Test

The specific result test attempts to determine whether a contract is to provide for a single service leading to a specific result or whether the payee is simply required to provide general efforts on behalf of the payer. Two criteria must be considered under the specific result test:

1. Specific work – if the payee is an independent contractor, it is agreed that certain specified work would be done for the payer as opposed to an employer/employee relationship, where the employee agrees, for either a period of time or indefinitely, either full or part-time, to work for the other party, i.e., the employer.

2. Personal service – a contract of employment normally requires a specific individual to place his or her own services at the disposal of the payer. Normally, however, an independent contractor's only obligation is to see that a certain agreed-upon task is completed. In other words, it doesn't necessarily matter who actually carries out the work.

An employee/employer relationship usually contemplates an employee putting his or her personal services at the disposal of an employer during a given period of time, without reference to a specified result and, generally, the work is accomplished on an ongoing basis. On the other hand, where a party agrees to perform certain specified work on behalf of someone else, it may be inferred that an independent contractor relationship exists.

A Recent Tax Case

Recently, the Federal Court of Appeal dealt with all these tests in the case of Wiebe Door Services Ltd. v. the Minister of National Revenue. The corporation was in the business of installing and repairing overhead doors. It carried on its business through the services of a considerable number of door installers and repairers, with the specific understanding that these people would be running their own businesses and would therefore be responsible for their own taxes, contributions to Workers' Compensation, unemployment insurance, and Canada pension. The Minister assessed Wiebe for unemployment insurance premiums and Canada Pension Plan contributions. The Tax Court of Canada agreed with the Minister that the door installers were employees rather than independent contractors. In arriving at that conclusion, the Tax Court applied the integration test, noting that the work performed by the installers was an integral part of the payer's business. The company then appealed to the Federal Court. The higher court found that *all* of the tests must be examined and that mutual dependency may only be a surface arrangement and is not necessarily expressive of the intrinsic relationship. On balance, the judge held that the installers were truly self-employed.

The decision in this case reinforces the fact that one must examine all factors in determining whether or not an individual is an independent contractor. Nevertheless, it would be difficult to use the Wiebe case as a precedent unless the facts in another dispute were almost exactly identical.

It is certainly important that any written agreements between the parties must be carefully drafted. It would appear that any payer should ask for an indemnification provision for any taxes and penalties that might become payable if a self-employment relationship is ultimately characterized as one of employee and employer. Then again, the individual payee might ask for the payer's assurance that the payer will assist in fighting any adverse assessment made against him or her by Revenue Canada authorities.

Incorporated Executives and Senior Employees

One important tax rule prevents incorporated employees from availing themselves of low corporate rates of tax. An incorporated employee is defined as an individual whose relationship with the person to whom services are rendered can "reasonably be considered to be that of an officer or employee and his employer." Such corporations are also prohibited from claiming *any* business expenses. However, professionals, independent sales agents, entertainers, and bona fide consultants are *not* affected by these rules.

Professional Corporations

As I mentioned previously, Alberta, British Columbia, and New Brunswick are the only provinces that allow all professionals to incorporate their practices in full. An Alberta professional corporation is somewhat of a hybrid between an individual and a corporation. By law, the only shareholder is the professional himself or herself. In other words, no splitting of shareholdings among spouses or other members of the family is permitted. In addition, the professional remains personally liable for all the debts and obligations of the corporation. The "unlimited liability" factor gives the public the same security as if it were dealing with the professional directly. This applies with respect to professional matters, trade debts, and any other obligations. In all other respects, the professional corporation is, however, a validly constituted entity. As such, corporate, and not personal, tax rates apply. In British Columbia, a spouse is permitted to own non-voting shares.

In general, tax planning for the professional corporation is rather simple. The corporation is set up to handle all billings, and it pays all expenses. The professional is paid a salary equal to his or her (pre-tax) living requirements. Wherever possible, the corporation also pays salaries to members of the professional's family for their assistance. Naturally, where such salaries are paid, the professional can thus afford to draw less money, thereby remaining in a lower tax bracket.

Corporate tax rates then apply to surplus profits. Usually, the corporate tax rate is significantly less than the marginal rate that would otherwise apply to the professional. Consequently, the corporation becomes an investment vehicle for after-tax profits. Some of the profits are used to finance the costs of business expansion, to pay for equipment, and to carry receivables from clients or patients. The balance can be invested in whatever types of investments the "owner" so desires.

Management Companies for Professionals

In cases where professionals may not legally incorporate, many doctors, dentists, lawyers, and accountants have formed service companies that perform many of the management functions connected with a professional practice. Revenue Canada has indicated that corporations may be used by practising members of the professions in certain circumstances. The services that such corporations can provide would include:

- Negotiating and signing leases for the premises from which the practice is carried on, and handling monthly rental payments.
- Hiring and training of staff and maintaining payroll and other personnel records.
- Purchasing supplies and acquiring or leasing all necessary furnishings, including equipment that may be required by the practitioner to carry on his or her professional practice.
- Providing accounting services, including billing and collection of accounts receivable.

In a typical situation, most of these services are provided by the corporation on a cost-plus basis. The corporation computes its cost of performing these services and adds a profit factor, which is charged back to the professional. Rates ranging from 10% to 15% have not been considered unreasonable. Ironically, the higher the overhead of the professional's operation, the greater the dollar amount of profit that can be transferred to the corporation.

Payment of an agreed fee to the corporation has the effect of reducing the professional's income by the amount of the profit factor. Where the individual is already in a high tax bracket, the result is an immediate tax deferral equal to the difference between his or her marginal tax bracket and that of the corporation. This is illustrated in Figure 11-1.

In addition, if one can justify a salary payable to members of the family, there is a tax *saving* equal to the difference between the professional's marginal rate and that of the other family members. Whether earnings are retained corporately or paid out as salaries depends primarily on the living requirements of the professional and his or her family. A management company can also be used as a vehicle to invest surplus funds not required for living expenses.

Figure 11-1   **Management Companies Reduce a Professional's Personal Taxes**

Without management company:

Gross income of professional	$120,000
Less: Expenses to operate practice	50,000
Professional's net profit subject to tax	$ 70,000

With management company:

Gross income of professional	$120,000
Less: Management fees paid	65,000
Professional's net profit subject to tax	$ 55,000
Fee income of corporation	$ 65,000
Less: Expenses "taken over" from professional	50,000
Corporation's net profit subject to tax	$ 15,000

$15,000 is "extracted" from the professional's highest marginal tax bracket and is taxed instead at lower coporate rates.

Professional Corporations Versus Management Companies

Using the management company concept in your business planning may not be quite as advantageous as having a professional corporation. This is because only a relatively small amount of profits can be transferred out of the professional's hands and into a corporation. The management company does, however, permit one specific form of income splitting that is not available through an *Alberta* professional corporation. The management company may pay dividends out of after-tax profits to members of the professional's family – as long as these family members own shares in the company. This is not permitted in the case of an Alberta professional corporation, since only the professional is permitted to be a shareholder. Nevertheless, the ability to incorporate one's *total* earnings and the opportunity to maintain only one set of records favours the professional corporation. I expect that several of the other provinces will eventually join those provinces that have already passed enabling legislation. Certainly, it would be worthwhile for professionals across the country to lobby for these privileges. It would be beneficial if other provinces were to follow the British Columbia model, which allows a spouse to hold (non-voting) shares, facilitating income splitting by way of dividends.

Before incorporating, however, a professional should make sure to determine the impact of the Goods and Services Tax on his or her business operation. It is extremely important not to lose the benefits of any available input tax credits.

Special Rules for (Professional) Partnerships

If corporations act in partnership, they must share between them one annual business limit of $200,000 which is eligible for a 20% corporate tax rate. Thus, in the case of a large partnership with many participants, the advantage of incorporation on a per-person basis may not be too significant.

I therefore recommend that, wherever possible, corporate partnerships be dissolved. Instead, the organization should be structured as independent practices sharing common overheads. In other words, wherever possible, each individual company should do its own billings to patients, customers, or clients and a formula should be evolved for prorating *overheads only*. Each corporation would therefore be a completely separate entity. This is probably feasible for many medical and dental practices. In addition, this idea may have merit for certain law practices as well. The larger accounting firms may have more difficulty in implementing such an approach since it may not be practical. In the case of accounting firms, different accountants often do work for the same client during a given year and it would be difficult to split the billings.

The Future of Service Corporations

With respect to entertainers, commissioned salespersons, and consultants, the 20% small-business tax rate applies *as long as the corporation is in fact carrying on a business*. If, on the other hand, the corporation is nothing more than an "incorporated employee," Revenue Canada will be justified in disallowing any low corporate tax rate entirely. The question of "what is a business" is the key question within the framework of tax planning. If a corporation has not got a business purpose and its only objective is to reduce taxes otherwise payable, the rules allow the Minister of National Revenue to look through the corporation and deem its owners to be earning personal employment income. The following sections examine the current status of specific types of service companies.

Athletes

It is difficult for most incorporated baseball, football, or hockey players to consider their sporting activities as an active business. Since athletes clearly earn their incomes through *personal* service, a corporation will not provide any benefits. However, what about other income, such as from advertising or endorsements? If a corporation earns significant income from other activities of this kind, it is likely that the corporation can show that it has a valid business purpose. If that is the case, it appears that the corporation will be allowed to stand and that the low tax rate of around 20% will apply. This results in a substantial deferral when compared to a personal rate of over 40%.

Entertainers

Canadian entertainers should be able to benefit nicely from the tax rules since, in most cases, they will have sufficient diversity of income to substantiate the fact that they are carrying on a business. To illustrate how arbitrary the rules are, however, consider the position of an entertainer who has a solo act and accepts a long-term contract to perform in one place. His or her company may become ineligible in that year for the small-business tax rate. However, where that same entertainer performs the identical nightclub act in several different locations during the year (even within the same city), his or her company would qualify for the small-business incentive.

Commissioned Salespeople and Other Consultants

For commissioned salespeople and other consultants, the service-corporation rules mean that special care must be taken in order to meet self-employment guidelines. Consider, for example, the case of two incorporated insurance agencies – one selling general insurance and the other selling life insurance. Assume that both have no outside employees. Because it sells insurance on behalf of several insurance companies, the general insurance agency would automatically qualify for a 20% tax rate. On the other hand, a life insurance agency typically sells insurance on behalf of one major insurance company. Since its commission revenue comes primarily from one entity, it may be classified as an activity that will not qualify for the low rate. Notwithstanding the law, one can argue that this is unfair. This is because both companies are independent agents and have basically similar business activities. Unfortunately, fairness doesn't count in this case.

As a further illustration, a structural engineer whose corporation services one major client in a given year could find his or her company blocked from the low rate of tax for that year unless he or she can clearly prove independence. This may suggest a merger with other unrelated companies within the same field, and if the engineer is not willing to merge, he or she would have to take into account the cost of higher taxes as a penalty for accepting one major client or contract. (Even a merger may not be advisable, since the problem here would be the requirement that the low-rate base of $200,000 be shared among otherwise unrelated parties.)

Incorporated Executives – Revisited

For an executive's management company to qualify for the small-business rate, it is imperative that the individual remove all signs of employment. If the individual is a shareholder, he or she may continue to retain stock, but should resign any directorship and cease to hold a position as a company officer. A bona fide attempt to achieve diversity of income is extremely important. In cases where a former employer requires the executive to carry out his or her activities solely for and on behalf of that company, the use of a personal service corporation is not viable. Revenue Canada will just look through the company and tax its income at top corporate tax rates.

While the legislation pertaining to incorporated employees has not been tested in the courts, I don't think that an executive will be able to "beat the system" by simply contracting his or her services to several different subsidiaries of the same employer. This will probably not constitute a reasonable diversity of income. Similarly, an executive will not be able to take advantage of the tax rules by taking a few employees onto his or her payroll who were previously employed by the ex-employer. Revenue Canada will deem this arrangement to be a sham.

If, however, the executive truly does have "outside" consulting income, a corporation may still be viable. The executive would be required to report his or her major income sources as personal employment income, but could still shelter miscellaneous fees through a corporation. In practice, a decision will probably depend on the dollars involved. Only the individual can judge if the tax deferral is worthwhile.

Organizing the Personal-Service Company

For most people, the question of whether or not to set up a personal-service company cannot be resolved without the assistance of professional advisers. Your accountant and lawyer should be able to explain your tax position to you, and also *quantify the benefits* that you may derive. Since each individual's income, expenses, family situation, and living requirements are different, you cannot simply rely on what your friends are doing when it comes to making your own business decisions.

Assuming that such a company is advisable, how is one set up? The steps would include the following:

- You must decide whether or not the company is to be exclusively concerned with one type of activity only, or whether it will undertake many different kinds of projects.
- You must then incorporate a company with the appropriate objectives and share capital – including the right to reinvest accumulated income in diversified investments.
- The shares must then be issued to the intended shareholders. (At this stage, estate-planning considerations should be taken into account by having, in some cases, the incorporator's spouse and/or children subscribe for shares in the corporation.)
- You must arrange for a management agreement between you, as the incorporator, and the company to be prepared in writing. The agreement should set out in detail the services to be provided by the corporation and the fees to be charged for such services.
- In the case of a professional practice, the present employees (other than those who are required to be employed directly by the professional) should become employees of the corporation. The change of employers should not be overlooked when preparing annual T-4 slips.

- The corporation should then proceed to do everything necessary to enable it to operate. These activities would include opening bank accounts, obtaining a telephone listing, ordering stationery with an appropriate letterhead, arranging with Revenue Canada to make required payroll deductions, and generally carrying out all steps necessary to perform its management contract.

Each step must be carried out in a proper and specific sequence in order to avoid problems at a later date. For example, the corporation should not begin to render services until after its charter has been obtained and the management and employment contracts have been duly and properly signed. In addition, if one is setting up a personal-service company *following* the severing of one's relationship with an employer, all signs of the previous employment relationship should be removed. For example:

- The individual should no longer be allowed to sign letters or contracts on behalf of the former employer – especially using the former employer's letterhead.
- The former employee should be removed from the former employer's group insurance and pension plans.
- If possible, the service company should operate out of different premises from those in which the former employer carries on its business.
- A company-owned or company-leased car should be surrendered and/or transferred by the past employer to the new service company.
- The executive's corporation must be permitted to carry on outside work as long as it is not in direct conflict with the contractual arrangements with the former employer. Again, if the former employer is unwilling to sever the employer-employee relationship completely, the corporation should probably not be formed in the first place.

CHAPTER 12

Tax Planning for
New Business Ventures

New businesses can make use of a number of strategies that maximize their returns and minimize the risks if the business turns out to be unsuccessful. There are different strategies for unincorporated and incorporated business ventures, so one of your major objectives should be to decide whether you should or should not incorporate.

How to Show You Are in Business

In many instances, a new business will produce a loss in its initial phases. Business losses are deductible against income, but only provided that *the business had at least an expectation of profit.*

Income-tax assessors are very strict about differentiating between a viable business on the one hand and a hobby on the other. There are certain steps that you can take from the very start to show that you are actually going to be carrying on a bona fide business. First, you should choose a name for your venture that is descriptive of the goods, services, or activities that you will be providing. Even if you don't incorporate, your business name should be registered. This is a relatively simple procedure but you would be well advised to seek some assistance in this area from your lawyer. Then, once your name has been accepted, a bank account should be opened in the name of that business. All income received from the business should be deposited to that bank account. Any expenses pertaining to your business should be paid out of that same account by cheque.

One of the biggest mistakes that beginners often make is to intermingle their business records with their personal records. Not only does this show that you don't really have confidence in the viability of your business but it also makes the record keeping for tax purposes at the end of the year that much more difficult to sort through.

Perhaps most important is that you must keep reasonable books and records of your activities. If your business is just starting out, you certainly don't need a sophisticated system. Basically, all that's required is a ledger in which you keep track of your receipts and disbursements. Even if you have no bookkeeping training whatsoever, a half-hour spent with a qualified accountant should be enough to show you how to keep these simple records. You will be able to total your figures on a monthly basis and balance your records against your bank statements. Then, at the end of the year, if you have no desire to learn accounting, you can get your accountant to make the necessary summaries and prepare your annual financial statements.

From the very outset, I believe that it is worth your while to invest a few dollars in order to print proper stationery, invoices, and any other forms that you require. If you don't want to go through the expense of printing, at least have some rubber stamps made showing your business's name, address, and telephone number.

While on the subject of telephone numbers, one of the key criteria in convincing Revenue Canada that you are involved in a viable business activity is a separate telephone line with a listing in your business's name, especially if you are going to operate out of your house.

Finally, I believe it's extremely important from the very outset (even before you commit yourself to any other expenditures) to prepare a budget for your first year of operations. This budget should show your anticipated revenues and also the types and amounts of expenses that you expect to incur. Then, you yourself will be able to determine whether or not your business does in fact have a reasonable expectation of profit. If you are counting on your business to provide a livelihood for yourself and your family, you should budget for a regular draw from that business to meet your personal and living expenses. Your budget should also take into account all capital expenditures that you may require, such as furniture, fixtures, equipment, special vehicles, and so on.

In most cases, a new business requires external financing from a lending institution. If you can convince your banker that you have a reasonable expectation of profit, that should also help you if you ever run into problems with Revenue Canada authorities.

One important word of caution. There are, of course, all kinds of potential business operations in which you can get involved. These range from wholesaling to retailing, manufacturing, construction, farming, and so on. One very popular business activity is to become a consultant and earn your income by rendering services either on a commission or fee basis. Generally, a business tends to get much more favourable tax deductions than does employment income. In addition, as I'll explain later in this chapter, if the business is profitable and you incorporate, you may be able to take advantage of corporate tax rates that are significantly lower than personal rates on equivalent amounts of income.

But, because businesses do enjoy favourable tax treatment, there has been an inclination over the last ten years or so for many people to incorporate service companies even in situations where they can be more readily considered to be earning employment income. One good example is the individual who is perhaps a middle-income executive with a large company. The executive resigns his or her position of employment and forms a personal consulting company through which he or she renders services back to the former employer. Another example is the commissioned salesperson who devotes perhaps all of his or her time and effort towards selling the products produced by one company only.

In the last few years, the Revenue authorities have begun to crack down on people who are really employees of another entity but who try to erect the façade of self-employment. If you are contemplating a service venture, you must be sure that you will truly be an independent contractor, regardless of whether you will be receiving fees or commissions. If your relationship with the entity that pays for your services can reasonably be considered employer-employee, then any attempt to take tax advantages from business expenses or from incorporating will be negated under the law. If you are in doubt as to your status, read Chapter Eleven carefully. You are also well advised to spend an hour or so reviewing your situation with your own tax adviser.

Do I Start a Business or Buy One?

Leaving aside the subject of service businesses, I suppose I can generalize and suggest that there are two ways of starting a business. Either you begin one by yourself or you buy the assets of somebody else's business.

If you are buying a going concern, you must make sure that your contract specifies exactly what you are buying. This is extremely important for tax purposes since the tax rules are quite different, depending on whether you are purchasing inventory, depreciable assets, customer lists, or what have you. In most jurisdictions, the purchase of property other than inventory will be subject to *provincial* sales tax considerations. Make sure that you acquire the necessary licences in order to claim sales tax exemption in the proper circumstances. For example, if you are buying property for resale, you are usually, if not always, exempt from provincial sales tax on your purchases. You should also spend some time with an accountant in order to review all of the relevant implications of the Goods and Services Tax.

Figure 12–1   **Tax Consequences of Purchasing Business Goodwill**

Cost of goodwill – $20,000		
Portion subject to amortization for tax purposes (75%)	$15,000	
First year's tax write-off	1,050	(7% × $15,000)
	13,950	
Second year's tax write-off	977	(7% × $13,950)
	12,973	
Third year's tax write-off	908	(7% × $12,973)
Unamortized tax cost of goodwill	$12,065	

If you buy someone else's business and pay more than the value of all tangible assets acquired, the difference is usually allocated to goodwill. This is because, if you are buying a going concern, you will be able to capitalize on the time and effort that were put in by someone else to help get that particular business established.

For tax purposes, three-quarters of the cost of goodwill can be deducted at the rate of 7% a year on a declining-balance basis. In other words, if you spend $20,000 for goodwill, your first year's tax write-off is 7% of $15,000. In the second year, you may claim 7% of $13,950, and in the third year, 7% of $12,973. This is illustrated in Figure 12-1.

The opportunity to write off only three-quarters of the cost of goodwill over an extended period of time is not particularly attractive. If, on the other hand, part of your purchase cost can be reasonably allocated to the value of a lease, or a franchise that runs for a specific length of time, then the tax rules will permit you to deduct your *full* cost over the time remaining before the lease or franchise expires. It is certainly worth your while to take that little bit of extra time to negotiate with the seller of the business to have part of your purchase price allocated to properties for which you can claim a full depreciation instead of a write-off based on only three-quarters of your cost.

What If I Incur Losses?

One of your most important tasks is to try to estimate whether or not your business will be profitable from the outset. If it is likely that your business will generate a loss for tax purposes, my general advice, subject to the comments I will make in the next few pages, is *don't incorporate.* Under the Canadian tax system, business losses can be carried back three years as an offset against prior years' income or forward up to seven years.

Let's assume that you have decided to go into business for yourself after many years of having been employed by someone else. If your business generates a loss, you can offset that loss against your other income for that same year and, if the loss exceeds your other income, you have, as I just mentioned, the option to carry back up to three years. If you take this option, what effectively happens is that you can recover prior years' taxes payable against your salary income.

If, on the other hand, you were to incorporate, the loss carry-over rules would be the same – except for one thing. A corporation is a separate legal entity and, as such, *the losses of that corporation cannot be used to recover personal taxes that you yourself have paid.* In other words, the corporation would have no choice but to carry its loss forward against future income – if and when profits are eventually made. In order to maximize your tax savings from a business loss, the object of the game is always to try to use that loss as quickly as possible. Thus, incorporating a new business can present a substantial disadvantage.

On the other hand, you must always keep in mind one of the greatest advantages of incorporation – that is, limited liability. If the business is unsuccessful, the unsecured creditors, such as your suppliers, cannot generally come back against you personally for amounts owing. The only time there is personal recourse is in cases where you have given a personal guarantee. So, to summarize, what you really have to do in a situation where a business loss is anticipated is weigh the two alternatives: the tax advantages of offsetting losses against personal income, compared to the danger that might exist if your business venture is totally unsuccessful and, in the final analysis, the business becomes insolvent.

Generally, the major creditor of any venture, new or old, is the business's lender. Today, it is very rare for any lending institution to provide financing without the personal guarantee of the principals. So, if your business is financed, for example, with a $50,000 bank loan and only owes, say, an average of $10,000 at any given time to other creditors, the corporate advantage of limited liability is not that substantial. After all, if the business turns sour, it doesn't make much difference whether you end up owing $50,000 under your guarantee or $60,000 to both your lender and your other creditors.

In any event, once you understand the principles involved, I suggest that you spend a few minutes with your own advisers before you decide whether or not to incorporate.

Husband-Wife Partnerships

One further option that you might consider, even if you don't incorporate, is having your business structured as a partnership between you and your spouse. One of the major advantages of such an arrangement is the opportunity to split income in order to take advantage of lower personal tax rates. This is an important concept that is quite unique to Canada and I have provided a detailed discussion of income splitting within the family business in Chapter Thirteen.

Setting up a husband/wife partnership has another major benefit beyond the splitting of income. There could also be an advantage if your business incurs losses in the initial stages. For example, let's assume your situation is such that both you and your spouse have full-time jobs. However, you've hit upon what you think is a good business idea and initially you believe you can operate that business on evenings and weekends. You expect, however, that in the first year or so, the business will generate losses for income-tax purposes. If both you and your spouse are in relatively equal tax brackets, you might be better off splitting the loss through a partnership arrangement rather than having the loss incurred by one person only. This would mean that the taxes recovered would be from the higher end of the scale. A partnership might then be very much to your advantage.

If you do set up a husband/wife business partnership, I make the strong suggestion that you prepare proper documentation – in other words, a *written* partnership agreement. If your arrangement is audited, the tax department will take the relevant documentation into account as well as the question of whether both parties are at risk of losing capital. For example, if you take a mortgage against your home, which is jointly owned, in order to provide funds for your business, this will show that both you and your spouse are sharing the risk.

Another important factor is the time and effort that is spent in administering the operations. If both spouses contribute equal amounts of capital and equal portions of time and effort, you would expect that profits should be divided 50/50. On the other hand, if one spouse operates the business exclusively while both spouses contribute equally to the required capital, perhaps a 75/25 or 60/40 split might be more appropriate. Again, these are matters that you might discuss with your own advisers. The profit-sharing ratio should also apply to losses as well.

Selecting a Year End

After deciding how your business is going to be structured, whether as a proprietorship, partnership, or corporation, your next step is to select your business's year end. Now, what are the various criteria for selecting a year end? First of all, as you probably already know, an individual is deemed to have a calendar year end for Canadian tax purposes. However, a business can pick any year-end date that it desires as long as there is consistency after the first year. The only other rule is that no business can have a fiscal cycle that is longer than twelve months in total.

For the first reporting period for tax purposes, it is permissible to select a year end less than twelve months after commencement of business operations. In theory, for example, if you start your business on March 30 of a given year, you can even take March 31 as your first year end. In other words, you could conceivably have as little as a one-day business year the first time around. However, after that first year end, you are committed to a March 31 year end each year subsequently. The only exception is if you apply in writing for a change of year end to your local District Office of Revenue Canada and permission for a year-end change is granted. Normally, you would require a good business reason for such a change to be accepted, such as a drastic shift in the nature of your products or services.

What I would like to do now is review some of the criteria for selecting your new business's year end. First of all, let's assume your business starts off as an unincorporated venture. You begin to carry on operations in mid-March 1993, on a part-time basis, while you continue to earn income from employment. If you select a year end any time in the 1993 calendar year, and your business is profitable, the income from that business would be added to your other income for the 1993 year. You would then have to pay your taxes on all this income no later than the end of April 1994. Conversely, if the business incurs a loss, as I indicated previously, you could offset that loss against your 1993 income.

On the other hand, what if you pick a year end in either January or February 1994? Even though your business will have operated for a period in excess of nine months in 1993, the business profits will only be reported when you file your 1994 income-tax return. In other words, you won't have to report your business profit until April 1995.

Figure 12–2 **Selecting a Year End for Your Business**

Individual is employed but also carries on a part-time business beginning mid-March 1993.

One alternative: Initial year end December 31, 1993
Income for 1993 (tax return due April 30, 1994)

Employment income	January–December 1993	12	months
Business income	March–December 1993	10	months

Income for 1994 (tax return due April 30, 1995)

Employment income	January–December 1994	12	months
Business income	January–December 1994	12	months

Another alternative: Initial year end February 28, 1994
Income for 1993 (tax return due April 30, 1994)

Employment income	January–December 1993	12	months
Business income		Nil	

Income for 1994 (tax return due April 30, 1995)

Employment income	January–December 1994	12	months
Business income	March 1993–February 1994	12	months

Business income taxable in 1995 (tax return due April 30, 1996)

Period from	March 1994–February 1995

In simple terms, selecting a year end in the next calendar year gives you an initial tax deferral in cases where your business is profitable. Moreover, the tax deferral is an ongoing business benefit. If, for example, you choose a January or February year end, your profits for the twelve months ended January or February 1994 will only be reported when you file your 1994 personal-income-tax return in April 1995. All of this is illustrated in Figure 12-2. On the other hand, if your business is going to sustain a loss in the first few months of operations, you may want a short initial year end sometime in 1993 in order to crystallize that loss so that you can offset it against your other income.

So, the first criterion in selecting a year end is the question of whether or not you want a tax deferral. Again, a few minutes with your accountant can help you make this very crucial decision.

In many cases, the year end of a business is selected on the basis of seasonal considerations. For example, let's assume that you will be in a lumber-supply business. You will supply wood products to the building trades and to people who are doing renovations to their homes. Assume that you intend to stock a substantial inventory of wood products at an outdoor location. In most places in Canada, you wouldn't want to pick a year end in the heart of winter. After all, how could you count your inventory if it's covered in snow?

Often, businesses pick their year ends at a time when their inventory is lowest. This is because often the biggest difficulty in preparing financial statements is physically taking inventory. A retail business will sometimes adopt a flexible year end, such as the last Saturday in January. This way, it can count its stock each year on the day following the year end – a Sunday – when the business is generally closed to trade and it becomes relatively easy to manoeuvre around the store. Always pay attention to your own circumstances before making a choice of a year end.

Capital Cost Allowances

Another point to consider is capital cost allowance or depreciation for tax purposes. Capital cost allowance under Canadian tax law is an optional deduction. You don't have to claim depreciation on machinery, equipment, buildings, or other assets owned by your business unless you want to. Most of the time, however, a profitable business claims the maximum capital cost allowance that it can in order to reduce income for tax purposes. Note that depreciation in the year any particular property is acquired is generally limited to one-half the tax write-off otherwise allowable. For example, while the ordinary depreciation rate on furniture and fixtures is 20% a year on a declining balance basis, in the year of acquisition you may only claim 10% of the cost of the property purchased.

What if your business is going to acquire substantial depreciable property right from the outset? You might consider selecting your first year end shortly after your major fixed-asset acquisitions are completed. You don't have to claim capital cost allowance unless you want to, but the point is that in your first complete twelve months of operations that follow, you will then get a *full* capital-cost-allowance claim, instead of only one-half. If you do choose to claim capital cost allowance, you should be aware that you would have to prorate even the reduced amount (i.e., one-half the normal rate) over the number of days in that first fiscal period as a percentage of 365.

Employing Family Members

Earlier in this chapter, I discussed setting up your new business as a partnership between husband and wife. Even if you don't choose to use that format, keep in mind that your spouse can qualify as a legitimate employee of your business, whether it is an unincorporated proprietorship or a limited-liability company. Not only can your spouse be an employee, but you are permitted to pay tax-deductible wages to any of your children who are active in your business.

The opportunity to split income by paying salaries and wages to a spouse and other family members is one of the major attractions of any business. It is such an important concept that it merits a much more complete discussion in the next chapter.

Incorporation

From the outset, it is important that you note that any business can be incorporated except (in some provinces) the professional practice of an accountant, lawyer, doctor, or dentist.

It really doesn't matter for income-tax purposes whether you incorporate your business to begin with or whether you incorporate perhaps several, or even many, years after your business is formed. There is a provision under Section 85 of the Income Tax Act that will permit an unincorporated business proprietorship or partnership to be transferred to a Canadian corporation without triggering income taxes in the hands of the transferor(s). Basically, the corporation assumes the assets and liabilities of the transferor(s) and continues operating from that time on.

I don't wish to imply, however, that the rules of application of Section 85 are necessarily simple. The concept of what is commonly called a "tax-free rollover" is easy to understand. After all, if you simply move a business from your left hand to your right – in other words, you retain beneficial ownership of that business both before and after incorporation – you can see the logic of why you should be able to reorganize without triggering income for tax purposes.

However, the actual application of Section 85 is fairly complex and, if you do choose to incorporate a business that has already been operating, you must make sure to seek professional legal and accounting advice before moving ahead.

Let me, however, highlight some of the major points that you should consider. First, the opportunity to transfer business assets to a corporation without triggering taxes only applies if the corporation is a Canadian corporation. In other words, if you live in Canada but your business venture is in the United States, you may not transfer your business to a U.S. corporation on a rollover basis for Canadian tax purposes.

Generally, most business assets are eligible for the rollover. The one exception is real estate inventory. If you are in the business of buying and selling real estate, you may not transfer your holdings to a corporation without doing so at fair market value.

Perhaps the most important consideration, though, is family involvement. Even if you were previously operating your business as a proprietorship, you can, if you so desire, incorporate the business and allow your family members to become shareholders in the corporation. In this manner, they may participate in the future growth and income generated by that business. However, you must be very careful in structuring your transfer under Section 85 so as not to convey any retroactive benefits to related family members. Your accountant and lawyer can help you so that you do not run afoul of the rules.

Advantages of Incorporation

One of the major advantages of incorporation from a tax point of view is that it allows you the opportunity to use a corporation as a vehicle to split income among family members. As I explained earlier, if you wish to have salaries paid to members of your family, these people must be active in the day-to-day business operations. However, if the business is incorporated and your family members hold shares, the company can be structured to pay dividends out of profits in the ratio of the shareholdings. In this way, it is possible to split income among the family, even in cases where family members do not take active roles. Moreover, if the business is ever sold, having involved the family in the ownership sets the stage for capital gains splitting as well.

In most cases, unless your children are actively involved or unless you as parents are very wealthy, it is unusual for a business, especially a new business, to be incorporated in such a manner that the children are shareholders. However, even if you choose not to involve your children as owners, bear in mind the advantages of splitting the shares with your spouse for the reasons mentioned in the previous paragraph.

There is one additional benefit of incorporation. Under the Canadian tax rules, if shares of an active business company are sold to third parties or are passed on to children or grandchildren, a transferor is permitted to tax-shelter up to $500,000 in capital gains. If a husband and wife are both shareholders, the $500,000 benefit is potentially doubled. The $500,000 amount applies on a per-transferor basis, irrespective of how many businesses one has and irrespective of how many children. You can take advantage of the opportunity to sell or pass on shares in a private business without triggering capital gains taxes *either* in your lifetime *or* on death. Of course, to double the advantage means that both husband and wife must be involved in the shareholdings.

Possibly the most important advantage of incorporating a small business, however, arises in cases where a business earns more than what the owners require on an annual basis to meet their living expenses. The schedule in Figure 12-3 gives you an outline of what the approximate 1993 tax rates are in various income brackets.

You can see that once you reach a taxable income of $30,000, the government will begin to take forty cents out of each additional dollar that you earn. By way of contrast, a Canadian-controlled private corporation that earns active business income pays taxes of around 20% on the first $200,000 of annual business profits. (The actual rate varies from province to province.) Thus, the theory behind proper tax planning should be quite evident. On excess profits not required by an owner-manager to meet living expenses, there is the opportunity to reinvest through the corporation eighty cents on the dollar, which is a lot better than reinvesting only sixty, or as little as fifty-five cents on the dollar after the payment of personal income taxes.

Figure 12–3 **Approximate Marginal Tax Rates for Individuals**

Taxable Income	*Tax + Marginal Tax Bracket*
$0 – 30,000	25%
$30,000 – 60,000	$7,500 + 40% on next $30,000
$60,000 – ∞	$19,500 + 45% on the remainder

You should note that the very generous small-business tax rate is designed to encourage and facilitate business expansion. However, after-tax profits can also be used to build up investment capital. A corporation can make whatever investments you might otherwise want to make personally. For example, a corporation can buy term deposits, invest in the stock market, or acquire real estate or even precious metals such as gold and silver.

One of the most underrated aspects of a corporation that qualifies for small-business tax rates is the ability it has to repay business financing liabilities with cheaper after-tax dollars. Almost any business requires at least a certain amount of funding in order to get started. Whenever money is borrowed for business or investment purposes, the interest is, of course, tax-deductible but repaying the debt itself requires after-tax money. Thus, incorporation does provide you with the opportunity to use cheaply taxed funds for that purpose, instead of income that is first subjected to much higher personal-income-tax rates.

In these uncertain economic times, we must be concerned, unfortunately, not only with business profits but with losses as well. If a corporation is used for business purposes, "allowable business investment losses" become deductible from a shareholder's or noteholder's total income. This type of loss arises when a share or debt investment is made in a Canadian-controlled private corporation and the investment subsequently loses its value or, in fact, becomes completely worthless. In the year such a loss is realized, three-quarters of the loss, instead of being treated as an ordinary capital loss, becomes deductible from the shareholder's or noteholder's total income, irrespective of whether or not he or she has capital gains. By way of contrast, advances made to a proprietorship or partnership, either by way of loan or capital, are not given this treatment. They are treated as ordinary capital losses and may only be deducted against capital gains from other sources.

Using a corporation to carry on business can also set the stage for using death-benefit programs in tax planning. In the event that a shareholder-manager dies, a death benefit received by his or her spouse, or perhaps even by other heirs, will be either partially or totally tax-free. The death-benefit concept is not available to the spouse of a proprietor or partner since the tax-free element is tied in to salaries previously paid. This was covered in Chapter Four.

Finally, by using a corporation, you may also introduce a retiring-allowance program (also dealt with in Chapter Four) and group life and health insurance plans, where these benefits are also tied in to salaries paid. These are matters that you should discuss with your own advisers once your business becomes profitable or if you are planning to retire within a short time.

Disadvantages of Incorporation

Of course, incorporation does have some disadvantages. I have already discussed some of these, such as the inability to use a corporate business loss as an offset against personal income. Another important disadvantage for a new business is the fact that a corporation carries with it the necessity of additional annual reporting requirements, including corporate tax returns. While this may not be a disadvantage from the standpoint of your lawyer or accountant, the cost is certainly a factor if you are an owner of a business.

Finally, recognize that incorporation is very much a one-way street. While, as I explained earlier, you can use Section 85 to transfer properties *into* a Canadian corporation, there is no rollover back to an individual shareholder on winding up the company. If assets are distributed in kind, the corporation will first be deemed to have disposed of its property at fair market value and this will trigger income. In addition, any distribution to the shareholders over and above the paid-up capital of the shares will be treated as a dividend. So, be careful. Don't transfer property into a company unless you want that company to keep that property until the property is sold to third parties.

CHAPTER 13

Tax Planning for the Private Canadian Business When the Small-Business Rate Applies

Under the Canadian tax system, only Canadian-controlled private corporations are allowed to pay taxes at a low rate. The low rate is also restricted to "active business income." Investment income earned by a private company is initially taxed at around 40%, but is subject to refundable-tax rules, which will be reviewed later in this chapter. We will see how involving family members in the structure of your business can help minimize the overall tax bite on profits from both business and investment activities.

The Canadian-Controlled Private Corporation

A "Canadian-controlled private corporation" is the only kind of company that has low-rate privileges. By definition, a Canadian-controlled private corporation (CCPC) is a company that is *not controlled* by one or more non-residents nor by a combination of non-residents and Canadian public corporations. Because this definition is phrased in the negative, a corporation will qualify for CCPC status even where non-residents or public companies own exactly 50% of the voting shares.

It is not uncommon to find joint-venture arrangements in Canada between Canadian individuals and either public corporations or non-residents. If the joint venture is carried on through a separate corporation, which is owned exactly 50% by each, this corporation will qualify for favourable tax rates. It would often pay the non-residents or public companies to relinquish control for the benefit of the lower rates of tax that would then apply to the joint-venture corporation, since the lower the tax rate on earnings, the greater the ability to pay dividends.

After 1987, CCPCs pay a federal tax of 12% on the first $200,000 of active business income earned annually. While provincial corporate tax rates vary from jurisdiction to jurisdiction, for purposes of this book, it is assumed that, on average, the provincial tax rate is 8% of this income. This results in a combined rate of 20%.

On active business income in excess of $200,000 a year or earned by a corporation that does not qualify as a Canadian-controlled private corporation, the federal rate is 28%. If we assume an average provincial corporate tax rate in these circumstances of 12%, this produces a combined tax rate of 40%.

If active business income is earned from manufacturing and processing *and* it is ineligible for the small-business rate, the federal tax is 22% (21% in 1994). If a 13% average provincial tax is assumed for rounding, this results in an effective combined rate of 35%.

Figure 13-1 summarizes the combined federal and provincial corporate tax rates that will be used from here on in this book.

Figure 13–1   **Combined Federal and (Estimated)
Provincial Corporate Income Taxes**

General Business – Federal	28%
– Provincial	12%
– Combined	40%
Manufacturing business – Federal	22%
– Provincial	13%
– Combined	35%
General small business – Federal	12%
– Provincial	8%
– Combined	20%
Small manufacturing business – Federal	12%
– Provincial	8%
– Combined	20%

Note that if two or more corporations are under common control they must share one allotment of the annual $200,000 limit. As mentioned in

Chapter Eleven, corporate partnerships are also required to share one annual low-rate limit as well.

When a corporation has a taxation year less than twelve months in length, the annual business limit of $200,000 must be prorated, based on the number of days in the particular year as a percentage of 365.

Definition of "Active Business Income"

Until about ten years ago, the Income Tax Act did not contain any definition of the term "active business income." Accordingly, by diversifying their activities, taxpayers were able to arrange their affairs so that interest income on mortgage portfolios and rental income on real estate properties could be deemed to be from active businesses. In addition, many individuals took advantage of the generous low rates to incorporate service companies. In late 1979, however, Parliament finally got around to passing legislation that tightened these loopholes.

The definition of active business income now includes manufacturing operations, natural resource activities, construction, logging, farming, fishing, wholesaling, retailing, and transportation. In addition, certain service corporation revenues now qualify, while rental and interest income may be deemed to be from an active business in some cases.

Rental and interest income only qualify as active business income of a CCPC when the company has a minimum of six full-time employees throughout the year. Thus, unless a corporation has six or seven rental buildings with full-time janitors, it is unlikely that the income will qualify. (Principal share-holders and members of their families will count as employees only if they are bona fide full-time workers.)

It is also unlikely that interest income will be eligible for small-business tax rates. This is because a portfolio of many millions of dollars of interest-bearing securities can be managed with fewer than six full-time employees.

In passing, you should note that interest income will, however, qualify for small-business tax rates if it is "incidental" to an active business. This would include interest received by a business on overdue trade receivables or interest on term deposits when surplus funds are held *temporarily* during a *portion* of the business cycle.

Where rental and interest income do not qualify, corporate taxes of approximately 40% will be levied, subject to certain "refundable-tax" rules that I will explain later. When a private corporation earns substantially more than $200,000 of profits from rental activities (or interest) after operating expenses, it in fact pays that corporation to try to carry on with fewer than six employees. You will see that, given the refundable-tax rules, dividend payments of 80% of earnings are potentially possible. Where the high rate of 40% applies on "active business income" and there is no refundable tax, dividend payments cannot exceed the remaining 60% of after-tax profits.

For service corporations, as I discussed in Chapter Eleven, a low rate of tax will only apply if the corporation is carrying on a bona fide business. An employee really will find no tax advantages in incorporating himself or herself and may, in fact, be penalized.

In this chapter and the one that follows, we will deal specifically with income that qualifies for the small-business tax rate, such as that derived from wholesaling, retailing, construction or manufacturing, and bona fide service companies.

Tax Planning for Public and
Foreign-Controlled Corporations

Before examining CCPCs in detail, however, let's explore the question of whether one can tax plan for *public* companies. For example, what if a public company shows a pre-tax profit on its draft financial statements of $10 million?

Since the low rate of tax does not apply to public corporations, one could anticipate taxes of approximately $4 million. Can these taxes be avoided? Perhaps. Consider, for example, the declaration of a bonus to the chairman of the board, the president, and five key directors in the full amount of $10 million. Naturally, these bonuses would become an expense of the corporation and would reduce the pre-tax profit to nil. This would have the effect of reducing taxes by the $4 million payable in the first place.

Of course, such a scheme would not be feasible. A public corporation is one that traditionally has an ownership that is separate and apart from management. Consequently, the share holders would be rather upset with any plan along the lines just described. They would certainly rather have $6 million of after-tax profits for themselves than have no profit at all. The purpose of this somewhat ridiculous example is, however, to indicate that tax planning is rather limited for public companies. You can never do anything for the benefit of management that is detrimental to owners, and vice versa.

What about the case of a *foreign-controlled* private corporation? Its owner is an American citizen who lives in Florida and never sets foot in Canada. Assume, as well, that the profit of the Canadian company is $100,000. Without any tax planning, it is obvious that taxes payable at 40% would amount to $40,000 (since no small-business deduction is available). In this case, could a bonus of the full $100,000 be paid to the non-resident to avoid all Canadian taxes? There would be no complaints from other shareholders because there aren't any. In addition, creditors would not complain as long as their claims were satisfied on time.

The only problem, however, lies with Revenue Canada. There is a nasty little provision in the Income Tax Act that prohibits the deduction of any outlay or expense that is "unreasonable in the circumstances." Faced with the possible loss of $40,000 in tax revenues, the authorities may just try to deem a good part of that $100,000 bonus as unreasonable. Assume that the full bonus was disallowed as an expense. This would result in Canadian taxes of $40,000 – the same amount that one tried to avoid in the first place.

The problem does not, however, end here. In the meantime, for U.S. tax purposes, an American citizen would have received a salary payment of $100,000. This would have to be included in his or her U.S. income. Assuming U.S. taxes payable of $35,000 on this salary, what would be the result? Out of the original $100,000 there would be Canadian taxes of $40,000 on a disallowed expense and U.S. taxes of $35,000 on a salary. *The net after-tax retention would be negligible.*

This scenario is not nearly as ridiculous as the first example involving the public company. The possibility of double taxation is quite real. In fact, the problem could not even be alleviated through an application of foreign tax credits. To obtain a foreign tax credit, one must always be dealing with the *same taxpayer* who is subject to tax under two different jurisdictions. In this case, $40,000 of tax would apply to a Canadian corporation on a disallowed expense, with the other $35,000 being levied against a U.S. individual. When separate taxpayers are being dealt with, no relief is possible. It is for this reason that accountants and lawyers must be extremely careful in advising their non-resident clients with respect to salary policies. Caution is advised in order to avoid the possibility of severe double taxation.

Tax Planning for Canadian-Controlled Private Corporations

What about the Canadian-controlled private corporation? Are there similar restrictions with respect to salary or bonus payments? Fortunately, the situation here is flexible. The corporate high rate of tax does not "cut in" until a CCPC has earned over $200,000 of profits. Where a company earns in excess of this amount, the chances are that the owner-manager is already drawing more than, say, $60,000 per annum. The reason for this is simply a function of the owner's standard of living. What good is it to earn a lot of money if you cannot live comfortably?

Assuming, then, corporate profits in excess of $200,000 (and a desire to avoid the high rate of corporate tax), and also assuming that the shareholder-manager is already drawing at least a $60,000 salary (which is deducted in arriving at corporate profits in the first place), I suggest that there is tremendous flexibility. Why should Revenue Canada care about losing the 40% corporate tax as long as it is going to get the same dollars as additional personal taxes? In fact, there have been no reported tax cases on the subject of excessive remuneration of an owner-manager of a Canadian private company.

Remuneration of Spouses

The only time that Revenue Canada raises the question of excessive remuneration is when the owner-manager attempts (in an unreasonable manner) to split income with members of his or her family. In such circumstances, there are two possibilities. Either the excess remuneration will be disallowed, or it will be tacked on to the income of the person who really earned it. In practice, the authorities would take the approach that yields the greater tax recovery.

When it comes to dealings with a spouse, you must be careful not to allow your corporation to overpay his or her salary. Revenue Canada assessors often question the degree of activity of the spouse within the owner-managed business and, based on industry norms, they are often in a position to assess at least a range of values. This range may, of course, be quite broad and, within reason, payments at the top end of the scale should be acceptable. For example, if a husband runs a manufacturing concern and his wife is the office manager, who is to say whether she is "worth" $12,000 or $20,000 per annum? Of course, you may even argue that, in some cases, controllers earn over $50,000 a year.

However, accountants and lawyers have evolved a rather interesting method of dealing with such an issue. The concept is called the "chicken threshold." In a layperson's language, this simply means the point beyond which one is afraid to plan aggressively because one is "chicken." While a slight overpayment of salaries may be tolerable, sooner or later everyone reaches his or her "chicken threshold" – and that is when you should stop. The hard thing to do is to balance your chicken threshold with Revenue Canada's assessment threshold! (The meaning of this latter term should not require any explanation.)

In dealing with spousal remuneration, there are always special circumstances. If, for example, a corporation manufactures dresses and Mrs. Shareholder is an expert in choosing designs, it may be that she works only the equivalent of three or four weeks a year. Perhaps Mrs. Shareholder is the one who visits London, Paris, and New York in order to decide on the styles to be manufactured each season. Clearly, if her choices are good, the company will prosper. Design services of this nature could be worth many thousands of dollars and may not be subject to the normal remuneration criterion of time spent on the work. Here, the key is the value provided, which is certainly not time-related. Each case is, of course, different and I strongly recommend that the business owner discuss these matters with his or her own advisers.

Before planning too aggressively, however, there is one particular case that is worth mentioning. In this situation, a corporation controlled by a husband paid a salary to the "owner's" wife. The Minister of National Revenue deemed the salary excessive and unreasonable and added it back to the husband's income. The husband objected and the case wound up in court. At that time, the lawyer representing the Minister put the wife on the stand and asked one question: What is the address of your husband's business? She didn't know. Guess who won the case? The moral to be drawn from that situation concerning business involvement is quite evident.

Loan-Guarantee Fees

As a result of losses incurred during the recessions of the 1980s, lending institutions have become much more cautious in granting credit. In dealing with small businesses, a lending institution will now often require a personal guarantee not only from the owner-manager but also from the owner-manager's spouse. Of course, whenever possible, the owner-manager should do what he or she can to avoid the spouse furnishing a guarantee to the lender. After all, even if an owner-manager has absolute confidence that the business will be successful, there are always unforeseen circumstances. No one wants to be in a position in which virtually all family assets are seized in order to meet the obligation of the business to its financiers.

Despite the advantages of avoiding spousal guarantees, these nevertheless tend to be a fact of life. The question then arises: why not pay the spouse a reasonable *fee* for providing this guarantee?

What is reasonable is, of course, a matter of conjecture. In my opinion, a fee in the vicinity of, say, 5% or 6% of the credit line would not be unreasonable. Thus, for example, if the average loan is, say, $200,000, a guarantee fee of $10,000 or $12,000 might be realistic. After all, if *you* were asked to guarantee a business loan for a friend or relative, what would you charge in order to justify the risk factor?

If a guarantee fee is then paid by the corporation it appears that the corporation itself should have no trouble claiming it as a tax-deductible expense to borrow money. The recipient of that fee would not treat it as a salary but as business income. (Even if the fee is a "one-shot deal" each year, the income would still be deemed business income under the wording of the Income Tax Act, as profit from an "adventure in the nature of trade.")

Thus, even in cases where a spouse (or other guarantor) is not active in the day-to-day operations of the business, it is certainly feasible to remunerate that person. It is also interesting that, as business income, the guarantee fee would qualify for tax sheltering within the normal limits of a Registered Retirement Savings Plan. It further appears that participation in such a program would make the guarantor eligible to contribute into the Canada/Quebec Pension Plan as well.

Again, I stress that you should not ever voluntarily offer to guarantee a corporate business loan. However, if a guarantee is required, why not make the best of the situation and take a tax advantage?

Remuneration Guidelines for One's Children

There is also a good deal of flexibility with respect to the role of your children within the CCPC. If the children are actively involved in the business, reasonable salaries can be paid. Once again, what is reasonable is a matter for conjecture. For example, if your son had just started working for your shoe-manufacturing business and you wanted him to learn the operation from the "bottom up," could you get the company to pay him $50,000 a year for sweeping the floors in the plant? This would not be reasonable. On the other hand, what if your son's title were Vice-President, Maintenance, and Director of Sanitary Engineering?

Over the years, I have not noticed Revenue Canada taking too vigilant an approach in auditing remuneration paid to children who are active in their parents' business on a full-time basis. However, a business owner might not wish to overpay in any event because of *non-tax* reasons. Many times, the owner would prefer to avoid "too much too soon" and would rather pay higher taxes than overpay his or her children.

One ploy that is definitely not recommended is the payment of salaries to children when the parent intends to take back the paycheques and deposit them into his or her own account. There was, for example, an interesting tax case that was heard a few years ago. In this situation, an Alberta farmer paid each of his ten children $1,000 for work allegedly done in that year on the farm. The Minister deemed the payments unreasonable and added them back to the farmer's income. The taxpayer objected and the case wound up in court.

In rendering a decision, the judge found that he had no difficulty accepting the idea that each of the children would have done enough work on the farm to warrant the payment of $1,000 apiece. However, the facts showed that the farmer paid each of the children a single lump sum and, on the next day, took the dollars back again into his own bank account. These transactions were alleged to be by way of loans, although no documentation was prepared. In addition, some of the children were minors and could not legally lend money to their father in any event. The judge therefore sided with the Minister and the taxpayer lost. The moral is quite clear. If you pay children, the payment should be bona fide and for services that are actually rendered.

Where many people fail to take advantage of income tax opportunities is in the area of remuneration to "dependent" children. Effective 1988, personal exemptions have been converted into income tax credits. This provides increased benefits to lower-income Canadians, while, at the same time, reduces the benefit of lower tax rates on upper-income individuals. No tax credits or deductions are given for dependants over age eighteen except for those who are infirm. Moreover, the federal dependancy credit for the first two children under age nineteen is only around $70 each. Even when provincial tax benefits are added, the total credit is only a little over $100. It thus becomes more important than ever before to find ways to legitimately remunerate one's children. All other tax incentives for having dependent children have been effectively eliminated!

The remuneration package should not, however, provide for an annual salary paid as a single amount on the night before Christmas. Rather, the payments should be made throughout the year commensurate with the services rendered by the child. In all cases, the child should actually work for his or her remuneration. I would be very unhappy, for example, about trying to defend a taxpayer who has paid salaries to a child when the child cannot describe in his or her own words exactly what was done to earn the income. It would also be somewhat difficult to explain away circumstances where payments are made and the parents then take back the money. All salaries paid should, in fact, be deposited in the children's bank accounts and expenditures for their benefit should be paid from these accounts.

Of course, if you are blessed with four teenage children, you may not have enough clerical, office, or maintenance work in the business to gainfully employ all four. However, in many circumstances, you can easily justify salaries to one or two children. From an educational perspective, let alone from a tax-saving standpoint, employment of the children can be most advantageous.

Directors' Fees

There is a common misconception that you can remunerate family members by simply making them directors of the company. Excessive directors' fees are, however, far more vulnerable to reassessment than excessive salaries. This is because there is an established market in Canada for the remuneration of a corporate director.

If a director of a *public* corporation receives between $3,000 and $10,000 for his or her efforts, how can the average Canadian *private* company pay similar amounts on a tax-deductible basis? A director of a public company must attend meetings, sit on committees, and is exposed to potential negligence suits. In the case of a private corporation, the meetings are very often a matter of formality only and may not, in fact, really take place.

Remuneration Guidelines for the Owner-Manager Where the Company Qualifies for the Small-Business Deduction

Having dealt with salaries to spouses and other members of the family, is it possible to evolve distinct guidelines for the purpose of determining the "best" remuneration package for the owner-manager himself or herself? Actually, such guidelines *can* be established by using simple arithmetic.

In the examples that follow, it is assumed that a shareholder-manager of a Canadian private corporation generally operates the business *primarily* in order to satisfy his or her personal or living requirements. This means that the first dollars earned by the corporation (after paying all other company expenses) must be drawn out one way or another (by salaries, bonuses, or dividends) for the shareholder-manager and family to live on from day to day. Thus, only dollars *over and above* personal living requirements can be devoted towards savings, and it is these *excess* dollars around which tax planning revolves.

For purposes of illustration, let us look at $100 of corporate profits from active business that remains after all operating expenses have been paid for out of revenues and *after* the remuneration needed for living expenses by the shareholder-manager has already been taken. The amount of $100 is very easy to work with, and we can easily convert from dollars to percentages where our base is 100; however, the *most* important point is that whatever holds true for $100 of business profits of a Canadian-controlled private corporation also holds true for *any* profits for which the small-business tax rate applies. In other words, the profit of $100 is representative of a range – all the way from the first dollar of earnings up to the annual business limit of $200,000.

In order to simplify the examples in this chapter and the next, the individual's other deductions and personal tax credits have been ignored in most cases. If you wish, you can assume that the shareholder-manager has other income which offsets these additional amounts.

The first possibility is that a shareholder-manager could draw the entire $100 profit by way of salary or bonus, even though he or she has already satisfied all personal living requirements. As such, depending on how much the individual has already drawn, we can estimate the taxes payable on an additional draw of $100 as follows:

Amount previously drawn as salary	$30,000	$60,000	$60,000+
Combined marginal tax brackets (approximate)	25%	40%	45%
Taxes payable on an additional bonus of $100	$25	$40	$45
After-tax retention on bonus	$75	$60	$55

As an alternative, however, the corporation can retain this profit after paying corporate taxes. Where the small-business deduction applies, the combined federal and provincial corporate tax payable will only be about 20%, leaving after-tax retained earnings of $80. Thus, *our first conclusion is that a corporation that is subject to the small-business deduction offers its shareholder-managers the opportunity for a significant tax deferral.* In other words, the company can reinvest significantly more after-tax dollars than the amount otherwise available to the owners them-selves.

It is evident from the comparison shown in Figure 13-2 that the mini-mum tax deferral is 5% based on the underlying income of $100 that was earned in the first place.

Figure 13–2   **A Comparison of Corporate and Individual After-Tax Earnings**

Corporation

Earnings	$100
Corporate Tax	20
Retention	$ 80

Individual

Income Level	$30,000	$60,000	$60,000+
Tax bracket	25%	40%	45%
Salary	$100	$100	$100
Personal tax	25	40	45
Retention	$ 75	$ 60	$ 55

Note: $100 is representative of a range between $1 and $200,000 each year as long as the company is a CCPC earning business income.

The opportunities for tax deferral do, however, extend to a possible 25% when the owner-manager is in the top tax bracket of 45%.

Meaning of Tax Deferral

In the previous discussion, I have consciously stayed away from refer-ring to the term "tax saving." Actually, there are three possibilities if you opt to allow a corporation to pay tax instead of the owner-manager.

First, where the corporate tax rate is only 20% and the company has $80 out of $100, it is certainly much easier to subsidize business expan-sion. Corporate retention would provide many more dollars than if the shareholders were to take out the funds personally and then lend back their after-tax proceeds.

Second, it is important to realize that the accounting concept of a pri-vate corporation being separate and apart from its owners is a pure fic-tion. You can never tax plan properly for a private company unless you look at the owners *and* the company as if they were, in effect, one entity. If, for example, a corporation does not need after-tax profits for business expansion, these same dollars could be used for a build-up of investment capital. The corporation could purchase term deposits, dividend-bearing securities, real estate, gold, silver, or, for that matter, any other kind of investment. All investment decisions would, of course, be those of the owner-managers. Thus, the corporation is simply an extension of its owners. The corporate low rate provides more funds for investment purposes than would otherwise be available to the owners themselves.

A third possibility is if the owner wants the after-tax profits for personal luxury items. This is the one area where, in a sense, the idea of a corporation being just an extension of its owners breaks down. Soon after a corporation takes its profits and uses them for the personal benefit of its owner-managers, individual taxes must be paid. (See Chapter Two for a discussion of loans to shareholders.) Thus, we do not refer to corporate retention of profits as providing a tax *saving*. It is just a *deferral*. The advantage of corporate retention lies in *reinvestment* of profits only.

The tax-deferral benefits are indefinite as long as the shareholder-manager can afford to leave the dollars inside the company without drawing on them for personal or living expenses. What happens, however, if a shareholder-manager does decide, in some future year, to draw out funds, which have been accumulated by the corporation, for personal or living expenses?

Salaries Versus Dividends

You must never try to compare a $100 salary to a $100 dividend. A salary is paid from pre-tax profits, while a dividend comes out of after-tax corporate earnings. Where the small-business deduction applies, you now must compare a $100 salary to a dividend of $80.

The example in figure 13-3 illustrates what happens when dividends of $80 are paid out to shareholder-managers. As discussed in Chapter Nine, a Canadian dividend is grossed up by 25%. This factor applied to a dividend of $80 always produces (for each of the taxpayers in the example) an income for tax purposes of $100. This income is then subjected to tax in the respective marginal brackets as indicated in the example. However, the tax otherwise payable is then reduced by a dividend tax credit.

The operation of the dividend tax credit is the key point to an understanding of how corporate taxes and personal taxes interact when dividends pass to shareholders.

Figure 13–3 **Tax Treatment of Dividends out of Small-Business Profits to Shareholder-Managers**

Income level	$30,000	$60,000	$60,000+
Marginal tax brackets	25%	40%	45%
Retention on $100 bonus	$75	$60	$55
Cash dividend = Corporate retained earnings	$ 80	$ 80	$ 80
25% gross-up	20	20	20
Income for tax purposes	$100	$100	$100
Federal and provincial tax in marginal bracket	$25	$40	$45
Dividend tax credit (combined)	20	20	20
Net tax	$ 5	$20	$25
Cash flow (cash dividend of $80 – net tax)	$75	$60	$55
Cash flow on $100 salary	$75	$60	$55

The Dividend Tax Credit

The federal dividend tax credit is 13.33% of the grossed-up dividend. Thus, in the example in Figure 13-3, the federal dividend tax credit on a cash dividend of $80 (grossed up to $100) is 13.33% of $100, or $13.33. However, when the example refers to marginal tax brackets, this means not only federal taxes but provincial income taxes as well.

In all provinces (other than Quebec, which has its own tax credit system), provincial taxes are levied as a flat-rate percentage of the federal tax otherwise payable. This percentage of provincial taxes is levied *after* the federal income tax has already been reduced by the federal dividend tax credit. Thus, in the example, if the federal tax otherwise payable is reduced by $13.33, the provincial tax is also reduced by the provincial percentage multiplied by $13.33.

Assume that a particular province levies income taxes at 50% of the federal tax. (Provincial rates outside Quebec currently vary between 44% and 64.5% of the federal tax.) A resident of that province who receives a cash dividend of $80 and who therefore reduces his other federal tax by $13.33 will then reduce the provincial tax by a further

50% × $13.33, or by $6.67. The total dividend tax credit (on a combined basis) is therefore $20. *In all provinces, the combined effective dividend tax credit is approximately equal to the dividend gross-up.*

Returning to the example in Figure 13-3, it is evident that the net retention on an $80 dividend is exactly equal to the net cash retention otherwise possible on a $100 bonus. The effect of the dividend gross-up is to bring the individual shareholder-manager into a position where he or she is subject to tax on the *underlying income that was earned by the corporation in the first place.*

The result of the dividend tax credit is then to give that same shareholder-manager an effective credit for the corporate tax that has already been paid on this income. Therefore, the individual shareholder-manager is only responsible for the difference between his or her personal marginal rate of tax and the corporate rate. The after-tax cash flow on a dividend is the *same amount* that he or she would have received had he or she taken a bonus or salary of $100 in the first place. This is called an "integrated tax system."

To summarize, the use of a corporation to retain active business income not required by a shareholder-manager for living expenses produces a substantial, indefinite tax deferral as long as the small-business deduction applies. The deferral provides excess funds for reinvestment until such time as the shareholder-manager decides to take out dividends. At that point, however, the total tax cost still does not exceed that which would have been paid had the deferral not been chosen.

Additional Implications of the Gross-Up and Credit System

The gross-up and credit system has another far more significant effect. As explained in Chapter Nine, when a Canadian resident has no other income and receives a $22,000 dividend from a Canadian corporation, he or she will pay *no personal income taxes at all.* (See Figure 9-3.)

Although there is no personal tax payable on dividends of up to $22,000 received by an individual, you should note that a business would still have to earn $27,500 in order to be capable of paying a $22,000 dividend (after corporate tax).

Corporate earnings	$27,500
Less: Income tax at 20%	5,500
Net amount available for dividend	$22,000

As an alternative to the $22,000 dividend, the corporation could pay a salary of $27,500, thereby saving the $5,500 of corporate taxes otherwise payable. The individual's tax position would be as follows:

Salary	$27,500
Less: Personal exemptions and	
other deductions (eliminated after 1987)	Nil
Taxable income	$27,500
On $27,500, federal tax @ 17% is	$ 4,675
Less: Personal tax credit in 1993 (estimated)	1,100
Subtotal	3,575
Add: Provincial income tax (50% × $3,575)	1,787
	5,362
Rounding difference	138
Total personal income taxes	$ 5,500

Thus, the combined federal and provincial income tax payable on a taxable income of $27,500 is also approximately $5,500. The retention on a salary of $27,500 is therefore the *same* $22,000 as if corporate taxes were first paid and a dividend was then distributed.

Tax Planning for a Proper Salary-Dividend Mix

From the foregoing examples, it would appear that it really doesn't matter whether a salary of $27,500 or a dividend of $22,000 is paid – at least when a CCPC is eligible for the low rate of corporate tax. However, whenever you tax plan, you must take into account different segments of the legislation contained throughout the Income Tax Act. In this case, specifically, tax planning should include provision for the Registered Retirement Savings Plan (RRSP), which was discussed in Chapter Five.

In order to obtain full benefits from an RRSP in *1994*, a *1993* earned income of $75,000 is required. This is because 18% of $75,000 is equal to $13,500, which is the maximum RRSP contribution limit for 1994. Figure 13-4 therefore proves that the first $75,000 earned by a Canadian-controlled private corporation should be extracted by way of salary. This is because a dividend is not considered "earned income" for tax purposes.

As I just mentioned, for a taxpayer to make use of an RRSP or even to benefit from the Canada/Quebec Pension Plan, he or she requires "earned income." Thus, if a shareholder-manager ceases to draw any salary, he or

Figure 13–4 **Some Earned Income Is Required for Effective
Tax Planning**

Alternative 1: The corporation pays income taxes on the first $75,000 of
profits (before shareholder-manager remuneration) and distributes the balance
as a dividend. The shareholder then retains $13,500 for investment purposes
(to provide ultimately for his or her retirement).

Income earned by corporation	$75,000
Corporate income tax at 20%	(15,000)
	$60,000
Less: Dividend paid	(60,000)
Retained earnings of corporation	$ —
Cash dividend	$60,000
25% Gross-up	15,000
Net income = taxable income	$75,000

Federal tax on taxable income:

$30,000 × 17%	$5,100	
30,000 × 26%	7,800	
15,000 × 29%	4,350	$17,250
$75,000		

Less: Personal tax credit	(1,100)
Dividend tax credit (13.33% × $75,000)	(10,000)
	6,150
Add: Provincial tax 50% × $6,150	3,075
	$ 9,225

Cash flow:

Income earned by corporation	$75,000
Corporate taxes	(15,000)
	60,000
Invested for retirement (income yield is taxable)	(13,500)
Personal taxes	(9,225)
After-tax disposable income	$37,275

Alternative 2: A salary of $75,000 is paid and an RRSP is purchased (to provide ultimately for the shareholder's retirement).

Salary	$75,000
Less: RRSP (18%)	(13,500)
Net income = taxable income	$61,500

Federal tax on taxable income		
$30,000 × 17%	$5,100	
30,000 × 26%	7,800	
1,500 × 29%	435	13,335
$61,500		
Less: Personal tax credit		(1,100)
		12,235
Add: Provincial tax 50% × $12,235		6,117
		$18,352

Combined marginal tax rate is now 45% (150% × 29%)

Cash flow:	
income earned by corporation and distributed as salary	$75,000
Corporate income taxes (salary is deductible)	Nil
Invested for retirement in RRSP (income is tax-sheltered)	(13,500)
	61,500
Less: Personal taxes	(18,352)
After-tax disposable income	$43,148
Advantage of salary (i.e., extra disposable income):	
$43,148 – $37,275	$ 5,873

Note:

Maximum tax on RRSP withdrawal is	
45% × $13,500	$ 6,075

she would have to forgo all benefits from these programs. The alternatives of choosing dividends or salaries are compared in Figure 13-4.

The reason a salary is preferable is that a corporation pays a tax rate of 20% on *all* profits (from the first dollar) before dividends can be paid out, while an individual does not reach as high an effective rate of tax on his or her income after RRSP contributions and a personal tax credit are deducted. The tax saving of a salary over a dividend can be, as illustrated, $5,873.

Even though taxes will eventually have to be paid on a withdrawal from an RRSP, these taxes would not amount to more than 45% on $13,500, or $6,075. If the extra disposable income of $5,873 were invested for just a few months, this would more than make up for any future taxes payable on the withdrawal from an RRSP.

A major advantage of a salary-oriented remuneration package involving RRSP contributions is the fact that RRSP funds will earn income that compounds on a tax-deferred basis. This is preferable to income earned on investment capital that is fully taxed when earned.

Note that this example does not take into account the fact that for 1995 the maximum eligible contribution to an RRSP is slated to become $14,500. Assuming that the formula for eligible contributions remains "18% of earned income," this means that an individual would have to draw a salary of $80,556 *in* 1994 in order to take advantage of the maximum RRSP in 1995. This is because allowable RRSP contributions are based on earned income for the immediately preceding year. The example also does not take into account the other advantage of receiving salary, which is participation in the Canada/Quebec Pension Plan.

Under the salary alternative depicted in Figure 13-4, the owner-manager has a net income of $61,500 after deducting an RRSP contribution. Since the corporate tax rate on retained income is then only 20% and since the shareholder-manager would now be in a 45% bracket, *no additional remuneration* should be paid *unless* the shareholder-manager requires such additional payments for personal or living expenses.

If the owner-manager does require additional remuneration, all additional payments could be made *either* by way of salary or dividend, depending on individual circumstances.

Summary

The current guidelines for what I consider the best remuneration package for a shareholder-manager of a Canadian-controlled private corporation can thus be outlined as follows where the small-business tax rate applies:

1. Draw as little income from the corporation as possible and make use of the tax deferral aspects of the small-business rate structure.
2. In 1993, the first $75,000 of gross remuneration should be taken by a shareholder-manager as a salary. This would make him or her eligible to contribute the maximum amount to the Canada/Quebec Pension Plan. Then $13,500 should be invested in an RRSP for 1994. Of course, the 1994 contribution would be funded out of 1994 earnings while the 1993 RRSP will be paid for using money drawn in 1993.
3. Since the shareholder-manager would then be in a 45% tax bracket (after step 2) while the corporation would pay taxes at only 20%, no additional remuneration should be taken out, if possible. This assumes that the shareholder-manager could meet all personal or living expenses on an after-tax retention of approximately $43,150. (The actual dollars vary from province to province.)
4. If additional remuneration is required for personal or living expenses, additional salary or a dividend may be extracted. If the shareholder-manager has a cumulative net investment loss as described in Chapter Six, dividends should be taken as an offset.
5. Dividends may also be paid to family members if salaries would be unreasonable.
6. For 1994, a salary of $80,556 will allow for a contribution of $14,500 to an RRSP for *1995*. The 1995 contribution will actually be funded out of 1995 earnings. The advantage of a salary in 1994 is similar to that illustrated in the previous example for 1993.

Of course, these are general guidelines, and it should be noted that extenuating circumstances may, in certain cases, warrant a deviation from the suggested pattern. For example, a difficult decision must be made in cases where an owner-manager finds that he or she can live quite comfortably on a salary of, say, $40,000 a year. If the business is profitable, this will allow the corporation to retain about 80 cents out of each dollar of profit (up to $200,000 annually) not taken out by salary, while additional remuneration to the owner-manager would require him or her to pay taxes at combined federal and provincial marginal rates of around 40%. The question therefore arises: would it pay to "draw" an additional $35,000 of salary in 1993 ($75,000 minus the salary already taken of $40,000) in order to contribute an extra $6,300 to RRSPs ($35,000 ×

18%) in 1994? The ability to shelter $6,300 from any tax at all may not warrant the penalty of paying an extra 20%-25% tax on the remaining $28,700 of salary that cannot be so sheltered.

In cases where an owner-manager draws a salary of $75,000 or more in 1993, the tax planning becomes simpler, as long as it is anticipated that there will be sufficient cash flow to warrant an increased RRSP contribution for 1994. As mentioned previously, the 1994 cash flow can be used to fund it. As RRSP maximum limits are adjusted upwards over the next few years (as explained in Chapter Five) additional salaries may become more advantageous.

Tax Planning for the Family

Logically, if a tax plan is advantageous for one owner-manager, it can provide twice the benefit in the case of two owner-managers. For example, if husband and wife are both active in the business, salaries of $75,000 should be paid to each of them for 1993 as long as this amount would be considered reasonable. Each would then contribute $13,500 to RRSPs for 1994. The cash flow and tax effect of this is illustrated below.

If the illustrated arrangement is feasible, the family's disposable income would be approximately $86,300 and the effective tax cost only 24.4%. *Any time taxes on earnings of $150,000 can be kept at this level, tax planning has been effective.* The corporation could then earn an additional $200,000 of active business income eligible for a 20% tax rate.

Figure 13–5   **Tax Planning for Husbands and Wives (Earned Income)**

	Earnings	RRSP Deferrals	Tax	Net Cash
Salary to husband	$ 75,000	$13,500	$18,350	$43,150
Salary to wife	75,000	13,500	18,350	43,150
	$150,000	$27,000	$36,700	$86,300
Effective tax cost	$\dfrac{\text{Taxes}}{\text{Earnings}}$	$\dfrac{\$36,700}{\$150,000}$	=	24.4%

What happens if husbands and wives do not contribute to a business equally – at least to the point where a salary of $75,000 could be justified for each? Consider, for example, the situation in which the husband is active while the wife is at home working hard to bring up children (without receiving any remuneration for this position). They might try this approach to tax planning:

- The husband should still draw $75,000 by way of salary and contribute to an RRSP.
- The next $27,500 of pre-tax profits should then be taxed at the corporate level. This would create an opportunity to pay dividends of $22,000 (after corporate taxes).
- $22,000 could then be paid out as a dividend to the wife. The example in Figure 13-6 shows how this would work.

In this case, the family's disposable income exceeds $65,100 and the entire tax bite is only 23.2% on a total income of $102,500. This too is quite inexpensive. Note that the $5,500 tax on the dividend to the wife is *not* really a tax payable by *her* but is the corporate tax payable initially in order to free up $22,000 of dividends on which no further taxes need be paid.

Figure 13–6   **An Alternative Tax Plan for Husbands and Wives**

	Earnings	RRSP Deferrals	Tax	Net Cash
Salary to husband	$ 75,000	$13,500	$18,350	$43,150
Dividend to wife	27,500	—	* 5,500	22,000
	$102,500	$13,500	$23,850	$65,150

$$\text{Effective tax cost } \frac{\text{Taxes}}{\text{Earnings}} = \frac{\$23,850}{\$102,500} = \underline{23.2\%}$$

*Corporate tax at 20%.

Separate Classes of Shares

At this point, you might question how one can pay dividends to a wife without also paying dividends to a husband who is (presumably) also a shareholder.

For several years, it was fashionable to set up the share structure of private businesses in such a way that different family members held different classes of shares. In many instances, the classes were identical in all respects, except that the board of directors was given the opportunity to declare dividends on one class without necessarily declaring dividends on another. Thus, if a husband owned Class A shares and his wife owned Class B shares, and the husband was active while the wife was not, the custom was to pay a salary to the husband and dividends to the wife.

Unfortunately, in several recent tax cases, Revenue Canada attacked such programs. In one case, the courts found that any arrangement in which dividends are paid on one class but not on another and where the shares are effectively the same is an indirect transfer of rights to income. In another case, the taxpayer won in an appeal made to the Supreme Court. As a result of the confusion, it may be wise to change existing arrangements that would give rise to such a problem. Specifically, it might be best for the husband in our example to own voting preferred shares only, which are redeemable, retractable, and even convertible, but do not necessarily bear dividends. These shares could also participate in the future growth of the business. Retractable means that these shares can be redeemed at the option of the holder, as well as at the option of the company. Then, if the wife holds all the common shares, dividends can be paid to her alone.

An arrangement to exchange the husband's capital stock for shares of another class can be structured using Section 86 of the Income Tax Act. I regret that a detailed analysis of Section 86 is beyond the scope of this book. However, suffice it to say that with qualified legal and accounting advice, a suitable share structure can be arranged that would accomplish income-splitting objectives.

Tax Planning for Corporate-Earned Investment Income

In Chapter Seven, I explained that investment corporations can no longer be formed as a vehicle to split investment income between a taxpayer and members of his or her family who are in low tax brackets. Instead, if the investment capital that is placed into such a corporation earns income and the income is distributed as dividends, the dividends paid to the low-bracket family members will be attributed back to the person who introduced the capital in the first place. These rules apply for investment corporations formed or receiving property after November 21, 1985.

There is, however, no restriction on having the shares of an *active business company* owned not only by an owner-manager but *also* by members of his or her family. If the corporation generates business profits and this income is not needed for business expansion, the corporation is then free to make investments. In this section we will examine how the investment income is taxed.

Overview of the Corporate Tax Structure for Investment Income

Investment income, such as interest, rents, royalties, and the taxable portion of capital gains, is initially taxed at approximately 40% (the actual rate varies slightly from province to province) when earned by a corporation. The Income Tax Act permits the remaining 60% to be reinvested. As I mentioned earlier in this book, a corporation is not eligible for the $100,000 lifetime capital gains exemption.

The theory behind this tax structure is that as long as 40% tax is paid initially, the government does not mind if a shareholder would otherwise pay a slightly higher percentage in personal taxes.

Although a privately owned corporation can "keep" only 60% of what it earns, any time dividends are paid out to shareholders, one-half of the 40% tax previously paid is refunded back to the corporation.

Therefore, the net permanent corporate tax is only 20%, and 80% of each dollar's earnings is available for distribution. These rules are summarized as follows:

Investment income	$100
Corporate tax	40
Net corporate retention (maximum)	60
Refundable tax (20% of $100)	20
Available for dividends	$ 80

As I explained earlier in this chapter, any time an individual receives a dividend of $80 out of $100 which was earned in the first place, the net after-tax retention will be the same as if that individual had received the $100 amount personally in the first place.

Thus, at first glance, there appears to be little advantage in earning investment income through a corporation. This is because the initial tax burden will be the same as if a high-tax-bracket individual had earned the income and, even when dividends are paid, the net retention will also be the same.

Income-Splitting with Family Members

The advantage of earning investment income through a corporation comes when this income can be split among low-tax-bracket family members. You will recall that up to $22,000 of Canadian dividends can be received by an individual *totally tax-free* as long as he or she has no other income.

The tax rules for investment income were designed to produce an equitable treatment where income is earned and is then passed on as dividends to the person who injected the capital into the corporation in the first place. Nevertheless, if the income can be channelled to family members, tax advantages do result. This is illustrated in the form of a diagram in Figure 13-7 and in the example in Figure 13-8, which outlines the advantages obtainable by putting together all the rules explained previously.

Figure 13–7   **Income Splitting Through a Corporation**

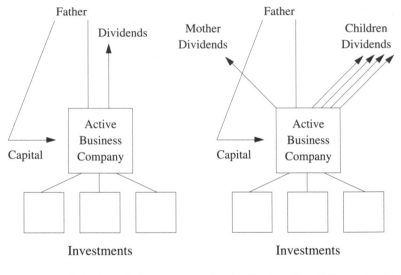

In the example shown, Father incorporates a private company to carry on a business that he could otherwise run as a proprietorship. He allows his family members to subscribe to shares so that they may receive dividends. In order to avoid "income attribution" (as discussed in Chapter Seven) it is important for the family members to invest their own funds or use money borrowed from outsiders.

The corporation operates very profitably for several years. Eventually, the company accumulates $1.4 million of after-tax active business income and the money is not needed for business expansion. Instead, the company invests its after-tax business profits to earn interest at, say, 9.8%. The annual yield is $137,500. As Figure 13-8 illustrates, if the investment income is retained corporately, total income taxes at 40% will amount to $55,000. On the other hand, if dividends are paid to the family members the effective tax will only be 20% of $137,500, or $27,500 in total. As you can see, there is a very substantial tax saving. This again assumes that Mother and the children have no other income and their net taxes payable after gross-up and credit on dividends would be nil. Mother and the children could then reinvest their dividends back into the corporation and the annual accumulation would be over $27,500 more than Father could have reinvested had he received all the dividends himself.

Figure 13–8 **Advantages of a Family-Owned Business Company Which Also Earns Investment Income**

Assumptions: Father, who is in a 45% tax bracket, is married and has four dependent children. His wife and children have no income but are shareholders in the business.

Alternative 1

• Investment income is retained corporately

Interest on $1.4 million at 9.8%	$137,500
Less: Income taxes thereon at 40%	(55,000)
Net retention (60% of total)	$ 82,500

Alternative 2
• Father holds shares with voting powers sufficient to control the corporation, but with no "growth potential."
• Mother and the children hold common shares and get dividends.

Interest on $1.4 million at 9.8%	$137,500
Less: Corporate tax at 40%	(55,000)
Retained earnings	$ 82,500
Add: Refundable tax to corporation when dividends are paid (20% × $137,500)	27,500
Cash available for dividends	$110,000
Less: Dividends to wife and four children	(110,000)
Remaining cash available for dividends	Nil
Dividend to each of wife and four children ($110,000 ÷ 5)	$ 22,000
Net tax payable by each	Nil
Net retention by family (5 × $22,000)	$110,000
Retention as percentage of gross income ($110,000 ÷ $137,500)	80%

Sheltering Capital Gains

While the previous example assumes an interest yield, income splitting through a corporation may be viable for all sorts of investment activity – *as long as the corporation was primarily an active business company when it was first formed.*

If the corporation holds marketable securities, the taxable portion of any capital gain is taxed as investment income, while the tax-free portion of the gain is not only tax-free to the corporation but can also be extracted by the shareholders personally with *no tax payable* on a special-dividend basis.

You should note, however, that earning capital gains through a corporation is not particularly useful unless the individual shareholders have already used up their lifetime capital gains tax exemptions. As explained in Chapter Nine, if the intent is to use active business profits for growth investments, you might be better off structuring a (short-term) loan from the corporation to provide *personal investment capital.*

Sheltering Public-Company Dividends

Investment yields in the form of public-company dividends can also be sheltered by funneling these earnings through a private corporation. When a private company receives dividends from Canadian public companies, these dividends are taxed at a flat rate of 25% *instead* of the regular 40% tax that applies to other forms of investment income. The 25% tax is *completely refundable* as soon as the private company in turn pays out these dividends to its shareholders. Thus, where Canadian public-corporation dividends are received by a private company and are simultaneously paid out, there is *no tax whatsoever* at the corporate level.

Again, given a spouse with no other income and four children, the opportunity exists for each one to receive $22,000 of dividends tax-free. On a combined basis, this amounts to $110,000 each year. If the average Canadian public company pays a dividend of 5% (computed as a percentage of the cost to acquire the shares in the first place), it is therefore possible to *shelter completely* the income yield from $2.2 million of share investments! ($5\% \times \$2.2$ million $= \$110,000$.)

Of course, the potential to tax shelter all kinds of investment income will vary from case to case and depends primarily on the number of family members one has available for this purpose. Remember, though, that after November 21, 1985, income attribution applies if investment corporations are formed by a high-tax-bracket individual in favour of his or her family members. *The idea is therefore to start off with a profitable business operation and make corporate investments only after business profits are no longer needed for business expansion purposes.*

Control of the Corporation

In most cases, if it is Father who is the "prime mover" of the business corporation, he would want to control investment policies and dividend-payment decisions. Presumably, he would hold voting preferred shares in the family company. The family members would own the common shares, which would participate in growth and which would facilitate income splitting.

How can Father ensure that his family members will reinvest their dividends in the company, short of using violence or other unsavoury methods of coercion? Actually, he has several alternatives. First, he can have the corporation capitalized with a special class of shares – non-voting redeemable preferred shares. Then, instead of having the company pay cash dividends to trigger a refund of taxes, he could have the company pay stock dividends to his family members in the form of these non-voting redeemable preferreds. The corporation would still obtain its 20% refund of tax, but all that the family members would receive would be pieces of paper. Although a stock dividend from a private company is technically taxable, as long as the amount is not more than $22,000 per person, the tax payable would be nil. Since Father would always have voting control of the company, he would decide if and when these special preferred shares would be redeemed.

The Formation of Discretionary Trusts

An alternative would be to create a trust to hold the shares of the children, while Father continued to control the flow of income and all business and investment decisions. Although establishing a trust is the most complicated method of ensuring dividends are reinvested in the company and it involves the greatest amount of legal and other documentation, it is the preferred route to take – especially if the children are minors.

Usually, a family trust involves three trustees, including Father, Mother, and a close family friend, relative, or adviser. Generally, if Father is in charge of the business, he would have the right to replace either of the other trustees, although they would not be able to replace him.

The trust would use borrowed funds to subscribe to the common shares of the corporation. This is done to avoid income attribution – especially where one or more of the children are minors. Dividends would then be paid by the corporation to the trust as illustrated previously.

When a trust receives a dividend, the trustees have two options. First, they could have the trust pay taxes on the entire dividend. Obviously, this would not be a good choice since there are significant taxes payable on dividends in excess of $22,000. As a second option, however, the trustees are permitted to enter into what the Income Tax Act calls a "preferred beneficiary election." The preferred beneficiary election is simply a decision to *allocate* the dividends to the children for tax purposes. The allocation makes the children's income taxable instead of the trust's. Of course, as long as the allocation per child is under $22,000, there are no personal taxes payable. In fact, however, no amounts need be paid out unless Father actually wants to give the children some money. The trustees can instead be in the position of holding money on which taxes have been paid. They can reinvest the funds back into the company to compound future growth.

If a trust is set up as being "discretionary," this provides even further scope for tax planning. The discretionary feature means that the trustees are permitted to distribute capital eventually (generally upon the dissolution of the trust) to whichever of the preferred beneficiaries (and in whatever proportions) the trustees, at their discretion, may at *some future time* see fit. Thus, Father may freeze his estate and pass on growth, even if he is unsure of exactly where he wishes such growth to go! Perhaps the children are relatively young and their capabilities and personalities are still not known.

The key point is that there is no requirement that the preferred beneficiary election (which allows for equal allocations of income amongst the children) be tied in to ultimate distribution ratios. As an extreme example, even though income may have been allocated to four children for many years, Father may decide that only one child should eventually receive *all* the funds. In fact, the rules permit a decision on distributions to be deferred for up to twenty-one years.

In order to discourage long-term *inter vivos* trusts (that is, trusts formed by living persons), there is a deemed disposition of trust property at fair market value if the trust is still in existence on its twenty-first anniversary. The deemed disposition would ordinarily trigger capital gains and this should be avoided. A deemed disposition can be avoided by simply winding up the trust shortly before its twenty-first anniversary and distributing the assets (the common shares of the corporation) to some or all of the children. Of course, if Father is still alive, he could continue to control the company, its operations and its portfolio, through his voting preferred shares. However, within twenty-one years, he should be in a position to know which of his children he wants to give an (eventual) inheritance.

Discretionary trusts giving the trustees the power to make annual preferred beneficiary elections are becoming more and more popular in tax and estate planning. Care must always be taken to comply with the particular laws of the jurisdiction in which the trust is being set up. Accordingly, it is always advisable to have the arrangement for such a trust documented by lawyers and accountants who have had experience in such matters.

Capitalization of the Company

A question usually arises in setting up a corporation as to how much money each of the shareholders must contribute in exchange for their shareholdings. For example, can a family member invest only one dollar in the common-share capital of a company and thereby receive dividends of up to $22,000 a year?

So far, there has been only one reported tax case on this subject. The case involves two Alberta optometrists who incorporated a management company in 1970 to administer their practice. The company was controlled by these two individuals through voting, non-participating shares, but their wives also held shares, which were non-voting but fully participating. The company paid management fees to the doctors and declared dividends to the wives that were very substantial in relation to their original investment. In fact, it appears that the wives literally invested pennies and, over a three-year period, received over $90,000 in dividends.

The Minister of National Revenue contended that an indirect benefit had been conferred by the doctors on their wives and that the whole set-up was a sham. The Tax Review Board upheld the Minister's treatment of the situation on the basis that although there was a business purpose for the incorporation of the company, the declaration of these dividends to the wives was not a sound business practice.

The judge showed no distaste for income splitting and estate planning as a *concept,* but, in his judgement, he gave the opinion that acceptable limits had been exceeded. He concluded that the scheme was simply intended to avoid income tax and that the dividends were rightly assessed as being income of the doctors. This case was appealed and eventually settled out of court.

In spite of this one case, many accountants and lawyers are still not overly concerned and companies are often set up with only nominal share capital. However, I personally recommend extreme caution in this area. If, for example, you are forming a corporation with the expectation of paying $22,000 a year of dividends to family members (either directly or through a trust), I think that the capitalization per person should be at least $10,000.

Thus, in a family corporation involving a wife and four children, common shares should be issued for a total consideration of, say, $50,000. To avoid income attribution, the father should not give these funds to the family members. Rather, they should take a bank loan, which, if necessary, could be *guaranteed* by him. The interest on the borrowed money would be tax-deductible, since the borrowings would be incurred for the purpose of earning income in the form of dividends from the corporation. In addition, the infusion of an extra $50,000 of capital into the corporation would result in additional income being earned by the company. There would be no economic loss. Finally, the bank loan could always be repaid by the family members out of dividends over a period of one or two years.

The advantage of taking all these steps is that the Minister of National Revenue would probably be hard pressed to allege that a transaction is a sham when $10,000 is invested for the purpose of earning $22,000. Unfortunately, there are no guidelines within the Canadian tax structure and any final decision as to capitalization of a company is a matter that must be resolved by each taxpayer together with his or her own advisers.

Associated Companies

Turning to the subject of corporate groups, you can see that without special rules it would be quite simple to "beat" the system that allows a Canadian-controlled private company to earn $200,000 a year at favourable tax rates. All one would have to do is incorporate a second company and arrange to have excess profits above this limit channelled into that other corporation. This type of planning is so obvious that special provisions are needed by the government to cope with it. The Income Tax Act therefore contains rules pertaining to "associated corporations": two or more corporations that are controlled by the same person or group of persons must share one small-business limit. Control, for tax purposes, always means ownership of more than 50% of the voting shares. Thus, for example, if Mr. Taxpayer has controlling interest in two or more companies, only one low-rate tax-base applies. This is the case even if the two companies are engaged in entirely different businesses.

However, what is the situation if there are two corporations, one of which is owned 100% by Mr. Taxpayer and the second is owned 100% by his wife? Are these corporations associated? In many cases, rules requiring these two companies to share one small-business tax rate would be unfair. For example, what if the husband's company is involved in manufacturing furniture while the wife's corporation operates a book store? It is clear that one spouse should not be penalized for the other's business activities.

On the other hand, what if the husband's corporation were set up for the purpose of providing income-tax consulting services and the wife's company was involved in bookkeeping? What if, by strange coincidence, the clients of both firms were the same? In this case, it would appear that the separate existence of the two companies might be primarily for the purpose of reducing taxes otherwise payable.

In order to accommodate different types of business circumstances, the rules in the Income Tax Act are therefore flexible. There is actually no automatic association of a husband's company with that of his wife. This is provided that the husband does not have a significant interest in his wife's company and that the wife does not have a substantial cross-holding in her husband's firm. However, the tax rules go on to say that, if the Minister of National Revenue is of the opinion that the separate existence of the two companies is not primarily for the effective conduct of business, but rather has as one of its prime objectives the reduction or avoidance of taxes otherwise payable, the two corporations can be *deemed* to be associated. This would require them to share the small-business tax rate.

In reality, situations are rarely black or white. In many cases, the separate existence of two companies, one owned by the husband and the other by the wife, can be justified for business purposes other than tax reductions. Under those circumstances, each company may utilize the small-business tax rate to its full extent. While a strict interpretation of the law would allow either husband or wife to have a small interest (up to 25%) in the other's corporation, the taxpayer is better off if there is no cross-holding whatsoever.

Planning for a Multiple Use of Corporations

In the most usual situation, a family unit of husband and wife starts out with one business. In most cases, it is advantageous for the shares of that corporation to be owned by both in relatively equal proportions. There are two major advantages:

- Even if one of the two spouses is not *active* in the administration of the business, that spouse can receive remuneration by way of dividends.
- If the shares of the business are ever sold, the capital gain can be apportioned between the spouses. The $500,000 lifetime capital gains tax exemption can also be doubled.

However, what if the family decides to start up a second business? Even if this new business is entirely different from the first, there will be an automatic association of the companies if the shares of the second company are owned by both husband and wife (even in different proportions).

Fortunately, however, there is an alternative. The alternative would require one of the two spouses to sell his or her interests in the first business to the second spouse *before* the second business is incorporated. Subsequently, whoever sells his or her interest in the first business would become the sole shareholder of the second. Then, as long as there is a good business reason for the separate existence of the two corporations, the family could enjoy a second small-business tax rate.

You should note that the sale of the shares in the first business can be made literally for "$1 and other valuable consideration" without necessarily requiring a price to be determined or a payment to be made. This is because, as described in Chapter Seven, transactions between a husband and wife are generally deemed to take place at cost in any event. This means that the fair market value becomes irrelevant. It is true that if the shares that are transferred bear dividends or are ever sold, the income will revert back to the transferor. However, a sale of shares in the first business does pave the way for the formation of a second corporation in order to take advantage of a second small-business tax rate.

In fact, as an additional planning mechanism, each and every corporation owned by a husband and wife should be set up in the first place with separate classes of shares. Not only does this provide the opportunity to pay dividends on one class without paying on the other, but also, if a husband's shares are ever transferred to his wife (or vice versa), one could then arrange *not* to pay dividends on that class in the future. This would avoid the income-attribution rules.

It is extremely important that the timing be arranged properly. If a husband and wife together own the shares of a first company, and then subscribe to the shares in a second, the corporations will automatically become associated. If share transfers are made later so that the husband disposes of all his shares in one company while the wife disposes of her shares in the other, the Minister, on audit, will recognize that this was done for tax purposes only. An ideal opportunity to avoid questions would arise in circumstances where the vendor of the shares of the first company sells out to a spouse in order to devote his or her entire attention to the operations of the new second company.

As a further extension of the foregoing, you should also note that it may be possible to get a *third* use of the small-business rate. This is when the children eventually grow up and (perhaps with financing from their parents) start their own business. As long as the parents have no share interests in the children's company and vice versa, *another* small-business tax rate may become available. Again, there must be a good business reason for this new company beyond just a reduction in taxes. Eventually, the children would presumably inherit the shares of their parents' companies. From that time on, the corporations would become associated and would no longer enjoy multiple small-business benefits, but there is no tax to recapture prior years' benefits.

You should note, however, that *minor* children cannot be "used" to obtain multiple benefits from the small-business deduction. A relatively new rule provides that shares of a corporation owned by anyone under the age of eighteen are treated as being owned by each parent for the purpose of determining whether that corporation is associated with any other corporation that is controlled by that parent or by a group of persons of which that parent is a member.

The subject of associated corporations has been dealt with in many court cases and, in practice, is one of the most complex areas within the small-business sections of the Income Tax Act. You are therefore strongly advised to consult with your own accountants and lawyers before setting up multiple business ventures.

CHAPTER 14

Maximizing Profits from All Private Canadian Businesses; The Taxation of Farming Operations

Taxation Guidelines for Business Income That Does Not Qualify for the Small-Business Tax Rate

A Canadian-controlled private corporation that earns more than $200,000 of active business income in a given year does not qualify for the small-business tax rate on its profits over this limit. Let us again use an example of $100 of active business income; this time $100 will represent all amounts that do *not* qualify for the small-business deduction. The range, in this case, is therefore any business profits from $200,001 (in a given year) and up. Again, whatever holds true for $100 will also hold true for all active business income that does not qualify for the low rate. (The exception for manufacturing and processing profits is dealt with later on in this chapter.)

Salary Versus Dividends

The shareholder-manager has the alternative of either taking a salary or bonus currently, or retaining the income in the corporation and later declaring a dividend for his or her class of shares. Figure 14-1 illustrates an important point. If the shareholder-manager is in a 25% tax bracket, allowing a corporation to pay taxes on profits at the high rate results in a tax *prepayment*. A taxpayer should therefore never put himself or herself into a tax bracket below that of the corporation.

Figure 14–1   **Tax Prepayment (Deferral) at Corporate High Rate**

Alternative 1: A bonus of $100 is paid, representing active business income that does not qualify for the small-business deduction.

Income level	$30,000	$60,000	$60,000+
Tax bracket	25%	40%	45%
After-tax retention on $100 bonus	$75	$60	$55

Alternative 2: The corporation pays tax on its "profit" of $100

Income of corporation	$100	
Corporate tax (high rate applies)	40	
Retained earnings	$ 60	

	$30,000	$60,000	$60,000+
Tax prepayment (deferral) where corporation pays the tax	$15	Nil	$(5)

In fact, there is not only a prepayment in cases where a corporation pays tax at rates higher than personal levels, but there are also severe penalties at the time dividends are later paid out, as we will see.

When a shareholder-manager reaches the 40% and 45% brackets, the choice between paying a bonus and letting the corporation retain the funds appears to be about equal. However, to assess the situation completely, we must chart what happens when a shareholder-manager decides to extract dividends at some point in the future. Here, the dividend will be $60 out of each underlying $100 of income and not $80, as is the case for income that qualifies for the small-business rate.

Once again, we must take care never to attempt to compare a $100 bonus to a $100 dividend. Where the small-business rate does not apply, the correct comparison is a bonus of $100 against a potential dividend (after corporate taxes) of only $60. The tax consequences when such a dividend is paid are shown in Figure 14-2.

The example indicates that there is a substantial tax penalty for individuals in *all* marginal tax brackets for having first allowed active business income to be taxed at high corporate tax rates before dividends are paid out.

Specific guidelines for tax planning can also be derived from this example. A shareholder in a 25% bracket should automatically draw a salary. This is because of the initial prepayment of $15 per $100, as well as the penalty of 19% that arises upon the payment of dividends.

Where shareholders are in 40% or 45% brackets, the original choice between personal and corporate tax was more or less equal. However, at the time of a dividend, there is a penalty of $14 – $15 on each underlying

$100 that had been earned initially. *Therefore, even an individual in the 40% or 45% brackets is better off receiving bonuses in the first place to reduce the amount of corporate tax otherwise payable.*

Figure 14–2 **Tax Penalties on Dividends Paid to Shareholder-Manager (No Small-Business Deduction)**

	$30,000	$60,000	$60,000+
Income level			
Tax bracket	25%	40%	45%
Retention on $100 bonus	$75	$60	$55
Dividend in cash = Corporate retained earnings	$60	$60	$60
25% gross-up	15	15	15
Taxable income	$75	$75	$75
Federal and provincial tax payable	$19	$30	$34
Dividend tax credit (combined)	15	15	15
Net tax payable	$ 4	$15	$19
Cash flow:			
Dividend	$60	$60	$60
Net tax	4	15	19
Retention on $60 dividend	$56	$45	$41
Tax penalty	$19	$15	$14

Effect of Tax Rules

Since personal income-tax brackets are not substantially above 40%, it is never worthwhile to pay corporate taxes of 40% on active business income. There is no significant opportunity to defer taxes through corporate retention. Moreover, there is a severe penalty if corporate profits are taxed at 40% and are then paid out as dividends.

All profits from active (non-manufacturing) business income that do not qualify for the small-business deduction should be paid out as salaries. The owner should pay personal taxes after sheltering as much as possible through an RRSP. If the owner's after-tax retention exceeds his or her living requirements, excess funds can either be loaned back to the corporation for reinvestment into the business or can be channelled into other investments.

A Canadian corporation should *never* pay taxes of 40% on active business income followed by *immediate* dividends to shareholder-managers, since there is an automatic penalty of at least 14%.

Planning for Public Corporations

There is now a brand-new planning technique for senior managers of public corporations that normally pay dividends. This strategy will be of use to the senior manager who is *also* a significant stockholder.

If possible, the senior manager should *waive his or her rights* to dividends in exchange for bonuses. A bonus of one dollar is certainly better than a dividend of sixty cents, and from the employer's standpoint the choice between (pre-tax) salaries and (after-tax) dividends is the same.

Income from Manufacturing and Processing

If a corporation earns business income from manufacturing and processing which does *not* qualify for the small business deduction, the federal tax rate becomes 22% (21% in 1994) instead of 28%. Assuming an average provincial tax rate of 13%, the combined tax rate is then 35%, instead of the 40% bite that would otherwise apply. A discussion on tax planning for business income is therefore incomplete unless we examine guidelines for such manufacturing and processing profits.

Although the phrase "manufacturing and processing" is not defined in the Income Tax Act, there are several industries, such as farming, fishing, logging, on-site construction, and certain exploration activities, which are specifically *excluded*. In addition, the rules require that at least 10% of a corporation's gross revenue for the year from all active businesses be from the sale or lease of goods that are manufactured or processed by that corporation in Canada.

Because there is no specific definition as to what is included, you are free to take a very liberal interpretation of the term "manufacturing and processing." For example, the activities of a restaurant could be eligible for this incentive since a restaurant processes food. Similarly, a newspaper or magazine processes paper, and even though the major revenue is derived from advertising, it can be said that publishing still qualifies.

Any time a business purchases goods in bulk and repackages them for sale in smaller quantities, it would appear advantageous at least to try to claim the reduced tax rate. Again, the "no-worse-off" principle would apply. I once had a client who was able to save $36,000 in taxes by mixing with water certain chemicals that had originally been purchased for resale to customers. This simple activity created a "processing" activity.

Calculating Manufacturing and Processing Profits

After it is determined that a corporation is engaged in manufacturing or processing, there is a formula to determine what percentage of active business income is deemed to be from these activities. The formula may be expressed as follows:

$$\frac{\text{Manufacturing}}{\text{and Processing}} = \frac{\text{Active}}{\text{Business}} \times \frac{\dfrac{100}{75} \times \dfrac{\text{Manufacturing}}{\text{Labour}} + \dfrac{100}{85} \times \dfrac{\text{Manufacturing}}{\text{Capital}}}{\text{Total Labour} + \text{Total Capital}}$$

This formula ties in manufacturing and processing profits as a percentage of active business income, based on a composite of both labour and capital (fixed assets) employed. The first part of the formula takes into account manufacturing labour and total labour for the year. The formula recognizes that even "pure" manufacturing companies require a certain amount of non-qualifying "support" labour. For example, every business must have salespeople, an office staff, and executive personnel. The fraction "100/75" allows for a 25% support factor. As long as not more than 25% of the total labour is devoted to non-qualified activities, the gross-up of 100/75 will produce no erosion in the amount of active business income that qualifies for the credit.

"Capital," as used in the formula, includes both fixed assets owned and fixed assets leased (other than land). The fraction "100/85" means that a corporation can have some non-qualified fixed assets without eroding its manufacturing and processing base – as long as these assets do not exceed 15% of the total. Thus, a capital investment in office and showroom furniture or automobiles will not necessarily reduce the availability of the special rate.

Tax Planning for the Manufacturing and Processing Incentive

Because of the arbitrary nature of the above formula, there are some excellent tax-planning ideas that can be adopted. For example, take the situation of a corporation engaged in both manufacturing and non-manufacturing activities. If the corporation's manufacturing profits are high while the non-manufacturing branch operates at just above the break-even level, you should consider splitting the business into two separate companies. You would transfer as much as possible of the non-manufacturing labour, fixed assets (such as office equipment), and overheads to the non-manufacturing company, and keep the manufacturing operations as "pure" as possible. Thus, the non-manufacturing activities would not diminish the use of the special deduction, as could be the case if the two types of operations were combined under one corporate roof.

Conversely, if manufacturing and non-manufacturing activities are carried on by two separate but related corporations, and the manufacturing business is marginally successful while non-manufacturing is very profitable, you should consider amalgamating the two corporations. Because of the arbitrary percentages in the formula, a portion of the non-manufacturing profits may end up qualifying for the deduction.

It is important to note that the manufacturing incentives apply to *all* large corporations, even if public or non-Canadian-controlled (and to Canadian-controlled private corporations on annual manufacturing profits over $200,000). There is ample opportunity in many instances to obtain substantial tax savings.

Tax Planning for Owner-Managed Manufacturing and Processing Operations – Salaries Versus Dividends

In order to complete our examination of the remuneration guidelines for corporations and their shareholders, we should now review the integration concepts as they apply to corporate tax rates in the 35% range.

Where the corporate tax rate is 35%, you would expect to find some tax deferrals, but nevertheless an ultimate tax penalty on payment of dividends. These points are illustrated in Figure 14-3 which covers the taxation of manufacturing income that does not qualify for the small-business deduction. This would apply in the case of a Canadian-controlled private corporation on annual profits in excess of $200,000 from manufacturing. From the example, it can be seen that only a taxpayer in a bracket below 35% would not get a deferral advantage by allowing the corporation to pay the tax. Of course, it is very unlikely that the owner-manager would be in a bracket below 40%, considering that we are dealing with income from an active business in excess of $200,000 per annum.

When the shareholder is in a 40% or 45% bracket, corporate retention

Figure 14–3 **Dividend Versus Salary Where a 35% Corporate Tax Rate Applies**

		$30,000	$60,000	$60,000+
Income level				
Tax bracket		25%	40%	45%
Alternative 1:				
After-tax retention on				
$100 bonus		$75	$60	$55
Alternative 2: The corporation pays tax of profit of $100				
Income of corporation	$100			
Corporate tax (after manufacturing and processing tax credit only)	35			
Retained earnings	$65			
Tax deferral (prepayment) where corporation pays the tax		$(10)	$ 5	$10
Payment of dividend:				
Cash dividend = Retained earnings		$65	$65	$65
25% gross-up		16	16	16
Income for tax purposes		$81	$81	$81
Federal and provincial tax in marginal bracket		$20	$32	$36
Dividend tax credit (combined)		16	16	16
Net tax		$ 4	$16	$20
Cash flow (cash dividend of $65 – net tax)		$61	$49	$45
Cash flow on $100 bonus		$75	$60	$55
Penalty for not having taken bonus of $100		$14	$11	$10

provides a potential tax deferral of 5% to 10%. On the other hand, when dividends are eventually paid the tax penalty is quite substantial.

As a general guideline, therefore, when business income qualifies for the manufacturing incentives but is substantially in excess of what is eligible for the small-business deduction, the loss of the small-business credit is now of serious consequence. The owner-manager (and members of his or her family to the extent that this is reasonable) should draw the excess earnings as salaries. The after-tax dollars can then be reloaned to the corporation for business expansion or can be retained for investment capital.

The Taxation of Farming Operations

Historically, farming operations have provided one of the most significant tax shelters under the Canadian tax system. This is because farmers were allowed to calculate both income and losses on the basis of cash accounting rules. Before 1989, for part-time farmers, whose chief source of income was neither farming nor a combination of farming and some other source of income, the deductibility of farm losses against other income was limited to $2,500 plus one-half of additional losses up to a maximum deduction of $5,000 a year.

It has long been recognized, however, that the old tax rules for identifying part-time farmers were very subjective and were difficult to comply with and administer. Moreover, start-up farmers often had problems in meeting the normal business test for the deductibility of losses – a reasonable expectation of profit. On the other hand, a full-time farmer could shelter other income by using cash-basis accounting and by writing off inventory purchases without reflecting the value of inventory at the end of each fiscal period.

In 1988, the government therefore introduced several changes to the treatment of farm income and losses. On one hand, the changes *increase* the amount of farm losses deductible in a year by a part-time farmer against other sources of income from $5,000 to as much as $8,750 ($2,500 plus half of the next $12,500). Part-time farming losses that cannot be claimed against other sources of income because of this rule may be carried back three years and forward up to ten years, and deducted against farm income in those years. The new tax rules maintain the benefit of cash accounting, but only in cases where there is *positive farm income*. This means where revenues exceed expenses. On the other hand, the new rules limit the opportunity for tax sheltering of other income through continuing farm losses. There is now a "mandatory inventory adjustment" in respect of purchased inventories on hand, in years when cash basis accounting produces a farm loss. Any inventory adjustment that reduces a loss of one year will be taken into account in determining the following year's income.

Objective criteria are being considered to allow most taxpayers to determine in advance whether they will be considered full-time farmers or part-time farmers in a given year. Some of these have not yet been implemented. Moreover, special provisions are being studied to ensure that start-up farmers will be in a position to claim start-up losses against other sources of income.

Generally, if a person is going to be involved in farming and expects to have losses from time to time, operating the farm as an unincorporated venture should be considered as long as the taxpayer has other income against which to offset these losses. On the other hand, if it is expected that a farm operation will be profitable on an ongoing basis, incorporation should be considered. This is because farm income of up to $200,000 a year qualifies for the small-business tax rate. There is then an opportunity to reinvest as much as 80 cents on the dollar for expansion on an after-tax basis.

CHAPTER 15

The Art of Buying a Business and the Use of Holding Companies

Introduction

From the point of view of taxation, one of the worst traps that you can possibly fall into is buying shares of a private business in your own name. Proper tax planning almost always involves the use of a holding company for business acquisitions. If you take the easy way out and transact directly, you could end up paying more taxes as a result of this one error than from all your other mistakes combined.

Holding companies have many other uses beyond being the ideal vehicle for business acquisitions. In fact, they are the key to "empire building." However, before we can fully appreciate the use of holding companies and their role in the tax system, a short review of some preceding material is in order. As described in the last two chapters, the Income Tax Act is designed so that corporate taxes are levied on business income at one of several different effective rates:

- Income that qualifies for the small-business deduction (including income of a Canadian-controlled private corporation from manufacturing below $200,000) is taxed at approximately 20%.
- Income that is from manufacturing but does not qualify for the small-business deduction is taxed at 35%.
- Income that neither qualifies for the small-business deduction nor is related to manufacturing is taxed at 40%.

When a dividend is received by an individual from an "operating company" (Op Co), the system of gross-up and credit at least partially compensates for the fact that the dividend is a distribution out of profits that have already been taxed once. The shareholder is credited for at least part of the corporate taxes previously paid.

It is, however, possible that an individual shareholder might not own an interest in Op Co directly but through a "holding company" (Hold Co). In such circumstances, dividends would pass from Op Co to Hold Co before the individual could receive any funds personally. (See figure 15-1.)

Figure 15–1   **Dividend Flow From Operating Company Through Holding Company to Individual**

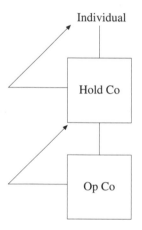

The Taxation of Intercorporate Canadian Dividends Out of Business Income

If dividends were taxed as they passed from one corporation to another (out of business income), in a *chain* of corporations, there would be less and less ultimately available for the person at the "top" of the chain. If that were the case, the individual would suffer double and triple taxation, depending on how many corporations stood between the individual and the source of income in the first place. This is illustrated in the example in Figure 15-2, which assumes (hypothetically) that intercorporate dividends out of business income eligible for the small-business deduction were subject to *even one dollar* of tax. Instead of receiving $80 (without Hold Co), the individual would receive only $79 (with Hold Co).

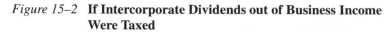

Figure 15–2 **If Intercorporate Dividends out of Business Income Were Taxed**

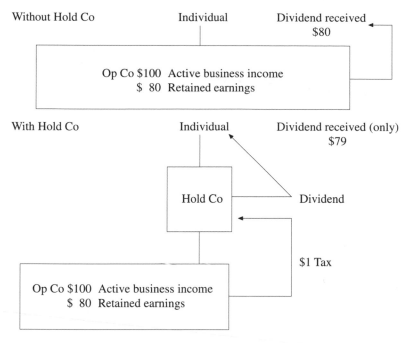

To avoid double taxation, the system was designed so that only the corporation that earns business income (i.e., Op Co) pays tax on that amount and type of profit. If there is any further tax to be paid, the rules were also designed so that this additional tax is not extracted until the *individual* (or individuals) who controls the holding company ultimately receives dividends. Thus, dividends out of business income have traditionally passed tax-free between a parent corporation and a subsidiary.

You should note that a holding company *itself* pays no tax as long as it owns more than 10% of the paid-up capital and the voting powers of the corporation that paid the dividend. If a top-tax-bracket individual were to receive a dividend *personally,* he or she would only retain about 55% of the underlying profits.

Where a holding company owns an interest of "10% or less," this is referred to as a "portfolio investment." Portfolio dividends are also subject to a special 25% flat-rate (refundable) tax, dealt with in Chapter Thirteen, which is repaid to the holding company at the time dividends are, in turn, distributed to the shareholders.

Figure 15–3 **The Flow of Dividends out of Small-Business Profits to Holding Companies**

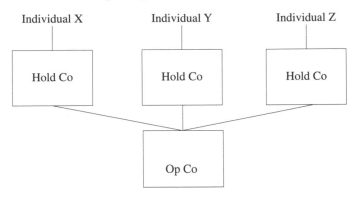

Op Co's pre-tax profit from active business		$100,000
Less: 20% corporate tax		20,000
Retained earnings		$ 80,000
Funds available for distribution		$ 80,000
Amounts received by each holding company ($80,000 ÷ 3)		$ 26,666

Tax-Planning Opportunities

If more than 10% of an operating business is acquired, the purchase should be structured through a holding company so that the acquired corporation can end up *paying for itself* by flowing dividends through to its new parent. The following example illustrates the advantages of using a holding company to make an acquisition of an operating business.

Assume that an individual, X, is an investor in the 45% bracket. X would like to acquire more than a 10% interest in Op Co. He negotiates with the prospective vendor, and the purchase price is settled at $100,000. Assume, as well, that X does not have the necessary cash to make the purchase. He does, however, know of a lending institution that is willing to finance the acquisition.

Effectively, the transaction can be structured in one of two ways: either X can make the acquisition personally, or he can use a holding company to do so on his behalf.

Presumably, X would not make an investment in Op Co unless he felt sure that the investment would ultimately pay for itself. In other words, he would expect that dividends from the newly acquired company would subsidize its cost. If X makes the purchase in his own name, he would have to draw dividends over a period of time so that his after-tax retention is sufficient to pay off the financing of $100,000. As described in the examples in Chapter Nine, an individual in the 45% tax bracket pays an effective tax of about 31% on Canadian dividend income – after the gross-up and credit. Thus, X would need $145,455 of *gross* dividends to retain a net amount of $100,000 for purposes of discharging his bank indebtedness.

Figure 15–4   **Individual Purchases Business**

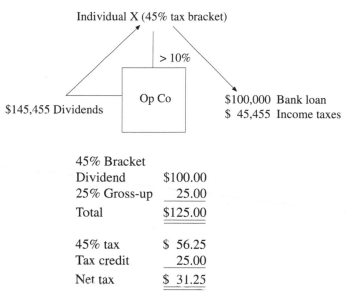

Individual X (45% tax bracket)

> 10%

Op Co

$145,455 Dividends

$100,000 Bank loan
$ 45,455 Income taxes

45% Bracket
Dividend	$100.00
25% Gross-up	25.00
Total	$125.00

45% tax	$ 56.25
Tax credit	25.00
Net tax	$ 31.25

Effective tax on dividends is 31.25%
Let D = Gross dividends needed to pay off bank
0.6895 D = $100,000
D = $145,455

In contrast, if a holding company is used to structure the purchase, Op Co will only have to generate $100,000 of dividends to its new "parent." As long as the parent holds more than 10% of the shares of Op Co, the dividend will be received tax-free and can then be paid over *directly* to the lending institution. To summarize, with proper planning, *it is possible for X to save over $45,000 for every $100,000 of purchase cost.*

Carrying this example one step further, if an extra $45,000 is not needed to pay taxes at the personal level, Op Co "saves" not only the dividend itself, but an even greater amount of "earning power." If Op Co is extremely profitable and pays taxes at the high corporate rate, the fact that $45,455 is not needed translates to an earning power of $75,758. This is illustrated in Figure 15-6.

Figure 15–5   **Holding Company is Used to Purchase Business**

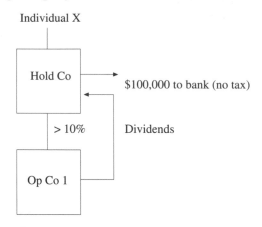

Individual X

Hold Co → $100,000 to bank (no tax)

> 10%   Dividends

Op Co 1

Only $100,000 is needed to pay off loan
Op Co "saves" $45,455 of dividends

Figure 15–6   **Op Co "Saves" $75,758 of Earning Power**

Earnings	$75,758
40% tax	30,303
Dividend (not needed)	$45,455

From the foregoing, it becomes evident that you *must* use a holding company as a vehicle to acquire shares of other companies, at least where the share interest is greater than 10%. *To do otherwise would result in unnecessary personal taxes that could be easily avoided with proper planning!*

Although the example assumes that the purchase price is borrowed from a lending institution, the same planning would hold true even if X acted as his own banker. He would want to be able to recoup his investment on a tax-free basis, without the necessity of extracting dividends subject to personal taxes. This can be achieved by lending his own capital to the holding company, which would in turn acquire Op Co. Dividends could then be paid from Op Cop to the holding company and the funds could be used to repay X's own advances.

Is there a catch? You might ask why the government has been so magnanimous in permitting such a wonderful opportunity to structure business acquisitions. Fortunately, there is no oversight in the law and the use of holding companies for such purposes is by no means a sham nor does it constitute undue tax avoidance.

The reason the government has beneficial rules on the flow of intercorporate dividends is that for every acquisition there is a corresponding sale. So far, we have only examined the position of the purchaser. For every purchaser there is a vendor who will (at least in theory) be paying a "capital gains tax" as a result of having sold his or her interest in Op Co. If the government gets its capital gains tax "up front" from the vendor, it may as well make it easier for the purchaser to buy.

You might also wonder whether the government is sacrificing substantial revenue by permitting a purchaser to structure his or her affairs to avoid taxes on dividends. Actually there is no significant difference from the treasury's standpoint, as we will see in the next section.

The Relationship between Dividends and Capital Gains

The next example depicts the relationship between dividends and capital gains.

	25%	40%	45%
Effective tax on $100 dividend (after gross-up and credit)	$ 6	$25	$31
Effective tax on $100 capital gain (taxable gain is $75)	$19	$30	$33

As discussed in Chapter Nine, the effective tax on dividends is only 6% to someone who is in the 25% bracket. Thus, taxpayers in 25% brackets will pay substantially less tax on dividends than they would on capital gains. However, where an individual is in a 40% or 45% bracket, the difference between receiving a dividend and a capital gain is not really significant. (It would be rare for a vendor of a business to be in a tax bracket below 40%.) Thus, the government has obviously decided that it really doesn't matter whether a tax on capital gains is paid by a vendor or whether a tax on dividends is charged to a purchaser!

Of course, no attempt is made by the government to publicize the advantages of using holding companies for business acquisitions. Presumably, Revenue Canada officials would not be too upset about receiving tax dollars *twice* – once from a vendor when he or she pays tax on capital gains arising from the sale, and again from the purchaser who struggles to pay for an acquisition that has been made personally.

As you might expect, the lifetime capital gains tax exemption may have a dramatic effect on a vendor's tax position. Barring any further rule changes, it may be possible for a vendor to sell shares of a Canadian-controlled private corporation engaged in an active business and effectively escape taxes, especially if the share ownership has been split among family members and the total capital gain per person is under $500,000. On the other hand, a purchaser, by using a holding company, can complete his or her acquisition without paying any personal income taxes at all!

Corporate Reorganizations

The use of holding companies also has advantages when it comes to reorganizing existing business situations. Assume, for illustration, that A, B, and C are unrelated individuals, each of whom owns one-third of the issued shares of an operating company. The operating company, for purposes of this example, has $80,000 in surplus cash that has been generated from business operations in which $100,000 had been earned and taxed at 20%. While A, B, and C get along quite well when it comes to administering the daily affairs of their company, they do not necessarily see eye to eye when it comes to investments. A is a big spender and would like to draw his share of the surplus funds as a dividend in order to meet his living requirements; B, on the other hand, wishes to invest his share of the money in term deposits; while C would like to acquire real estate. Under the existing structure of the company, illustrated in Figure 15-7, a problem exists, because the diverse objectives could not be realized without paying out taxable dividends.

Figure 15–7 **Before Reorganization**

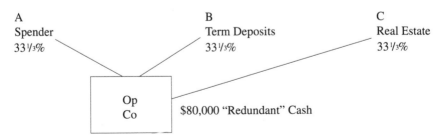

Figure 15–8 **Holding Companies Can be Used to Meet Shareholders'
Diverse Requirements**

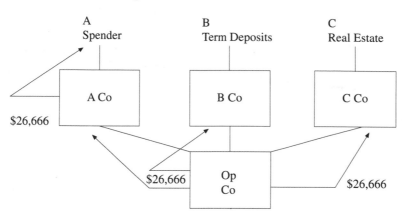

If, however, the shareholders each had personal holding companies, the problem could be solved. Using special provisions of the Income Tax Act, A, B, and C could each transfer their shares to their own holding companies (on a tax-free basis) in exchange for shares of the holding company. Op Co could then pay three dividends of $26,666 to each of the "new" shareholders. A could draw his portion as a further dividend and use the after-tax proceeds for living expenses, while B and C could cause their holding companies to invest in term deposits and real estate respectively.

A could obtain a further advantage by dividing the ownership of A Co among his family. If the Op Co dividend of $26,666 were split between the family members, it is possible that the tax bite could be eliminated completely.

Another advantage of the holding-company structure just described is that A, B, and C would each be free to involve his family in the ownership of his personal holding companies without necessarily consulting the other "partners." In cases where the shares of Op Co are held directly, B might (for example) object to A's spouse being a shareholder. No similar objections could be voiced by B with respect to A Co's share structure.

In summary, holding companies can be very effective in segregating the diversified spending or investment desires of business owners from their common operating objectives. There are also other advantages. By keeping Op Co free from excess or "redundant" assets, if business ever turns sour, there is less for the creditors to seize – although this does not mean that a corporation can pay large dividends when bankruptcy is already imminent. In addition, Op Co becomes far more saleable if it does not own assets that a prospective purchaser would not be interested in acquiring. Investments out of excess profits could be made by the holding companies just as easily, and there is no need for any prior payment of personal taxes.

While holding companies have their advantages as a vehicle to reorganize business situations, the complexities of rearranging one's affairs should not be understated. For example, specific tax rules must be followed in order to transfer shares in a business to a holding company without attracting tax. In addition, if A, B, and C had owned their shares in Op Co before 1972, certain other tax problems could arise with respect to capital gains considerations. These complexities would have to be handled by qualified legal and accounting professionals.

Finally, I must stress that the use of holding companies is primarily for the benefit of flexibility. The fact that A Co is owned only by A, and B Co by B, etc., will *not* provide for a multiple use of the small-business deduction. For all practical purposes, the entire group of companies will only be permitted to earn $200,000 annually at low corporate rates. (An exception would be where one or more of the holding companies is *independently* involved in operating an active business.)

Certainly, the use of holding companies for the purpose of reorganizing existing structures is worth exploring, and they should almost always be used for business acquisitions.

Bringing Buyers and Sellers Together

A comparison of the net tax costs of dividends and capital gains for taxpayers in various marginal brackets lends itself to some excellent planning opportunities when buyers and sellers are being brought together. An adviser working with both parties and without any personal involvement can help greatly to facilitate business acquisitions.

For example, if a prospective vendor of a business is in a low tax bracket and has already used up his or her capital gains tax exemption, it may be advantageous for that individual to take a dividend *before* selling his or her shares. Of course, if he or she takes a dividend, this would reduce the tangible net worth of the company and would result in a corresponding decrease in the purchase price. If the purchase price is reduced by the same amount as the dividend, the vendor's capital gain would become that much smaller and the tax thereon is decreased as well.

Very often, good timing can help a deal progress much more smoothly. If a business sale is being negotiated towards the end of the year, it may be advantageous for the vendor to take a dividend before December 31. He or she would then sell the shares (for a smaller price) on January 2, and in this manner, the dividend and the capital gain would be reported in different years.

The Ideal Corporate Structure

Under what I consider the "ideal" corporate structure, X should own his shares in Op Co through a holding company. It doesn't really matter whether the holding company has been used to acquire Op Co from someone else, or whether the business of Op Co was *started* by X in the first place.

As long as Op Co earns active business income that qualifies for the small-business deduction, it should float its after-tax profits up to Hold Co by way of dividends. The involvement of X's spouse in the ownership of Op Co (indirectly through the holding company) is optional. If the family only has one business, it is generally advantageous for both X and X's spouse to participate in the ownership. If there is a second business operation *unrelated to the first,* it would usually be more advantageous for X to own all of the shares of the first corporation and for X's spouse to be involved only in the second business. In this manner, it may be possible to obtain two low-rate tax bases instead of one. (See the last few pages of Chapter Thirteen.)

As Hold Co receives dividends (tax-free) from the business income of Op Co, the dollars that are not needed for business expansion could be retained corporately for investments or could be paid out as dividends to the shareholders.

Expanding the Business Empire

As an offshoot to the "ideal" corporate structure, there is also the opportunity to use the profits of Op Co as capital to invest in further business acquisitions as shown in Figure 15-9. If X (the indirect owner of Op Co 1) becomes interested in a new venture, the holding-company structure would enable him to acquire the new business without any personal tax penalty. Again, the source of the funds would be Op Co 1, which would first pay dividends to Hold Co. The holding company would then reinvest these funds to acquire Op Co 2. The shareholders of Op Co 2 can actually be any combination of family members. Wherever possible, you would consider creating a structure under which the two businesses are not associated for tax purposes.

Figure 15–9   **Structure for Further Business Acquisitions**

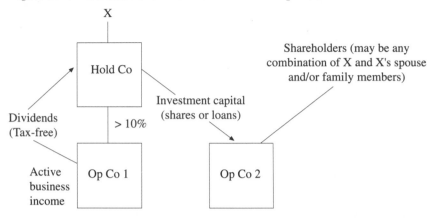

The advantage of having the businesses of Op Co 1 and Op Co 2 in separate corporations goes beyond the potential of doubling up on the small-business tax rate. This structure also facilitates a sale of *either* business and the retention of the other. If separate businesses are under one "corporate roof," a sale becomes much more difficult. In addition, X may consider involving key employees in the ownership of one business without necessarily having them participate in the growth of the other.

From Figure 15-9 you should also be able to visualize the benefits when Op Co 2 happens to be a company whose only asset is real estate used by Op Co 1 as business premises. Keeping the real estate in a separate corporation generally facilitates business arrangements. It may be possible to sell the real estate without disposing of the operating business and vice versa. In addition, you can involve key employees in the business activities without also making them equity holders in the real estate.

The Era of the Holding Company

We are now well into the era of the holding company in Canada. There are many who feel that a multitude of companies tends to be somewhat cumbersome and may diminish the effectiveness of business operations. This could be true. You must always weigh the business advantages and disadvantages of two alternative approaches before making *any* decision. Prior to incorporation, you must determine in each case whether or not the dollars to be saved warrant the existence of a new company.

If the owners of Op Co are not looking to expand and all profits are needed for their personal living requirements, a holding company may not be useful. On the other hand, for substantial share acquisitions, a holding company is mandatory. In practice, decisions can only be made on the basis of specific facts and with the aid of your professional advisers. Of course, an understanding of the tax system helps.

CHAPTER 16

A Commonsense Approach to Estate Planning

Your major concern in estate planning should be to ensure that your assets eventually pass on to your designated heirs – preferably without Revenue Canada taking too large a share. The first step in minimizing taxes is to know what you are up against. The current tax system is designed so that wealth is taxed as and when it is accumulated. Subject to the lifetime capital gains exemption, each time you realize a capital gain, three-quarters of your profit is taxed on a pay-as-you-go basis. This is the opposite of the rules prior to 1972, under which capital growth accumulated during an individual's lifetime and was not taxed until death. At that time, the old Estate Tax Act applied, with calculations based on a person's net worth.

Under the present system, since capital gains are only taxed when realized, you can always postpone the necessity of sharing profits by not selling your property. In Chapter Seven, for example, we explored the idea of borrowing against increases in values to extend your investment holdings.

Can capital gains be avoided completely? In the absence of specific tax rules, there are only three ways that come to mind: giving property away, becoming a non-resident, and death. Provisions have, however, been designed to prevent an easy escape. We have seen, for example, that a gift of property to anyone other than a husband or wife is a deemed disposition at fair market value. A gift will thus trigger accumulated capital gains, although future growth will pass to the benefit of the recipient.

Rules have also been designed to prevent anyone from avoiding taxes by becoming a non-resident. At the time of departure from Canada, the Income Tax Act deems a disposition at fair market value on many kinds of capital property, such as publicly traded securities. The deemed disposition forces a taxpayer who is giving up Canadian residence to include in his or her income the taxable capital gains portion of the difference between the cost and the fair market value of property at the time of departure. Taxpayers are permitted to request a postponement until an actual sale is made – provided they furnish adequate security to the tax collector.

Deemed Dispositions on Death

Even if there were tax advantages, not everyone wishes to leave Canada or give away property. Eventually, therefore, everyone encounters the "ultimate" of the deemed dispositions – that which takes place upon death. The tax rules are summarized in Figure 16-1.

Figure 16–1   **Deemed Dispositions Upon Death of a Taxpayer**

Beneficiary	*Type of Property*	*Deemed Proceeds*
Spouse or Spousal Trust	Non-Capital	– No Tax Implications
	Capital	– Cost (Adjusted Cost Base)
	Depreciable	– Undepreciated Capital Cost (UCC)
Anyone Else	Non-Capital	– No Tax Implications
	Capital	– Fair market value (FMV)
	Depreciable	– Fair market value (FMV) after 1992

Non-Capital – Cash, Government of Canada Savings Bonds, term deposits, life insurance proceeds

Capital – Most corporate bonds, land, personal effects (jewellery, art, etc.), shares in public and private corporations

Depreciable – Buildings

From the schedule, it is evident that the consequences of death depend on two factors: to whom the property is bequeathed and the kind of property the deceased had. For non-capital property such as cash, Canada

Savings Bonds, and life insurance benefits, there are no income-tax implications whatsoever – no matter who the individual's beneficiary happens to be. This is because cash, Canada Savings Bonds, and other non-growth assets represent income on which taxes have already been paid. In the case of life insurance, the proceeds are not taxable since policy premiums are not deductible.

With respect to all other property, husband and wife are considered as the equivalent of one person. No tax need be paid until the last of the two dies. Thus, whenever capital property is bequeathed to a spouse, there is a (tax-deferred) transfer at cost. No gain is recognized until the recipient spouse either sells the property or, in turn, dies and passes it on to someone else. Similarly, depreciable property passes at undepreciated capital cost (cost minus accumulated depreciation for tax purposes).

If capital property or depreciable property is passed to heirs other than a spouse, there is deemed disposition immediately before death at fair market value. This will trigger all accrued capital gains on the deceased's last tax return. To the extent that the deceased still had all or part of the lifetime capital gains exemption yet available, no taxes will become payable.

The Use of Spousal Trusts

The concept of the husband-wife unit is perhaps the most important factor when it comes to estate planning. To repeat, there is complete "rollover" (that is, a tax-deferred transfer) when property passes from either spouse to the other. The rollover applies not only to outright bequests, but, as well, whenever property is left to a *trust* for the benefit of the surviving spouse.

The "spousal trust" may have two advantages. The first pertains to situations in which an individual feels that his or her spouse is either not interested in administering property or does not have the necessary expertise. Instead of leaving property directly to the spouse, the person drawing up his or her will can create a trust. This gives the "testator" (the person making up his or her will) the opportunity to appoint outside executors and trustees. In this manner, the responsibility for investment and business decisions can either be taken away entirely from the other spouse or the burden can be shared with the spouse. The second advantage of a spousal trust is even more important. Leaving property in trust, instead of outright, gives the testator the opportunity to control the *ultimate* disposition of his or her property – even after death.

If, for example, you were preparing your will today, you should start by estimating your current net worth in the event of death. Let us assume, for purposes of illustration, that this amounts to $500,000. Now, before you assume that this is an unrealistic amount, note that most business owners, professionals, and executives are worth much more dead than alive because of life insurance. Estates ranging from half a million dollars and up are therefore not uncommon. Returning to your situation, assume you have one spouse and four children. Your objectives are, first, to protect your spouse and, second, to provide for the children. If you were to leave all your property directly to your spouse, he or she could then do whatever he or she wanted with the assets. Your spouse could remarry and give all the property to the new spouse. Your spouse could spend all the money, lose all the assets in the stock market, gamble away everything in Las Vegas, have more children and disinherit your children, or, conversely, take the capital and triple it.

The point is, you don't know what would happen. Thus, by leaving your property in trust, you could control the ultimate disposition. You would have the opportunity to appoint trustees and executors so that your spouse could not act alone. If you followed standard practices, you would nominate three trustees or a trust company. If individual trustees were appointed, the power to make all decisions would usually be left to the majority.

If you made these arrangements, the trustees would have a dual responsibility after your death – to your spouse and to the children. Your will would provide for the assets to be maintained for your spouse's benefit with the residual amount to be divided among the children upon your spouse's death.

You would instruct the trustees to pay out capital amounts (in addition to income) upon reasonable request only. For example, if your spouse remarried and proceeded to ask the trustees for $200,000 out of the estate to finance his or her new mate's business, the request would presumably be refused. After all, the trustees could not agree to anything that might jeopardize the position of the children.

On the other hand, if your spouse were to approach the trustees after your death for $5,000 towards the purchase of a new car, the trustees would probably sanction such a withdrawal of capital. After all, one of the objectives of building an estate is to ensure that a spouse can maintain a certain lifestyle.

The trust-will therefore allows for the fulfillment of two basic objectives: protecting a surviving spouse and also (ultimately) providing capital for your children.

In many cases, a trust-will is *not* necessary – especially if the holdings of an estate are not complex. However, such an arrangement becomes almost mandatory where a husband and wife have children by previous marriages. *A trust arrangement is the only way to guarantee that the children of the deceased eventually inherit their parent's assets.*

Income-Tax Requirements for Spousal Trusts

For assets to pass into a spousal trust on a tax-deferred basis, the trust must meet two specific conditions:

- The surviving spouse must get all the income earned by the trust in his or her lifetime.
- No one other than the surviving spouse may encroach upon the capital of the trust before he or she dies.

The first rule requires the surviving spouse to receive all *income* earned *without any strings attached.* If you put a clause into a will prohibiting your spouse from deriving income from the trust if he or she remarries, or reducing the amount of income that he or she would be entitled to receive, this would negate the rollover benefits of the trust for tax purposes. You would still have a valid trust from a legal standpoint, but all assets passing into that trust would be received at fair market value. This would trigger the taxes on death that you are presumably trying to postpone.

The second rule contains another restriction and the difference is rather subtle. You can have a perfectly valid trust for tax purposes even if your spouse is *not* permitted to touch any of the *capital* (provided he or she receives all the income), as long as no one *else* can encroach on capital *either.*

Capital-Encroachment Powers

What is the advantage of a complete prohibition against capital encroachment? If you make up a will prohibiting your spouse from encroaching on capital, you can be quite certain that your children (or other heirs) will inherit at least the same amount of assets as went into the trust in the first place – even if your spouse spends or otherwise disposes of all the income received in his or her lifetime.

Returning to your $500,000 estate, I think it would be nice for you to be able to ultimately give $125,000 of assets to each of your four children. If you forbid your spouse to encroach on capital, this "objective" is easily attainable. On the other hand, is a blanket prohibition against capital encroachment really wise? If you left your spouse $500,000 of assets, today it may be reasonable to project an annual return of about 10%, or $50,000. While this might be more than adequate for his or her current needs, what about inflation? Of course, a lot depends on your spouse's age, spending requirements, the ages of the children, and so on. To completely prohibit capital encroachment can be somewhat risky in the long run unless an estate is very large. The term "very large" is itself subjective and each person must evaluate the meaning of this independently. Yet to allow your spouse an unlimited capital encroachment would negate the value of having a trust in the first place. You should therefore try for a flexible arrangement. The flexibility is achieved by appointing several trustees (generally including your spouse) and having each decision on capital encroachment left to the majority.

"Overprotecting" a Spouse

While providing adequately for a spouse is probably the prime objective of estate planning, I think that there is such a thing as "overprotection." In the classic case, a man dies leaving an estate of $5 million to a trust for his wife, with instructions that on her death, the assets are to pass to the children. At the time of the man's death, his wife is seventy years old. He, of course, has wrongly assumed that she will be dead within two or three years of his own death. He has forgotten that her life expectancy from age seventy is still *another fifteen years* (see Chapter Five). If the wife had her children when she was around the age of twenty-five, the children will then be in their sixties before their mother dies. In novels and movies, the children become disgruntled and "help" Mother along on her way to the pearly gates. In "real life," however, the family relationships often simply disintegrate.

When there are more than enough assets to go around, I think that it might be better social planning to divide these assets either during an individual's lifetime or at the time the first spouse dies. Even if taxes do become payable, the social benefits could outweigh the tax disadvantages. For instance, several years ago, a friend of mine asked me to provide some tax and general investment counselling to his widowed mother. My friend's father had recently died, leaving a will under which all assets were to be held in trust for his wife until her death, at which time there would be a distribution between his two children (both were in their mid-thirties at the time). My friend gave me a list of the available assets to work with.

I determined that the value of the estate was approximately $450,000 and that the anticipated income yield was $45,000 a year. When I met with my friend and his mother, the first question I asked was how much she needed for living. She answered, "About $3,000." I made some quick calculations and suggested that if her living requirements were $36,000 per annum, and the investment yield was only $45,000, she had best invest rather conservatively. She interrupted, however, and told me that she meant $3,000 *a year,* not each month. When she saw the look on my face, she began to explain. She told me that her house was paid for, she had never learned to drive a car, she didn't have expensive tastes in clothing, never took vacations, treated herself to a movie only once a week, and spent her other leisure time visiting her grandchildren. She assured me that $3,000 was more than adequate for her annual needs.

Under these circumstances, if my friend's mother does in fact live to be eighty-five years old, the $450,000 estate could be worth at least three times that amount. This is a good example of "overprotection." With all due respect to the deceased (whom I had never met), an estate of $450,000 is not large by today's standards. I really don't know whether I would have advised him to prepare his will any differently if I were in a position to do so. Perhaps if before his death he had had a frank discussion with his wife on the subject of her living requirements, he himself might have thought differently when making up his will. It might not have been such a bad idea to leave $50,000 directly to each of the couple's two children so that each one could pay off his home mortgage. If this had been done, "only" $350,000 would have passed to the wife.

The worst example of bad estate planning that I have ever seen involves the family of another friend. This friend has one brother and one sister and in each case the family income is approximately $50,000 a year. All three are therefore comfortable but are by no means wealthy. My friend has a father in his early seventies who is a widower. This man is now retired, having made about $2 million in real estate transactions over the years. In fact, a good deal of his assets today consist of vacant land.

My friend's father has informed his children that under the terms of his will, the assets are to bypass them completely and will vest, on his death, in the grandchildren. His reasoning is that, although he cannot avoid capital gains on his own death, by passing the assets to his grandchildren, there will be no further deemed dispositions for the next sixty years. (After all, if the assets were only to pass to his *children,* the next deemed disposition could conceivably take place thirty years sooner!) Needless to say, my friend and his brother and sister are a little upset with their father's version of estate planning.

One might argue that a father does not owe his children anything once they are out on their own and that, if he wishes to pass his assets to the grandchildren instead, he has every right to do so. However, the motivation here is not that the grandfather does not get along with his own children, but rather a somewhat paranoid desire to reduce taxes otherwise payable. What upsets my friend most is not his own disinheritance, but the fact that his children stand to be considerably wealthier than *he* is within a few short years without having earned anything on their own. This is a clear case of the tax tail wagging the social and economic dog.

Sometimes, it may be necessary to pay more taxes than might otherwise be possible just to maintain good family relationships. Certainly "overprotection" and unnecessary tax avoidance should be considered when estate planning.

Appointment of Executors

One of the most difficult tasks that we all must face is choosing proper executors. It is more than just an honour to be an executor of an estate; it is a responsibility. Executors must be given broad powers and must have good administrative abilities. They must make sure that the deceased's wishes are carried out and that all assets are collected together and allocated properly. There are various "tax elections" that may be made in the year of death in the course of filing final tax returns, and they must be aware of all options. The executors must often deal with matters such as selling property and negotiating the best possible prices. Most of all, there is the responsibility of maintaining a balance between the relative rights of the various beneficiaries. Wherever possible, an attempt must be made to avoid potential conflicts of interest. Often, people appoint their accountants and lawyers as executors because of professional competence but without considering possible difficulties.

One of the most interesting cases that I ever worked on involved such a situation. I received a call one day from an accountant friend of mine who asked me to help him solve a conflict of interest. He had been appointed as an executor of an estate by one of his clients, who then died leaving behind a mentally handicapped son as his sole heir. The client also left a thriving business and it was his intention (although not specifically mentioned in the will) that certain key employees be given the opportunity to acquire this enterprise at a "fair price." The employees were more than happy to exercise their option and asked the same accountant to stay on as their auditor and adviser as well. The accountant thus found himself in an awkward position. He could not possibly allow himself to be in a position where, in negotiating a purchase price for the business, he would have to choose between his first client's son and the prospective clients.

In this case, the conflict was resolved rather nicely. The accountant asked me to act on behalf of the key employees and represent them in formulating a bid. He, in turn, represented the estate. The purchasers of the business understood the necessity of such an arrangement and cooperated fully. An agreement was reached within a short period of time as to the purchase price and method of payment and everybody wound up content. Unfortunately, this does not always happen.

Potential conflicts of interest are not the only problem with which you must contend in appointing executors. In another recent situation, I was asked to help a client reorganize his business holdings and to do some estate planning. The estate was rather complex and the work took several months to complete. By the time of our final meeting in the lawyer's office, the will had already been prepared and had been reviewed several times. All that was left was to fill in a few of the details and sign it. At one point, my client's lawyer asked him to name some executors in addition to his wife. The client thought for a moment and named his brother-in-law – who lived in Lima, Peru. The lawyer and I looked at each other in amazement and then explained to the client that the choice of a brother-in-law in a far-off country as an executor is just not feasible. Fortunately, the client saw the logic behind our arguments and appointed a more suitable substitute.

The most common problem, though, occurs when parents appoint their children as executors. I have often been involved in cases where a client says to me: In the event my spouse predeceases me, I would like my oldest son, John, to be the executor.

The client usually thinks he knows what he is doing. He can give you all the right reasons. Not only is John the oldest child but he is a university graduate, has a good "business head," and gets along well with his brothers and sisters. The problem, however, is that any time you appoint one of your children as an executor, if you don't take other steps with which I will deal shortly, you set the stage for a life-long enmity between that child and his or her brothers and sisters.

Let me explain with an example. Let's assume, as we did before, that your net worth is $500,000 at the time of your death and that you have four children. Assume that your spouse predeceases you. I suggest that if your only asset were cash, you could almost get away with appointing a chimpanzee to act as the sole executor of your estate. One really doesn't need several college degrees to divide $500,000 by four and distribute $125,000 to each child.

And yet, no estate is that simple. There are always assets that are not divisible. Who, for example, will inherit your car? Who gets the family jewellery? What about the Group of Seven painting that hangs in your living room, or the gold pocket watch that you inherited from your grandfather?

As I mentioned before, executors must be given very broad powers. In fact, the clauses in a will prepared by most attorneys that deal with executors' rights and responsibilities tend to run perhaps three or four pages. This is more than just boiler-plate, designed to increase legal fees. Executors must be protected from lawsuits initiated by disgruntled beneficiaries. If an executor had to live in constant fear of getting sued, no one would ever accept such an appointment.

So the standard clause in the will states that an executor's decision is binding, and unless he or she has committed fraud, there is no recourse against his or her decision.

The problem basically is that anybody who picks one of his or her children as an executor must consider the types of properties that I just referred to which are not easily divisible and may have sentimental value to *several* of the children.

So, what can be done? There are really two choices. The first is to deal with all of these personal items specifically in the will. This is the textbook approach, but one which is frankly difficult to carry out in real life. This is because there may be literally hundreds of personal properties and a family's personal holdings tend to change from time to time.

What I recommend instead is that periodically you should have a family-council meeting with your children. For these purposes, the children do not all have to be adults. Children as young as eight or nine can understand this kind of subject as long as you use simple language. The idea is to sit down with your children and explain to them that, in the event that you and your spouse die, you have decided to appoint your son, John, as an executor. This means that he will have the job of distributing all your property. You can explain that the idea behind your will is to make the distributions equally, but that certain properties cannot be divided. Then, you can express your specific wishes. For example, John (being the only one old enough to drive) will inherit the family car. Mary, your only daughter, would receive the family jewellery, while Tom, who always liked the Group of Seven painting, would be able to keep that for himself. The gold pocket watch would then go to George.

If any of the children are unhappy with what you have decided, there are two possibilities. The first is that you can encourage the children to voice their opinions and, if expedient, to make trades between themselves. For example, what if Tom tells you that he really doesn't like the painting but he would rather have the gold watch, while George prefers the painting instead of that watch? Having the children resolve their differences in your presence might be better for all concerned.

Alternatively, even if the kids walk away unhappy, the point is that they are angry with *you* and not with John who is the executor of the estate. After all, once you are dead, it really doesn't matter whether your children are slightly angry at something that you may have done. On the other hand, you must count on their living with their brothers and sisters for most of the rest of their lives.

To summarize, whenever possible, avoid conflicts of interest. Think about this problem before you finalize the appointment of your executors – especially in family situations, keep the lines of communication open.

Special Rules – The Family Farm

So far, this chapter has only dealt with the general rules pertaining to transfers of property on death. However, there are special rules that apply whenever a family farm is transferred from one generation to another. As long as the farm is located in Canada and is transferred to either children, grandchildren, or great-grandchildren, a transfer can take place with no capital gain being realized. (This is quite apart from the special $500,000 capital gains exemption.) These rules apply as long as the recipients of the farm are resident in Canada and the property had been used in farming by either the deceased, his or her spouse, or one or more children immediately before death.

Over ten years ago, the Income Tax Act was amended to extend the family-farm "rollover" (which originally applied to only unincorporated farms) to interests in family-farm partnerships and shares in the capital stock of family-farm corporations. In most situations, it would now be advantageous to reorganize the structure of one's farm holdings to take advantage of the corporate tax rules for small businesses.

The Family Farm – Recent Changes

In 1984, the government made more significant changes with respect to family farms. First, on the death of an individual, it is now possible to elect to transfer farm property, including an interest in a family-farm partnership or shares in a family-farm corporation, to a child or children at any value between the cost amount of the property and its fair market value. Thus, if a farmer dies and has losses available for carry-forward at that time, or dies early in a given year and has little income otherwise taxable, it may pay to trigger some capital gains. The advantage of an election at an amount in excess of the deceased's cost would be to provide a higher cost for tax purposes to the heir or heirs who receive the property.

For the purposes of the rollover rules, the definition of the word "child" has been expanded for transfers of farm property to include any person who, at any time before he or she attained the age of twenty-one years, was in law or in fact in the custody and control of the transferor and was wholly dependent on him for support. This would include, for example, foster children who were not legally adopted.

In addition, the farm rollover was extended to include property leased by an individual to his or her own family-farm corporation or to a family-farm corporation or partnership of the spouse or child. Such property will be deemed to be used by the owner in the business of farming for the purposes of providing a tax-deferred rollover. This measure gives farmers far more flexibility in organizing the structure of their farm holdings.

In the past, much concern had been voiced about the situation in which farm property is transferred by a taxpayer to a child in the transferor's lifetime and the child subsequently dies. Under the prior income-tax rules, there was no provision for a rollover if the farm was then passed back to the parent who made the transfer in the first place. After 1983, this problem has been resolved. Thus, if a parent reacquires an interest in a family farm (incorporated or otherwise) upon the death of a child, there is an election to deem the transfer back to take place at any value between the cost amount to the deceased child and the fair market value.

Finally, in cases where a family farm is sold to third parties, the special $500,000 lifetime capital gains exemption is also available. As with any other small business, if interests are owned by several family members, the opportunity arises for multiple use of this special incentive.

Tax-Free Transfer of Small-Business Holdings

The concept of the family-farm rollover was also extended, several years ago, to shares of a "qualified small business" that are left to children or grandchildren. A qualified small business is any Canadian-controlled private corporation that earns active business income. Thus, qualified businesses include (among others) companies engaged in wholesaling, retailing, construction, manufacturing, natural resources, and transportation, as well as certain service companies.

Under the special tax rules, every owner of shares of a qualified business is given a (maximum) lifetime $500,000 exemption from capital gains.

The $500,000 limit applies irrespective of how many businesses an individual owns and/or how many children he or she has. An individual is free to allocate his or her $500,000 amount in any way that he or she desires, and the allocation can take place either during one's lifetime or upon one's death.

Assume, for example, that you have shares in a Canadian private business with a cost of $100,000 and a fair market value of $1,350,000. If you die without having previously taken advantage of this special provision and leave these shares to one or more of your children, your capital gain will be $750,000 (instead of $1,250,000).

There are several opportunities for effective planning. First, you need not wait until death to take advantage of your $500,000 limit. If, for example, you wish to admit your children into your business, the special rules will help you greatly in meeting your objective. Using the above numbers, it is possible for a father or mother to literally give 40% of a business "tax-free" to one or more children. This would be especially advantageous when the children are already active in the business. The 40% factor just happens to be the percentage that would apply in this particular case:

Portion of business transferred to son/daughter		40%	
Fair market value	$1,350,000	$540,000	
			$500,000 gain is "exempt"
Cost for tax purposes	$ 100,000	$ 40,000	

As long as the difference between the cost of the interest sold and its fair market value is under $500,000, no gain need be recognized. In the preceding case, however, the child or children would pick up 40% of all future growth.

Effective tax planning also involves taking advantage of the potential to double up on the $500,000 exemption by *initially* involving both husband and wife in the ownership of a business. It is inappropriate to have a Canadian private business capitalized with only a few shares. To take an extreme position, what if a company were owned equally by husband and wife, each of whom had only one share? The problem is that, no matter who dies first, the surviving spouse would not have control of the business if the deceased leaves his or her share to the children. Fortunately, this problem can easily be corrected by simply subdividing the shares (ten for one, or a hundred for one, etc.) as soon as possible. The splitting of shares would *not* attract any income taxes.

What is even more inappropriate is a case in which a company is owned 99% by husband and only 1% by wife. If the wife dies first, all she is capable of transmitting to the children is her 1%. Unless the company is worth somewhere in excess of $50 million there is no possibility that her 1% could have appreciated by $500,000 since its acquisition.

A disproportionate ownership is also not well suited to splitting income by way of payment of dividends – even where separate classes of shares are held. I have dealt with this in previous chapters. The only time I would suggest that a company be owned completely by a husband (to the full exclusion of his wife) would be where separate businesses exist, each of which would qualify for the small-business tax rate. In these circumstances, if the husband owns 100% of the first company, his wife should own 100% of the second. If the family's intention is to own one business only, the ownership should be spread fairly equally.

If you are faced with a grossly disproportionate ownership among shareholders of a single family business, a reorganization of capital can be carried out. This is quite technical and requires professional assistance. The reorganization would allow the wife in the previous example to participate in *future* growth, which she could pass on to the children as part of her $500,000 exemption if she were to die first.

Transfers of Small-Business Corporations – Recent Changes

The opportunities of transferring property on a tax-deferred basis to a foster child or from a deceased child back to his parents, recently provided for family farms, have also been extended to shares of other Canadian-controlled private corporations engaged in active business. However, the tax which may be deferred in conjunction with family-farm rollovers remains unlimited, while the maximum capital gains which may be eliminated on the transfer of shares of other small-business ventures is limited to $500,000.

Estate Planning and Life Insurance

The topic of estate planning couldn't possibly be covered without some reference to the role of life insurance as part of the overall picture. As a bare minimum, you should insure your life so that there need be no forced sale of assets at the time of death solely for the purpose of paying income taxes. For that purpose, some kind of permanent insurance is necessary and term insurance will not usually be sufficient. (A term policy will not help if it expires before your death.)

Basically, you should determine the tax consequences resulting from deemed dispositions on death for bequests to beneficiaries other than a spouse. Your accountant can assist you in putting together the figures. You would then apply combined federal and provincial marginal tax rates to the anticipated income. In order to be fairly conservative, you might assume taxes of about 40%–45% on taxable gains after available exemptions have been used up.

Of course, the tax implications of death depend largely on the time of year in which you die. If you die early in a given year, the income arising from deemed dispositions might be taxed all by itself at favourable rates. However, if you die late in the year, the income from deemed dispositions is then added to all your other income of that year and the tax burden could be significant.

You should next calculate your available cash, Canada Savings Bonds, and "near cash," such as marketable securities. In addition, liquid assets realizable from the sale of a family business would be relevant if there is a buy-sell agreement between yourself and one or more partners. The minimum insurance you would then require would be that needed to discharge your tax liabilities after applying the liquid assets towards that purpose. Taxes arising from deemed dispositions may be spread over ten years, but each instalment would currently bear interest at 8%. This instalment interest is not tax-deductible and the financing therefore is expensive.

Of course, life insurance has additional uses beyond just paying taxes.

Its role is also to provide a larger income to your heirs, especially for a spouse and dependent children. If your estate is tied up in either vacant land that yields very little income or growth stocks that do not pay dividends, your spouse may be in a rather embarrassing financial position without proceeds from life insurance with which to generate a future flow of income. If you own a part-interest in a private business, life insurance is almost mandatory to assist the surviving partners in buying out the estates of those who die first.

For individuals who maintain liquid estates and who require the bulk of their protection in the early years, perhaps term insurance would be advisable. When it comes to a business situation, however, many advisers would opt in favour of a more permanent type of coverage. This is because most term policies are calculated to expire at age seventy, whereas the average individual will probably not die until one or two years later. Term insurance therefore provides protection for your early needs while your children are young, but it is not adequate for long-range business planning and the preservation of property that is not liquid, such as real estate. When it comes to estate planning, a good insurance agent is just as important a member of the team as your accountant or lawyer.

The Time for Planning Is Now

Unfortunately, people tend to postpone estate planning, the preparation of their wills, and similar matters, because the contemplation of death tends to be a bit distasteful. However, ask yourself, what would happen to your family if you died today? If you spend a few minutes thinking about the consequences, tax and estate planning will become much more important. *The time for effective planning is now.*

CHAPTER 17

How to Deal
with the Tax Collector

Reporting of Income

An individual is required to file a Form T1 for each year in which he or she owes tax before April 30 of the following year. An individual is also required to file this form within "a reasonable time" if a demand is made by the Minister. If an individual does not owe any taxes and does not receive a demand, he or she is generally not compelled to file. However, if an individual realizes a capital gain or loss that affects the lifetime exemption, he or she must file a return even if no taxes are payable.

If you receive a substantial portion of your income from salary, and tax deductions at source are large enough so that you have a refund owning, it is, of course, in your interest to voluntarily file a return to get back your overpayment. In addition, a tax return is required if a claim is made for the child tax credit.

Although not all individuals are required to file, the law provides that *every* corporation must file an income-tax return (Form T2) within six months after the end of each fiscal year. This return must show how income has been calculated as well as all taxes payable. In addition, if the company is exempt from tax, the return must indicate the reasons. A set of financial statements must accompany each return, together with schedules setting out such things as capital cost allowances, capital gains, and an explanation of differences between accounting income and income for tax purposes. All amounts owing should be paid on or before the due date for the filings to avoid (non-deductible) interest charges.

Contact with Revenue Canada

Your first contact with Revenue Canada is usually shortly after the required income-tax return is filed. In most cases, you will receive a Notice of Assessment stating that the return has been assessed as filed and a statement indicating the balance of tax owing either by you or by the government. Additional correspondence with Revenue Canada can usually be avoided if all required receipts, vouchers, forms, and documents are filed with your return.

Aside from the usual mathematical errors, which are picked up by computer, the most frequent cause of rejection or delay in processing a return is a form or voucher that is missing. You can never assume that Revenue Canada will know that you, in fact, have the missing document. For instance, assume that you were in full-time attendance at a Canadian university during the year and you submitted an official receipt for tuition fees for the fall session with your return. However, you also claimed the education credit for the same four months without submitting Form T2202 or Form T2202A. In this case, Revenue Canada will allow only your tuition fees and disallow the education credit.

Revenue Canada may contact you by telephone or letter, concerning your assessment or reassessment. Since anyone speaking on a telephone can state that they are from Revenue Canada, it is usually advisable to have all communication in writing. On the other hand, as long as a Revenue Canada official has identified himself or herself to your satisfaction, you may wish to reply by telephone in cases where the information is not confidential or crucial. Nevertheless, in many cases, it is preferable to deal with a written query so that you may analyse the information requested and formulate a precise answer. Your reply to any queries from Revenue Canada is very important because they would not be asking for additional information or explanations if they were totally happy with the information that you had submitted in the first place.

Analyse the information that is being requested and determine why it is wanted. Something that may seem quite logical to you may, in fact, trigger a rejection by Revenue Canada because of a specific section of the Income Tax Act. Then again, there may be another section which overrides the restriction and it then becomes your responsibility to inform the officials. Remember that not all employees of Revenue Canada have the same knowledge, expertise, or experience and you may be dealing with someone who has had only a few weeks of training and has a very limited knowledge of the Income Tax Act. It is in your interest to be patient and courteous at all times.

Assessments and Reassessments

You should note that Revenue Canada does not have to accept any return as filed and may assess or reassess the taxes for the year generally within three years from the date of an original assessment, or at any time if the authorities can prove fraud or misrepresentation or if a waiver has been signed by the taxpayer for that particular year. The subject of waivers will be covered later on in this chapter.

A Revenue Canada Audit

A request by Revenue Canada to examine your records, vouchers, receipts, cancelled cheques, deposit slips, bank statements, sales invoices, etc., is usually referred to as an audit. The audit may be restricted to only a few of your records or may encompass all of your records for one year or even several years. Some people take the attitude that something should always be left for the tax auditor to find. This is, however, a rather dangerous position because if the auditor finds one thing, he or she may continue looking until something else is found as well. Therefore, if your records are kept properly and only deductions that are permissible are taken, the audit should be of very short duration and no reassessment will be issued.

The auditor will complete the examination in as little time as possible if he or she is not unduly interrupted. The auditor may during the course of the examination make notes and if he or she cannot find certain answers while doing the examination, he or she will request explanations from you. Most audit queries can be satisfied by supplying a copy of a purchase invoice or a cancelled cheque or a receipt of some sort.

Don't be paranoid even though the tax auditor is usually there to try to extract more taxes than you would otherwise pay. Usually there is a specific reason for the audit. Possibly your entertainment and promotion expenses are too high. Sometimes Revenue Canada is simply investigating the particular industry that you are in or you have claimed a tax-shelter deduction and the validity of this is being questioned. In other cases, Revenue Canada may be looking at your records simply to see if payments you made are being reported by other people. On the other hand, they might also be checking to see if you have reported payments made by others who have already been audited.

It pays to cooperate. Remember that the tax auditor has extensive powers. He or she can obtain any information to determine whether or not you are complying with the law. An auditor is also permitted to examine the records of a third party to substantiate a particular fact, and if the auditor disagrees with your treatment, the onus is on you to prove he or she is wrong.

How to Prepare for the Audit

The tax auditor will normally telephone in advance to arrange an appointment. If the time requested is inconvenient for you, you need simply ask for an extension. As long as you are reasonable, the tax auditor will cooperate. State your reasons for asking for an extension. For example, if you are in the midst of your busy season or plan to be out of town and would rather be available during the course of the audit, explain your position calmly.

Find out exactly what is being audited and prepare accordingly. Usually the tax auditor will look at two or three taxation years. If you know what he or she wants, this will save you the trouble of digging out records that are unnecessary. Remember that a tax auditor can usually only go back three years unless fraud is suspected.

Try to adopt a friendly manner. If you have the space, provide a clean desk and a good working environment. It is important to discourage your staff from unnecessary contact with the Revenue officials. Specific people should be delegated to discuss the different matters. If a business is being audited, it is usually necessary to have only three people talk to the assessor. You, as principal owner of the corporation, will want to be available to provide general information as to how the business operates. Your bookkeeper should be the one who explains how the records are kept, especially if there are any unique features to your particular business. And finally, your public accountant should be on hand to answer questions pertaining to the actual preparation of the financial statements or tax returns.

The fact that you should make yourself available does not mean that you have to babysit. In fact, if you hover around the auditor and keep him or her from doing the job, this will create unnecessary ill will. I recommend that you arrange with the auditor to have a daily question-and-answer period. Ask the auditor to write down all of his or her questions and set aside a half-hour to an hour each day so that you can deal with these matters. This is preferable to interrupting everybody's schedule several times a day as the auditor comes up with different questions.

Following the Audit

When the audit is finished, take the initiative to ask the auditor in a straightforward manner if he or she is going to make any adjustments. If changes are going to be made, obtain full and complete explanations of each and every proposed change. Tell the tax auditor you would like an opportunity to consider these changes and that you will get back to him or her within a reasonable period. Then, assess these changes very carefully. Make use of the government's own published tax information so that you can get a better idea of what the official Revenue Canada position is. Actually, this is not a difficult thing to do.

In 1970, Revenue Canada inaugurated a series of Information Circulars and Interpretation Bulletins. The Information Circulars are aimed at informing the general public about procedural matters relating to the Income Tax Act. The Interpretation Bulletins provide Revenue Canada's interpretations of the various sections of the law it administers. Both of these sets of information are available to the general public. There are now over five hundred Interpretation Bulletins. An Interpretation Bulletin does not have the force of law. It simply reflects Revenue Canada's opinion as to how specific matters in the Income Tax Act should be dealt with. From time to time, disputes are taken to the courtroom and if Revenue Canada loses its case, an Interpretation Bulletin may be retracted and reissued. Nevertheless, it is important to know what Revenue Canada's opinion is. In general, Revenue assessors are bound by policy to follow the dictates of the official interpretations.

Once you know where you stand, go over each change with your public accountant and decide whether you are in agreement or whether you wish to challenge the change. Some changes might appear to be insignificant but you should realize that you may be setting a precedent for future years and there may be more serious consequences later on.

Waivers

In most cases, you will not be pressured by any time constraints as long as you are open and forthright with the Revenue officials with whom you are dealing. If it is taking you more time to assemble a defence for your position than you thought it would, try to set a reasonable deadline and you will find that the officials will cooperate.

Sometimes, however, you may encounter problems. Specifically, this is in cases where the actual audit and its aftermath take place as the normal "statute of limitations" approaches. As mentioned before, Revenue Canada cannot generally reassess after three years have passed following the date of a previous Notice of Assessment unless fraud or misrepresentation is alleged.

If the three-year limit is rapidly approaching, the Revenue authorities may feel pressured into issuing an arbitrary assessment adjusting your taxes just to keep the particular year open. To avoid this, it is usually in your interest in these circumstances to file a voluntary waiver of the statute of limitations. In this manner, you will be able to defend your position on an informal basis without having to cope with an official assessment until all the facts are in. Generally your accountant can advise you on whether a voluntary waiver is in your interest.

Resolving Contentious Issues

It is always important to resolve as much as possible before an actual reassessment is issued. This is because interest claimed by the authorities accumulates until all liabilities have been settled. You should note that, if the amount of tax requested is large, you may find that it is feasible to furnish security to the Minister in lieu of an actual tax payment. Proper security would include an assignment of a term deposit, a bank guarantee, or perhaps, in some instances, a mortgage against real estate that you own.

Make sure that your public accountant meets with the Revenue Canada auditor and presents your position as clearly and as emphatically as possible. Then, if the auditor and your accountant cannot agree, arrange a meeting with the auditor's superior to try to convince Revenue Canada that your original treatment was correct. It is important for you to persist at the audit level. If you find (in rare cases) that the tax auditor is abusive or expects your entire business to stop while you hunt down a receipt, touch base with your accountant to decide whether or not you should request a change of auditor. Certainly you will have the right to appeal if an assessment is eventually issued, and this may turn out to be the only solution. However, it is far less expensive to settle the matter at the initial audit level and, sometimes, to effect a compromise.

Special Audits – The Net-Worth Assessment

A Revenue Canada audit may not be restricted to the mere verification of a few vouchers, cheques, deposits, or sales. From time to time, the Department will proceed on what is called the "net-worth method." This type of procedure applies in instances where Revenue Canada officials suspect that a taxpayer has unrecorded income.

Here is how a net-worth assessment works. First, a Revenue Canada assessor will attempt to determine your assets less liabilities at the beginning of a certain year. To that, he or she will add your income declared since that time and deduct a reasonable allowance for your cost of living. These cost-of-living expenses will include anything from a toothbrush to your monthly mortgage payment. The result will then be compared to your assets less liabilities at the end of a certain period.

If the balance obtained at the end is greater than your opening assets minus liabilities plus your reported income after deducting your living expenses, Revenue Canada will assume that you have earned other income and will tax you on that amount as if you, in fact, had earned it. It is then up to you to show that certain amounts were received during that period that increased your net worth but did not constitute income for tax purposes, such as an inheritance, a windfall, or the non-taxable portion of capital gains.

Dealing with a Notice of Assessment or Reassessment

If you receive a Notice of Assessment or Reassessment with which you disagree, your first step is to file a Notice of Objection which must be submitted within ninety days from the date of mailing of the Notice of Assessment or Reassessment. You should note that late-filed Notices of Objection do not have to be accepted by the Minister and all taxes will then have to be paid without any further recourse.

The Notice of Objection must be prepared setting out all the relevant facts and reasons for the objection. It must be signed by the taxpayer or an authorized representative and sent by registered mail to the Deputy

Minister of National Revenue for Taxation in Ottawa. A separate Notice of Objection should be filed for each taxation year under dispute.

When the Notice of Objection is received in Ottawa, a copy is then sent to the local District Taxation Office of Revenue Canada for an independent review by the Appeals Section. Officials from that section will contact the taxpayer or an authorized agent, who may make further representations concerning the objection. There is the opportunity to discuss the facts and possibly resolve the contentious issues. If successful negotiations can be concluded at the District Office level, this will save the costs of further appeals and court appearances.

If the dispute cannot be resolved at the District Office level, the Appeals Section must report to the Minister who is then obliged to inform the taxpayer by registered mail that the Assessment or Reassessment has been confirmed.

I strongly advise you to put a great deal of effort into dealing with the Appeals branch to avoid a costly courtroom battle. Produce proof to support your position and evidence to corroborate your facts. Be prepared to have your accountant quote specific sections of the Income Tax Act and Regulations or to refer to Information Circulars and Interpretation Bulletins. It is generally also advisable to see what jurisprudence is available to help you substantiate your position. In other words, make use of the expertise and knowledge that you can get from professional help. Although the objection stage is fairly informal, keep in mind that much of the information gathered will be useful if you choose to pursue the matter later on through the courts.

Appeals to the Courts

After the Minister replies to an objection and either confirms it or reassesses (but not to the complete satisfaction of the taxpayer), the taxpayer has the right to appeal to the Tax Court of Canada or to the Federal Court of Canada. Under the law, an appeal must be made within ninety days from the mailing date of the Minister's reply. If the Minister fails to reply to the Objection within ninety days, the taxpayer may take the initiative and appeal to the courts instead.

The sittings of the Tax Court of Canada are generally in the spring and fall in all larger cities. The different judges are not restricted to sitting in any particular area, so that the person who presides over the hearings in any particular location will vary from sitting to sitting.

When a case is set down for hearing in a particular location, solicitors in the employ of the legal branch of the Taxation Division will generally arrive a short time in advance of the date of the hearings in order to review the Crown's case with the officials of the District Office and to prepare the Crown's arguments.

During this period, which may be only a few days, it is common for discussions to take place between the Department's solicitors and the taxpayer's representatives, and often settlements of the points involved are made at this time. Consequently, it is not uncommon for the Court to have a lengthy list of cases to be heard, only to find that the docket has shrunk to as few as two or three cases when the hearings actually begin. Cases that have already been conceded or settled in one way or another are either withdrawn by one or other of the parties involved, or a consent to judgement is filed, allowing the appeal in part.

Several factors must be considered before appealing to the courts. First, you must decide whether instituting an appeal will be cost effective. Are the additional dollars assessed worth the time, effort, and inconvenience involved? What are the costs of presenting an appeal, including the prospects of being forced to absorb court costs if you go to the Federal Court and lose? What are the costs of obtaining professional legal assistance? Although proceedings in the Tax Court of Canada are less formal, the Federal Court operates under strict rules of presentation and process and any failure to prepare and present a position properly may result in a losing case.

Summary

These factors add up to a time-consuming and expensive undertaking. I therefore cannot stress enough the need to negotiate and compromise whenever feasible at each step along the way, beginning with the audit itself. To whatever extent possible, every available avenue of objection and appeal should be taken, short of going to court.

Your main defences are good records, logical reasons for what you did, and competent tax planning. The best way to prepare for a tax audit is by sound thinking when your financial statements and tax returns are prepared in the first place.

EPILOGUE

Taking the "Ax" Out of Tax

If you have gotten this far without skipping too many chapters, you should now be quite familiar with just about every legitimate technique for effective tax reduction. Now it is time to apply these suggestions to your own situation. So, start again from the beginning. Open this book to the Table of Contents, and start making notes. Be brief. All you have to do is list some of the areas where you can take the "ax" out of your tax.

Begin with Chapter Two. List the fringe-benefit plans that you think are reasonable for you. The next time you are due for a raise, be ready for some serious negotiations. Remember, very often valuable benefits won't cost your employer a penny extra when compared to salary. If you earn your income from commissions, reread Chapter Three.

Are you ten years or less away from retirement? Is there any chance that you may be leaving the country soon? Are you thinking of selling your business? If the answer to any of these questions is yes, reread Chapter Four and make sure your boss (or accountant) buys a copy of this book and reads it too. If the answer to all these questions is no, go on to Chapter Five.

Do you have a Registered Retirement Savings Plan? If you do, continue to contribute. Keep in mind the advantages of spousal plans. If you still don't believe in RRSPs, reread Chapter Five – *slowly*. Study Chapter Ten and learn why you must plan carefully for your own retirement. You can count on government to help you, but not for your full support.

Do you have a program geared toward generating investment income? If not, start saving your pennies! Do you have more than $50,000 of capital and are you in a 40% bracket or higher? Do you have a son or daughter attending university? Remember, income splitting isn't difficult.

Are you separated or divorced or contemplating an end to your marriage? Protect yourself. If you don't look after your own interest, you will be the loser. Study Chapter Eight. Then seek professional advice geared towards your own circumstances.

Are you reading this book in the den of your Westmount or Forest Hill home or on a cruise ship bound for warmer weather or on the beach outside your Hawaii condominium? If your answer is yes, consider the benefits of the lifetime capital gains exemption and organize your investment portfolio accordingly.

Do you receive fees for services? Can you *diversify* your consulting activities so that you can be paid by several different customers or clients? If so, make an appointment with an accountant – even if it costs $100 or $150. After about an hour he or she will be able to tell you if incorporation is feasible.

If you own your own business or are planning to start one, reread chapters Twelve through Fourteen. I know they have lots of numbers and very few jokes and anecdotes. But they are worth the bother. Then, spend a morning with your accountant planning your strategy.

Are you about to buy or sell a business? See your advisers *before* you finalize a deal. Improper tax planning here can be the worst mistake you will ever make. Don't forget – this is the era of the holding company – don't fight progress. It's your money.

Don't ignore the inevitability of death. If you have a spouse, is he or she adequately protected? Is your spouse "overprotected"? Does your spouse know what you have and where it is? Communicate. Your lifestyles may depend on it.

Finally, if you are having problems with Revenue Canada, reread Chapter Seventeen. Keep your cool and make sure you have a good case. Remember, Revenue auditors are just people trying to do their jobs.

Looking Ahead

Certainly, some of the incentives, loopholes, and other opportunities to reduce taxes have been eroded by recent federal budgets and by former finance minister Michael Wilson's Tax Reform. As you probably know, the current investment climate in this country is somewhat uncertain. If you are like most people, you are concerned with personal financial and tax planning. What should you buy? For the time being, perhaps nothing. A bad investment may be worse than no investment at all. Remember, however, that the investment market never stands still. The person who jumps in at the right time can do extremely well. There is an old Chinese curse that says "May you live in interesting times." These are definitely interesting times.

GLOSSARY

Active Business Income Income from manufacturing, wholesaling, retailing, logging, farming, fishing, natural resource exploration and development, transportation, and in certain instances, services. This income qualifies for a low rate of corporate tax when earned by *Canadian-controlled private corporations.*

Adjusted Cost Base The cost of property for tax purposes. This may be either the cost to the taxpayer or the value as of December 31, 1971, subject to any adjustments required by the Income Tax Act.

Amortization The allocation of an expense or debt over a period of time.

Annuity A series of regular (and usually equal) payments consisting of interest and principal.

Arm's Length Where the parties to a transaction are unrelated by blood, marriage, or adoption.

Asset A property that is owned and has value.

Attribution Rules A series of tax provisions whereby income generated from property transferred or loaned by one spouse to the other will be reallocated for tax purposes to the person who made the transfer. Similar provisions also apply for transfers to minors.

Beneficiary A person who receives or is named to receive money or property from an insurance policy or *will.* A person for whose benefit a *trust* exists.

Buy-Sell Agreement An undertaking among owners of a business whereby those that remain agree to acquire the interest in the business of an owner who dies, retires, or becomes disabled.

Canadian-Controlled Private Corporation (CCPC) A company incorporated in Canada where the majority of the shares are not held by non-residents or public companies or by any combination of non-residents and public companies.

Capital Cost Allowance A provision for depreciation as permitted under the Income Tax Act to recognize wear, tear, and obsolescence and to allocate the cost of an asset over the period for which it is useful in generating revenue.

Capital Gains The profit realized when certain assets such as real estate and shares of a public or private company are sold for proceeds in excess of cost. A taxpayer's capital gain is measured as the difference between the selling price of property and its *adjusted cost base.* Subject to the lifetime capital gains tax exemption, three-quarters of a capital gain is taken into income when proceeds are received. This is called a taxable capital gain.

Classes of Assets For tax-depreciation (*capital-cost-allowance*) purposes, assets are divided into pools or groups. Each pool has its own depreciation rate, which is usually related to the useful life of the assets that it contains.

Collateral Stocks, bonds, or other property pledged as security for a loan. A lender has the right to sell collateral in the event of a borrower's default.

Combined Individual Tax Rates Rates (usually expressed in percentages) that take into account the effect of both federal and provincial taxes.

Controlling Shareholder Usually, a shareholder who owns more than 50% of the voting shares of a corporation.

Deemed Disposition An event such as death, departure from Canada, or the making of a gift, where an individual is considered for tax purposes to have sold his property for consideration (generally) equal to its *fair market value.*

Deferred Annuity An *annuity* under which payments of principal and interest will only begin some time after the annuity is acquired.

Deferred Compensation An arrangement under which income is postponed until some future time, usually until retirement from employment.

Dividend A distribution out of after-tax earnings or profits, which a corporation pays to its shareholders.

Dividend Tax Credit A reduction from taxes otherwise payable by an individual who receives a dividend from a Canadian corporation. The tax credit takes into account the fact that a dividend is a distribution by a corporation out of previously taxed profits.

Earned Income The sum of incomes from employment, self-employment, pensions, rentals, and alimony minus losses from self-employment and/or rentals and alimony paid. Up to 18% of earned income qualifies for an annual investment into an individual's *Registered Retirement Savings Plan* (subject to certain maximum dollar limitations).

Effective Taxes Combined federal and provincial taxes as a percentage of total income. (Compare *marginal rate of tax.*)

Equity Capital The funds in a business, which have been invested by the owners and not loaned by others.

Estate Freezing An exchange of assets whereby properties with growth potential are exchanged for properties whose value remains constant through time.

Estate Planning The orderly arrangement of one's financial affairs so that assets may be transferred on death to persons designated by the deceased, with a minimum loss of value due to taxes and forced liquidations.

Executor A person named in a *will* to carry out the provisions of that will.

Fair Market Value The price for property that a willing buyer would pay to a willing seller on the open market in circumstances where both parties deal at *arm's length* and neither is compelled to transact.

Front-End Load An administration charge for handling investment capital that is levied against the initial contribution(s) to a savings plan, such as a *Registered Retirement Savings Plan.*

Grossed-Up Dividend When an individual resident in Canada receives a dividend from a Canadian corporation, the amount that is taxable is one and one-quarter times the actual payment received. The individual is then allowed a *dividend tax credit* approximately equal to the 25% gross-up.

Guaranteed Term A minimum term under which annuity payments are guaranteed. In the case of a life annuity with a guaranteed term, the payments will continue through the guarantee period even if the recipient of the annuity dies before the end of that period.

Management Company A corporation set up by professionals such as doctors, dentists, lawyers, and accountants to provide administrative services to the professional business of the practitioner(s).

Manufacturing and Processing Profits Deduction A special reduction from corporate income taxes otherwise payable, computed at 6% (7% after 1993) of taxable income from manufacturing and processing activities which does not also qualify for the small business deduction.

Marginal Rate of Tax The combined federal and provincial tax rate that would apply to the next dollar of taxable income earned by a taxpayer in a given year. Compare *effective taxes.*

Net Income Gross income from all sources less expenses to earn this income, but before loss carry-overs from other years and taxes.

Non-Resident Withholding Tax A flat rate of tax imposed on investment income such as interest, rents, dividends, and annuities paid to a non-resident recipient. In Canada, the rate of withholding tax is generally 25% unless reduced by a tax treaty with the country in which the non-resident lives.

Participating Shares Shares in a corporation, which participate in the growth of a business and its assets and on which (theoretically) unlimited dividends may be paid.

Pension-Income Credit A provision under which the first $1,000 of annual pension income (other than the Canada/Quebec Pension or the Old Age Pension) qualifies for a $170 federal tax credit.

Personal-Service Corporation A corporation formed to earn fees for services or commissions where the income can be attributed to the personal efforts of one or a few individuals.

Principal Residence A housing unit ordinarily occupied by an individual during a given year and designated as being his or her principal residence. Only one such residence may be designated for each year. Where an accommodation that was a principal residence throughout the period of its ownership is subsequently sold, the *capital gain* thereon is exempt from tax. A family unit of husband and wife can designate only one property at a time as a principal residence.

Recaptured Depreciation *Capital cost allowances* previously claimed, which are determined (in the year that depreciable property is sold) to be in excess of the actual amount by which the property in question has depreciated.

Refundable Tax A portion of corporate taxes previously paid by a private corporation on its investment income. Initially, the investment income is subject to a 40% tax rate, although an amount equal to 20% of the investment income is refundable back to the corporation upon payment of dividends to shareholders. The net corporate tax on investment income is thus reduced to 20%.

Registered Retirement Income Fund (RRIF) One of the settlement options available to taxpayers who wish to draw an annuity from their *Registered Retirement Savings Plans.* Under this option, payments received generally increase annually until the recipient is age ninety.

Registered Retirement Savings Plan (RRSP) A government-approved program whereby individuals may make tax-deductible contributions with annual maximums as a savings towards retirement.

Replacement Property In certain circumstances, gains on the disposition of property may be deferred for tax purposes if other property (i.e., replacement property) is acquired. The tax cost of the replacement property is reduced by an amount equal to the deferred gain.

Retiring Allowance A payment made by a former employer to an employee in recognition of long service or for loss of employment. In some cases, retiring allowances may be transferred to *Registered Retirement Savings Plans.*

Rollover A transfer of property from one person to another where the tax rules permit a deferral of gains at the time the transfer is made.

Small-Business Tax Rates A special incentive available to *Canadian-controlled private corporations* earning *active business income.* The first $200,000 of annual profits is taxed at approximately 20% (the rate varies from province to province).

Spousal RRSP An option available under a *Registered Retirement Savings Plan* whereby a taxpayer may earmark all or a portion of his or her annual contributions into a program for his or her spouse. This option is designed to ensure future *annuity* benefits for that spouse.

T-4 Slip A form prescribed by the Canadian government for employers to use in reporting salaries, wages, and benefits paid to employees.

Tax Credits A direct deduction against taxes otherwise payable. Among others, tax credits are available to individuals with respect to Canadian dividends received and to all taxpayers with respect to foreign taxes previously paid on foreign-source income.

Tax-Deductible Describes amounts which may be subtracted in arriving at one's income for tax purposes.

Tax Deferral A situation in which taxes on income or benefits are postponed until some future date.

Tax Depreciation See *capital cost allowance.*

Tax Loss Versus Tax Shelter A *tax loss* is a loss from business or property that is deductible when determining income for tax purposes. A tax loss becomes a *tax shelter* in circumstances where it is created by claiming *capital cost allowances* and does *not* involve an actual outflow of cash or a reduction in the value of one's investment. As a result of recent income-tax amendments, the use of tax shelters has been severely restricted.

Tax-Sheltered Describes income that is not taxable currently but will be taxed at some future time.

Taxable Benefit A benefit provided by an employer to an employee where the value is taxed in the hands of the employee as additional remuneration received.

Taxable Income Net income from all sources minus a few miscellaneous deductions including losses carried over from other years. For Canadian corporations, taxable income is computed after deducting dividends received from other Canadian corporations. Taxable income is the base on which income taxes are levied.

Term Insurance Life insurance that only pays if death occurs within a specific time period. There is usually no cash value under such a policy. Compare with *whole life insurance.*

Testator A person who makes a *will.*

Tracking Earmarking the flow of borrowed funds to clearly indicate the purpose for which these funds have been used.

Transferee A person to whom a transfer of title, rights, or property is made.

Transferor A person who makes a transfer of title, rights, or property.

Treasury Shares Shares that a corporation has the authority to issue but that are still unissued.

Trust An arrangement made in a person's lifetime or effective upon death whereby legal title and control of property is placed in the hands of a custodian (*trustee*) for the benefit of another person or group of persons who are known as *beneficiaries* of the trust.

Trustee A person who acts as custodian and administrator of property held in *trust* for someone else.

Undepreciated Capital Cost The cost of depreciable assets minus accumulated *capital cost allowances* previously claimed.

Vesting The process whereby a right to property passes unconditionally to a particular person, such as where an employee becomes entitled to the full benefits from contributions previously made by an employer to a pension program.

Will A legal statement of a person's wishes about what shall be done with his or her property after death.

Whole Life Insurance Life insurance that remains in force until the insured dies, irrespective of when this occurs. Whole life insurance policies usually have cash values, which increase over time and which may be borrowed against, or for which the policy may be surrendered.

Year End The end of the business cycle each year. For tax purposes, a business must file an annual report disclosing its profits. Initially, the year end may be selected to fall on any date. However, no change in the year end may be made subsequently without the permission of Revenue Canada authorities.

Yield Return on investment, usually computed as the percentage of the anticipated (or realized) annual income relative to the capital invested.

THE AUTHOR

Over the past fifteen years, **Henry B. Zimmer, CA, CFP,** has lectured to thousands of Canadians on income tax and financial planning. He formerly taught the taxation course at the University of Calgary and at McGill and Concordia Universities in Montreal. Mr. Zimmer has lectured for the Canadian Institute of Chartered Accountants in their professional development programs and in student preparation programs across Canada.

Before moving to Alberta in 1977, Mr. Zimmer was a tax partner in a Montreal accounting firm. He qualified as a Chartered Accountant in 1967 and is a member of The Canadian Tax Foundation, the Institutes of Chartered Accountants of Alberta and Ontario, the Order of Chartered Accountants of Quebec, and the Canadian Association of Financial Planners.

Mr. Zimmer has published numerous books on tax and financial planning, investment strategies, and real estate investment, including *The Canadian Tax and Investment Guide,* which has been a bestseller and regularly updated since its first edition in 1980/81. He has also written four textbooks on Canadian taxation for students in accounting.